1989 David R. [illegible]

University of St. Francis
GEN 364.36 P544
Phelps, Thomas R.
W9-ADV-289
3 0301 00070346 8

JUVENILE DELINQUENCY: A CONTEMPORARY VIEW

THOMAS R. PHELPS
DEPARTMENT OF CRIMINAL JUSTICE
CALIFORNIA STATE UNIVERSITY, SACRAMENTO

Goodyear Publishing Company, Inc.
Santa Monica, California

LIBRARY
College of St. Francis
JOLIET, ILLINOIS

Library of Congress Cataloging in Publication Data

Phelps, Thomas R.

Juvenile delinquency.

Bibliography: p.

Includes index.

1. Juvenile delinquency—United States. 2. Children's rights—United States. 3. Rehabilitation of juvenile delinquents—United States. I. Title.

HV9104.P46 364.36 74-31511

ISBN 0-87620-500-7

Copyright © 1976
by Goodyear Publishing Company, Inc.,
Santa Monica, Ca.

All rights reserved. No part of this book may be reproduced in any form or by any means without permission in writing from the publisher.

Library of Congress Catalog Card Number: 74-31511

ISBN: 0-87620-500-7

Current printing (last number):

10 9 8 7 6 5 4 3

Y-5007-3

Printed in the United States of America

364.36
P544

In memory of Leo J. Robinson, S. J. (1899–1968) whose course in juvenile delinquency transformed a brief summer's learning experience into a lifetime concern for juvenile justice.

132,670

CONTENTS

PREFACE

In the last few years there has been a renewed interest in the rights of juveniles and related delinquency problems. College students and older people are volunteering to supplement the services of overworked juvenile court and institutional staff personnel; law students concern themselves with the youngster in the courts; laymen in general are asking what they can do to influence local government. This new level of involvement calls for usable texts with corresponding emphasis on contemporary application of existing knowledge and an eye toward future trends. I have tried to organize the book around this greater awareness of students and citizens. Emerging careers in the juvenile justice field, of real interest to the student, I felt deserved more practical attention. The failure of juvenile institutions gives this priority a compelling urgency.

The first chapter introduces current issues in delinquency prevention and control—the rights of children, youth involvement, the impact of the U.S. Supreme Court on juvenile justice, federal legislation and agencies providing direction for innovative programs; Great Society and New Federalism programs including general revenue sharing. The second chapter gives the legal and nonlegal definitions of delinquency, and in the process shows how delinquency is measured. The third chapter summarizes historical and current views about what causes delinquency. Youth service bureaus, a community response to delinquency, are explored in Chapter 4. Delinquency control is explored in Chapters 5, 6, 7, and 8. Topics include the police role in delinquency prevention and control, the use of detention, and the tendency to jail juveniles. Juvenile corrections is emphasized (i.e., the juvenile court, probation, institutions, and aftercare). Chapter 9 points up the need for community action, based on a comprehensive state plan for delinquency prevention and control. Youth employment and school problems are examined in the tenth chapter. Recommendations of the National Advisory Commission on Criminal Justice Standards and Goals are reviewed in the final chapter. In conclusion the book tries to suggest ways of building an effective knowledge base to meet the problems of youth. Extensive footnotes accompany each chapter; a general bibliography (Appendix D) lists and organizes sources not identified in the footnotes.

I wish to thank several people who have been helpful in setting the mood for this book: Dr. Vernon Fox, School of Criminology, Florida State University, who pioneered in training personnel to work with troubled youth, and Professor Paul B. Weston of California State University (Sacramento) for his friendly encouragement and thoughtful comments.

In addition, special thanks are due Mr. Joseph Clark Schmidt whose incisive comments and careful reading of the material provided many suggestions for improvement. My gratitude, also, to Mrs. Helen Duvall who typed the manuscript and sacrificed much of her leisure time in order to meet the deadlines.

THOMAS R. PHELPS

ISSUES IN DELINQUENCY PREVENTION AND CONTROL

Turmoil and change. The emerging problems of the unmanageable cities. Public anxiety over crime exerts enormous pressure on an already overburdened police. The juvenile court is expected to be a stern and protective parent with unlimited resources. The institutions are admonished to retrain their charges. The community is asked to provide a full range of alternatives to incarceration.

These images of delinquency contain many contradictory elements. The police can hardly calm the streets until the community responds to the restless concerns of youth. Local government must become responsive to its neighborhoods. Delinquency prevention and control programs fail because of the barriers youth encounters in achieving recognition and respect.

THE MEANING OF PREVENTION AND CONTROL

Everyone supports the general idea of preventing delinquency without having an exact idea of what it means. Delinquency prevention occurs when community services meet the current needs of youth; ideally, noncoercive social services are made available to the youngster not yet adjudged delinquent by the police or courts. Therefore, when the juvenile justice system diverts youth very early from police contact or from juvenile court intake, it is engaging in delinquency prevention. The police and the courts are saying, "You do something for this juvenile in your community." Delinquency prevention programs are effective when the juvenile who misbehaves gets help outside the formal social control agencies.

When a juvenile tangles with the law, the responses taken on his behalf by official agencies are delinquency control measures.

These programs are effective when the youth satisfies police, courts, or corrections that he is conforming.

The police officer and the juvenile court worker know that contact with the formal system of delinquency control puts a stigma on the youth.[1] Stigma is not a high priority concern if the juvenile is charged with an adult crime and his presence in the community constitutes a real danger. Then, it is best to confine him in the hope of changing his behavior. However, when a juvenile commits a non-adult crime and is more dangerous to himself than to the community, then processing through the juvenile justice system may be of less value than diversion.[2] Diversion is screening out of the justice system those juveniles who do not require the formal restraints and compulsory services of the juvenile court. Anxious parents believe that the juvenile court experience itself will somehow produce the desired, modifying effect. In fact, the future of a juvenile in trouble is not determined by the process but by the manner in which remedial strategies are applied.

Since the formal juvenile justice system is aware of the meaning of stigma, it follows that the police and the courts are deeply interested in delinquency prevention. However, when the formal agencies use diversion to prevent delinquency, an important question must be asked—to whom do we divert and under whose jurisdiction do we place the youth? There must be a path for re-entry into the community because when a delinquent returns to the school, the social agency, or place of employment, he meets difficulties; some schools exclude juveniles with delinquent histories. Because most agencies file cases alphabetically or by an index number, they do not know where the juvenile lives. To meet his needs, it is necessary to know something about his neighborhood. Matching juvenile with agency is not enough. The agency must offer a treatment strategy that responds to the youth in his world: the neighborhood, the family, the peer group, and the formal agencies of control that govern him in his day-to-day activities.

Character-building organizations and activities—such as scouting, church related youth groups, and boys' clubs—commonly assume that their programs and activities keep young people from misbehaving and from becoming delinquent. Such programs should examine their target population (i.e., the youth they serve) in order to determine whether the activity schedule serves juveniles in danger of becoming delinquent. When the target population consists of already conforming youth who will probably continue their non-delinquent pattern, it is best to omit reference to delinquency prevention when stating the goals of the organization. When the target *is* delinquent youth, we then do need to refer to delinquency prevention. A definition of delinquency, however, explains little when used in connection with concepts like prevention of recidivism, rehabilitation, or deterrence. These terms are noble but also too general to assist us much. So we must review the areas and concepts that do determine the meaning of delinquency prevention.

We start with the realization that each youth deserves a valid ticket to competency in the adult world, that this achievement occurs when he can acquire respect and power in the community. The juvenile struggles for this command within his home community. Therefore, to understand him, workers must observe him interacting among the several groups in his neighborhood: police, law-abiding people, delinquent youth, and the agencies. How does one observe what is occurring in the daily arena of juvenile action? It is important to assess how the youth perceives his needs. Then, we seek remedies where needs are not being met, and evaluate operating programs and personnel from this point of view.

It is difficult to appraise most delinquency prevention personnel—they are trying to do their best, but unfortunately, the desire to prevent or control delinquency does not ensure success. When these workers create a program based on their "deep concern for youth," and process youth through it, they have probably done little to reduce the tensions that lead to delinquency. Rather, they should first identify the aggravations, provocations and pressures toward delinquency and attempt to reduce these. Specific programs that ignore such daily experiences cannot develop meaningful strategies for prevention. To expect youth to conform is realistic only when adults permit them to participate in the ongoing operations of viable social institutions. Otherwise, what is their reward for conforming and adhering to the values of the adult world?

Progress in the prevention, control, and treatment of juvenile delinquency will be more likely to occur when citizens as well as administrators familiarize themselves with the following widely held views:

1. Diversion is the most appropriate community response when juveniles misbehave.

2. The juvenile offender should be treated in the home community when resources are available and when the youth himself has agreed.
3. Juveniles should be confined within an institution as long as needed to protect the community—but no longer. Release from the institution should be predicated upon a professional prognosis that a resumption of delinquent activity is unlikely.
4. The forms of treatment appropriate for different types of delinquents can be distinguished and applied.
5. As the juvenile goes step by step through the justice system, each decision about him influences the selection of treatment strategies and the imposition of restraints. Therefore, thoughtful attention should be accorded this decision-making process.

In conclusion, delinquency prevention meets the needs of youth by diverting them from the formal system of juvenile justice when possible. Local agencies such as mental health, public welfare, and the schools prepare the juvenile population for responsible roles in the adult world. Further, delinquency control will be easier if the community provides for delinquent children in the same way it provides for children who are not in trouble. The task might be even simpler if *juvenile delinquency* is redefined to include only the serious transgressions of youth, namely, adult crimes committed by juveniles.

MINIMUM SERVICES FOR CHILDREN

The costs of youth crime are compiled annually; community wrath follows the reports. But anger hardly provides motivation for the specialized community services needed by troubled children. A recent study shows that little money is put into preventing delinquency in young children. In 1967 nearly $37 billion were spent on the family car and auto parts, over $9 billion on alcoholic beverages, and $2 billion on pets. The money for prevention programs was a small fraction of any one of these.[3]

George Edwards argues that he knows no state or community which claims it possesses adequate facilities for delinquency prevention and control. According to Edwards, the minimum services required by a community include:

1. Police youth bureaus trained in methods of delinquency prevention and detection. Such a bureau would be headed by officers of high enough rank to be able to demand full use of community facilities for predelinquents and, where necessary, arrest and detention methods suited to juvenile cases.
2. Family social casework services capable of aiding both court and community by carrying needed help into the homes of delinquents and predelinquents.
3. Probation services for the juvenile court, with sufficient trained personnel to hold caseloads below 50 so that the probation officer can actually get to know and to help his charges. Half of the counties in America have no juvenile probation service and, where it does exist, 60 percent of all the probation officers have no professional training whatsoever.
4. Modern detention facilities where youngsters can be handled in small groups. If the detention home is so understaffed that the primary program is enforced idleness and troublesome children must be handled in large groups, the detention period can do more harm than good. Only a small minority of detention homes currently can afford modern facilities and trained staff. In addition, for lack of juvenile detention facilities, 100,000 children each year are held in jails.
5. Shelter facilities to insure separation of delinquent juveniles from nondelinquents. To place a nondelinquent child, taken into custody because of parental neglect, into a detention home where he will be surrounded by delinquents, is as irrational as putting a patient suffering from malnutrition into a TB ward.
6. A specialized Juvenile or Family Court, headed by a judge (or judges) with adequate court time and concern for rehabilitation of their young charges.
7. Psychiatric and psychological service for the Juvenile Court, preferably in a court clinic, to guarantee accurate diagnosis at court hearings.

8. Foster home services. Many of our most difficult delinquency cases can be handled well simply by providing decent homes.
9. Adoption services, which really seek to place the hard-to-place child. There is no room in the case record form of the good adoption service for the notation: "not suitable for adoption." The only children not suitable for adoption are those for whom institutionalization is mandatory.
10. Good, open-type boarding schools for both boys and girls available for Juvenile Court placements.
11. State vocational schools for delinquent boys and girls for whom custody is required, manned not by ex-wardens of penitentiaries, but by teachers, counselors, and social workers who have had training in treatment work and are interested in and like youngsters.
12. State mental health clinics and hospitals for mentally and emotionally disturbed children, oriented not toward custody but toward cure.[4]

Many communities offer a few of the services recommended by Edwards. There is a growing awareness of how much can be accomplished by offering community-based rehabilitation as an alternative to traditional corrections. The needs are enormous, particularly when we look at them from a perspective advocating the children's rights movement.

THE RIGHTS OF CHILDREN

A substantial number of children are unable to secure the basic rights presumed to accrue to them under our Constitution. There each child is given:

1. The right to be wanted.
2. The right to be born healthy.
3. The right to live in a healthy environment.
4. The right to continuous loving care.
5. The right to satisfaction of basic needs.
6. The right to acquire the intellectual and emotional skills necessary to achieve individual aspirations and to cope effectively in our society.[5]

Renewed attention focuses on the legal accountability of those charged with improving and guarding the rights of children. It might seem that all children receive these basic rights. Not true. Neglect and abuse are among the recurrent problems reported by public agencies dealing with the troubled child. A large number of referrals also emerge from parent-child conflict. The hostility of parents toward their own children is seen every day by police officers, judges, and school officials. Children often run away from an unsatisfactory home, from parents who do not want them.

An adolescent ward of a training school, an acquaintance of mine, received a letter from his parents informing him that they were moving to another state. He was not to learn their destination. The terse letter ended, "So good by and Good Luck forever. Once was Mom, & Dad."[6] Many times parents talk about the "welfare of the child," but instead use their children to work out personal problems, ventilate anger, or merely to meet some short-term adult interest. The home situation for many youngsters today resembles that of sixteen-year-olds in the Massachusetts Bay Colony in 1646. At that time, it was decreed that if a man had a stubborn or rebellious son, he need only bring him to the magistrate's court where he would be put to death.

Since then, we have accepted the view that the state is the benevolent protector of the child, but this concept, known as *parens patriae* (that the court will act as an ultimate parent), is not effective in assuring children's rights. The principle that the parent knows best is in question. A movement in the 1970s suggests that the parent, the school, and the courts will function more adequately if assisted by persons or agencies assigned to enforce the rights of children. This new specialization, concerned with securing justice for all younger citizens, is known as the child advocacy movement.

Child Advocacy

The advocacy role is most effective because it involves so many people—the concerned parent, the state and federal agency, and all who support the need to provide our younger citizens with a legacy for competency. Child advocacy has been defined as:

> . . . a consumer-controlled outreach system with two major objectives: to obtain more responsive, adequate and effective service from child and family service agencies; and to develop the strengths, skills and initiatives of families and communities to solve their own problems.
>
> . . . a service program or approach directed toward changing systems and designed to improve life conditions for children by assuring that service delivery systems and institutions bearing most on children work *for* these children, rather than against them.[7]

The child advocate will be committed to the interest and welfare of children and families and will offer assistance to the school, the police, and the juvenile court, as well as public and private child-serving agencies. The 1970 White House Conference on Children recommended the establishment of an independent Office of Child Advocacy on the federal level. The national agency would be supplemented with programs in the states, local communities, and neighborhoods. In response to this request, a National Center for Child Advocacy was established within the Office of Child Development of the U.S. Department of Health, Education, and Welfare in 1971. Among the child advocacy projects funded by this agency are the following: a twenty-four-hour emergency service for children in crisis; a counseling program and medical clinic for teen-agers; family day care programs; an adoption project focused upon the black child; and a statewide program to influence legislation and coordinate public child welfare services.[8] (A list of state and local child advocacy programs appears in Appendix A.)

New York state established an Office of Children's Services in 1972 to assume an advocacy role for children brought before the New York City Family Court. This special project of the New York State Judicial Conference, if found to be successful on the local level, may lead to a statewide operation. The office hopes to give judges and appropriate government agencies factual information to help plan for the care, supervision, and treatment of children; to identify existing and needed services; and to determine responsibility for executing programs. The Office of Children's Services was formed from recommendations of the Committee on Mental Health Services for the Family Court; this committee discovered, in its 1971 fact-finding report, that little information existed for determining the needs of children who appeared before the family court.[9]

Minnesota has established a Youth Advocacy Corps within its Department of Education. The program will help the 449 independent school districts work toward the establishment of school or community resource centers. These resource centers operate on the premise that schools do not cause delinquency but often compound the problem by failing to make socially desirable roles accessible to students. The resource center is a part of the school system and it tries to provide a number of services: an adolescent treatment center; a foster home placement service; individual, family, and group counseling; community volunteer tutoring programs; and a youth employment service. Many criticize the program because it places all helping services under the control of the local public school system. The chronic financial problems of school districts, with their often drastic curtailment of educational services, suggests nothing optimistic for their advocacy potential. Is the local school district effective enough to mobilize and operate the many kinds of services recommended for the school or community resource center? Furthermore, can a social institution, which has so long operated on the premise of compulsory attendance, accept the noncoercive nature of services? However, on the positive side, the schools recognize their responsibility to juveniles. Each community should have an advocacy center. The most promising model for a community advocacy center is the youth service bureau (see Chapter 3).

Children's Lobbies

Many private citizens have organized themselves into groups for the purpose of lobbying for the rights of children at the local level. Since 1966, San Francisco's Citizens for Juvenile Justice has won many battles in its struggle for children. This non-official organization of over 600 people, under the courageous guidance of Jean Jacobs, has awakened local public officials to the plight of children who are neglected, dependent, and delinquent.

Although lobbyists are a common sight in the halls of the state legislature, until recently the interests of children went unnoticed there; youngsters seldom went to the legislature except as members of a guided tour. However, this situation changed with the establishment, in 1971, of the California Children's Lobby. Concerned about adoptions, delinquency, malnourished and battered children, etc., it is a political voice for California children under age 18—the voteless minority. Don Fibush, who helped found it, has realized a 30-year dream in his new role as a volunteer children's lobbyist. While most lobbies are financed and staffed by the interests they represent, the Children's Lobby operates on a nonprofit, nontaxable structure and exists on contributions from over 500 donors. It has been successful in familiarizing elected officials with specific legislation affecting children. Because the executive branch of a state government often vetoes 50 percent or more of all legislation dealing with child welfare, this program needs to be expanded into other states.

Youth is learning more about its rights; a number of books give young people a working knowledge of law. An objective guide to the problems of the law is the carefully written *Growing Up Clean in America* by Joseph S. Lobenthal, Jr. He discusses the operations of the legal system as viewed by the youngster in trouble; the risks associated with various actions which can appear reasonable when peers support them; the attorney-client relationship; the rights of the student at school. Michael Dorman, in *Under 21: A Young People's Guide to Legal Rights,* explores legal rights in such areas as dress and hairstyle; self-expression; employment, driving, contracts and legal agreements, money, voting; and home and parents. A small number of these writings, available in underground bookstores, dwell on the constraints of law and overlook the fact that youth live under the law and enjoy freedom without undue hassle. The popular publications help prepare students to serve as child or youth advocates. The courses in elementary- and secondary-school juvenile law further acquaint students with the sometimes unclear line between conforming and delinquent (or criminal) behavior. The changing nature of law will require a host of other publications in this area.

YOUTH INVOLVEMENT

Accompanying the renewed interest in juvenile rights are increased opportunities for youth to participate in local and state government. Young people between the ages of 15 and 25 are becoming more important in making decisions about programs and policies that have direct impact upon their lives.

In 1969, the National Council on Crime and Delinquency held two workshops dealing with how to involve youth in the planning and operating of delinquency prevention and control programs. The meetings were held at Bass River, Massachusetts, and Decatur, Georgia. The participants included planners, persons associated with state planning agencies funded by the Law Enforcement Assistance Administration; managers, those who administer direct services to youth, such as police, judges, probation and parole administrators, or institutions personnel; and a youth delegation, made up of high-school and university or college students, delinquents, and nondelinquents. Adult participants outnumbered youth; and this problem was compounded in one city where the secondary-school principals would not excuse their students to attend the workshop.

A number of important conclusions were reached: (1) youth welcome the opportunity to be heard and they would like to influence decisions in a positive way; but (2) they are seldom heard by planners and managers because they lack power; (3) young people do not discuss delinquency on the abstract level that delights their elders, so communications between them are sometimes strained; (4) therefore, conferences including youth, planners, and managers should focus on specific issues rather than on the more general topic of delinquency prevention and control (e.g., how might we handle the runaway problem without juvenile court referral?); and (5) the purpose of the meetings is to formulate a more enlightened delinquency control program, not to give youth token notice of their needs.

Young people have met with little success in their struggle with the older generation.[10] Adults find it hard to listen, and the youth themselves are apathetic, as noted in recent elections. However, adolescents are very good at helping each other. Many university students, for example, volunteer to tutor juveniles in correctional institutions. Perhaps the most important reason for their involvement lies in the contemporary view that rehabilitation cannot be forced upon a delinquent. A program for changing behavior must permit the youngster to participate to some extent in his own improvement.

This attitude is part of the twentieth century crusade for the child. Not only have we emphasized children's rights, child advocacy, and youth involvement but we have also seen the establishment of a special court for the young.

THE JUVENILE COURT

In 1899, concerned citizens fought for the child in need of protection against a criminal justice system which treated the youngster in trouble as if he were an adult. These reformers were doubtful about the entire process of criminal justice and the emphasis upon conviction, punishment, and release. In this atmosphere, the first juvenile court was established in Illinois in 1899. It was civil rather than criminal.

Unfortunately, relaxing procedural safeguards meant the loss of constitutional guarantees. The juvenile court adopted the notion of *parens patriae*, a concept borrowed from English common law, known as the principle of chancery. Under English law the king served as mediator in cases where the law was excessively harsh with children. The king's chancellor, who served as the administrator of the judicial system, was entrusted with carrying out this task. Thus, in England the power of the king was delegated to the court of chancery, and in this country the power of the court was delegated to the juvenile court. Therefore, two important concepts arose: *parens patriae* and *in loco parentis*. The latter refers to the fact that, in individual cases, the king acts in lieu of the natural parent. By assuming this role in the United States, the juvenile court has endeavored to help the youngster in a setting free from the conflict and drama characteristic of the adult criminal court. Cohen imples that the law relating to juvenile delinquency has developed the following characteristics:

1. Extremely broad and ambiguous statutory language;
2. Wide discretionary powers vested in the administrators of the system as to the formulation of basic policy and the resolution of concrete issues;
3. The duration of confinement governed by the "response to treatment" and age factors rather than assessment of the gravity of the "offense";
4. The consignment of more legally relevant issues to matters of *privilege* rather than *right;*

5. The relaxation of procedural safeguards normally associated with judicial proceedings;
6. A quite narrow score of judicial review in deference to the presumed expertise of the authoritative decision-makers.[11]

The juvenile court has sought to consider the welfare of the child and carry out the goals of rehabilitation. While the traditional criminal courts try to determine whether the defendant is guilty or innocent, the juvenile court asks why there was misbehavior, under what circumstances, and what can be done to help the juvenile. Unfortunately, the benign efforts of the juvenile court have not been an unqualified success. When the state supreme courts are asked to respond to critics of the juvenile court movement, they usually agree with the classic Pennsylvania decision, *Commonwealth* v. *Fisher*, in 1905:

> To save a child from becoming a criminal, or from continuing in a career of crime, . . . the Legislature surely may provide for the salvation of such a child, if its parents or guardian be unable or unwilling to do so, by bringing it into one of the courts of the state without any process at all, for the purpose of subjecting it to the state's guardianship and protection. The natural parent needs no process to temporarily deprive his child of its liberty by confining it in his own home, to save it and to shield it from the consequences of persistence in a career of waywardness; nor is the state, when compelled, as *parens patriae*, to take the place of the father for the same purpose, required to adopt any process as a means of placing its hands upon the child to lead it into one of its courts. When the child gets there, and the court, with the power to save it, determines on its salvation, and not its punishment, it is immaterial how it got there. The act simply provides how children who ought to be saved may reach the court to be saved . . . No constitutional right is violated, but one of the most important duties which organized society owes to its helpless members is performed.[12]

This court opinion upholds the doctrine of *parens patriae*, in which the state acts in the best interest of a child in a non-adversary proceeding. The issue is proper treatment for the child rather than the matter of guilt or innocence. Nonetheless, whatever attention may be given the child by juvenile court judges and their staffs, they cannot supply the loving care of a good parent on a continuing basis.

The "Golden Years," 1966–71

A number of decisions by the U.S. Supreme Court, testing the constitutionality of routine procedures in the juvenile court, were heard between 1966 and 1971; the opinions dealt with due process and the right of counsel for juveniles. In 1966, our highest court concluded:

> There is much evidence that some juvenile courts . . . lack the personnel, facilities and techniques to perform adequately as representatives of the State in a *parens patriae* capacity, at least with respect to children charged with law violation. There is evidence, in fact, that there may be grounds for concern that the child receives the worst of both worlds: that he gets neither the protections accorded to adults nor the solicitous care and regenerative treatment postulated for children.[13]

This decision, *Kent* v. *United States,* was from an important juvenile court case in the District of Columbia, and was the first of five to reassess the founding premises of the juvenile court movement. These important U.S. Supreme Court decisions are:

1. *Kent* v. *United States,* 383 U.S. 541, 16 L.Ed.2d 84, 86 S.Ct. 1045 (1966).
2. *In re Gault,* 387 U.S. 1, 18 L.Ed.2d 527, 87 S.Ct. 1428 (May 15, 1967).
3. *In re Whittington,* 391 U.S. 341, 20 L.Ed.2d 625, 88 S.Ct. 1057 (1968).
4. *In re Winship,* 397 U.S. 358, 25 L.Ed.2d 368, 90 S.Ct. 1068 (March, 1970).
5. *McKeiver* v. *Pennsylvania,* 403 U.S. 528, 29 L.Ed.2d 647, 91 S.Ct. 1976 (June, 1971).

There was no desire to dismantle the juvenile court but rather to make it function more satisfactorily. Although the case of Morris A. Kent, Jr., was applicable only to the District of Columbia, the others have reshaped the juvenile court movement in this country.

A characteristic of the juvenile court is its informality. A hearing has two parts: first, the adjudicative hearing or fact-finding phase, which determines whether a youngster is a delinquent; and, second, the dispositional hearing in which a determination is made about the delinquency.

Kent* v. *United States. Informal proceedings, many find, can be oppressive because a judge at his discretion can transfer a case from the juvenile to the adult court without giving a reason to the juvenile or his parents. In the case of Morris Kent, Jr., the U.S. Supreme Court concluded that a juvenile has certain constitutional rights when the juvenile court is deciding whether he will be tried as a juvenile or prosecuted as an adult. For sixteen-year-old Morris, the decision to try him as an adult rather than a juvenile held great importance because the offense in the juvenile court could bring a five year sentence while as an adult he might receive the death penalty. As it was, he received a sentence of 30 to 90 years in prison for the crimes of burglary, rape, and robbery. When he was 14, Morris had been placed on probation for purse snatching and housebreaking. The juvenile court judge decided to waive this case to the adult criminal court without conferring with Morris, the parent, or the lawyer retained by the boy's mother. The judge gave no reason for the waiver to adult court even though requested to do so by counsel and the juvenile. In fairness to the District of Columbia, it should be stated that the juvenile court at that time had only one judge, who was overburdened with a workload that no judge could properly manage.

In *Kent* v. *United States* the U.S. Supreme Court ruled that a juvenile is entitled to: (1) a full hearing in the juvenile court on the issue of transfer of his case to an adult criminal court; (2) the assistance of counsel at the hearing; (3) permission of the counsel to have access to the social records prepared by the court personnel in determining whether transfer to the adult court is appropriate; and, (4) a statement of the reasons formulated by the judge in reaching the decision for the waiver action. This decision does not question the validity of the laws permitting the transfer of juvenile court cases to the adult courts for criminal prosecution. The U.S. Supreme Court merely questioned the procedure used in effecting such transfers since the constitutional rights of the juvenile were in question.

This 1966 decision, even though applicable only to the District of Columbia, does represent the entrance of lawyers into juvenile court proceedings; it accelerated the children's rights movement.[14] State legislatures probably will not alter the existing statutes, which permit concurrent jurisdiction of adult and juvenile courts in felony cases, because so many young people use violence when committing offenses. Such violence increases the tendency of the community to "make an example" of certain children as criminals. If this does not effectively reduce violence, it does seem to dispel the anxiety of fearful people. The *Kent* decision, however, is a useful safeguard; judges may be more reluctant to transfer juvenile cases to the adult court except in cases determined to be exceedingly serious; they know that reasons for the waiver must be stated and that a full hearing is required for the action.

In re Gault. The *Kent* decision was followed one year later by a most important case in the juvenile justice revolution. The *In re Gault* opinion affords the juvenile the same rights as those granted the adult offender. The juvenile receives the procedural protections guaranteed by the Bill of Rights and the Fourteenth Amendment. Thus, the U.S. Supreme Court ruled that the juvenile adjudication proceeding will provide the following principles of due process which are so important for the protection of individual freedom. (1) The child and his parents or guardian should be notified in writing of the specific charges to be considered at the hearing. Such written notice should be given in sufficient time to permit thoughtful preparation for the hearing. (2) Right to counsel. The juvenile needs the assistance of counsel and the child and the parent must be notified of this right. Counsel will be appointed by the court if the child or the parent cannot afford it. (3) The right to confrontation and cross-examination of complainants and other witnesses in accordance with constitutional requirements. And (4) the privilege against self-incrimination. The right to remain silent will assure that admissions or confessions are reasonably trustworthy and have not been taken under duress or coercion.

The Court did not rule upon two additional issues dealing with the rights of the accused; namely, the right to a transcript of the proceedings and the right to an appeal from a determination of guilt. However, the Court clearly indicated that both were desirable practices. Progressive juvenile courts in many states (especially

California, Illinois, Minnesota, New York, and Oregon) had substantially met the requirements of *Gault* long before 1967. Such juvenile courts implemented the recommendations of the Standard Juvenile Court Act prepared by the National Council on Crime and Delinquency some years ago.[15] It might be added that many courts have long accepted the right of counsel to be present in court but some had not furnished counsel when the youngster or parent were unable to provide such service.

The *Gault* decision is based upon the case of Gerald Gault, who in 1964, at age 15, was adjudicated a juvenile delinquent in the Gila County (Globe), Arizona, juvenile court. He was charged with making an obscene telephone call to a neighbor. Gerald—then on probation for being in the company of another youngster who had stolen a wallet—was taken into custody by his probation officer on June 8 after the neighbor, Mrs. Cook, complained about the lewd message. The contents of the telephone call would hardly be considered obscene by the standards of the 1970s. Kittrie reports the conversation: "Did you give any? Are your cherries ripe today? Do you have big bombers?"[16] Gerald was picked up while his parents were at work. No message was found when they returned home later that day. Gerald, his mother, his elder brother, and two probation officers met at the court hearing the following day, June 9. The complainant, Mrs. Cook, did not appear. The adjudication hearing was completed without a formal notice of the charges, without counsel, without the right to confront and cross-examine witnesses, without the preparation of a transcript or recording of the hearing, and no one was sworn at this hearing. Gerald was returned to detention afterward.

The dispositional hearing was scheduled for June 15th; he was released from detention and driven home on June 11th or 12th after having been confined since the day of the alleged offense. At the June 15th hearing, the court probation officers filed a "referral report," listing the charge as "lewd phone calls" although Gerald's parents had no knowledge of this report. At the conclusion of this hearing Gerald Gault was committed to the State Industrial School at Fort Grant, Arizona, until he became 21. If Gerald had been 18 at the time of the offense, the maximum punishment would have been a fine of $5 to $50 or a jail sentence of no more than two months. But as a juvenile, the punishment for the offense was six years. This landmark decision focuses strongly on the child's need for counsel; the individual whose rights are in jeopardy cannot always understand the complexities of the law.

Opponents of the *Gault* decision felt that the privilege against self-incrimination has introduced the adversary system into our juvenile court system. They assume that the informal, civil proceedings of the juvenile court emphasize only treatment objectives, and that there is, therefore, little need to provide juveniles with procedural safeguards equivalent to those afforded adult defendants. Unfortunately, this benign atmosphere of the juvenile court setting can be used in an unscrupulous manner. Juvenile court personnel say such an environment encourages children to tell the truth; some are even known to boast that they can solve more crimes than the local police departments. Improper use of the juvenile court is not widespread, but there is a distinct need for additional procedural protection such as that provided by *Gault*. The juvenile can no longer be deprived of his basic rights by adherence to a *parens patriae*, the "best interests of the child" doctrine.

Following the *Gault* decision, the California legislature required police to notify a child of his right to counsel and of his right to remain silent when taken into custody. In addition, the probation officer is required to give the same notification to a child brought to a detention facility or to the juvenile court.[17] The *Miranda* decision, another Arizona case referred to the U.S. Supreme Court, is also applicable to the juvenile and refers to the free exercise of the privilege against self-incrimination. It requires that the youngster be instructed that whatever he says may be used against him in court. This is critical in situations where "confessions" are taken by police or court personnel under the guise of friendship and without benefit of prior legal counsel.[18] Ferguson and Douglas, in their study of youngsters' awareness of the privilege against self-incrimination, found that 96 percent failed to understand their rights and voluntarily waived them.[19] These constitutional rights include the right to remain silent, the right to have counsel present during an interrogation, and the right to have counsel appointed if unable to afford counsel.

In re Whittington. Following the *Gault* decision a number of lawyers in the various state courts requested that the *Gault* decision be retroactively applied to those cases in which the requirements of due process had not been met. *In re Whittington* is such a case, and a remand for a new hearing was carried out.

Buddy Whittington, age fourteen and an only child, was arrested in early August 1966 after a complaint was filed in the juvenile court of Fairfield County, Ohio, alleging that he was a delinquent child by virtue of having murdered a Mrs. Willard. The victim was reported missing by her relatives on July 29, 1966. Late in the evening the citizens of the small community of Baltimore, Ohio, searched the area; Buddy and his father joined them and Buddy discovered the body under his own bed. She had been strangled. It was discovered that Buddy was the last to see Mrs. Willard alive because she had visited the Whittington home on the morning of the crime when she returned some hair curlers to Buddy's mother. The juvenile court stated that there was probable cause to believe the youngster had committed the crime. Since there was no juvenile detention center in the small community of Baltimore, Ohio, Buddy was kept in solitary confinement in the Fairfield County Jail for 78 days.

The case presented the following issues: (1) the standard of proof to be used in a delinquency adjudication; (2) the right to trial by jury in the juvenile court; and (3) the applicability of the *Miranda* warning to juveniles. None of these considerations were acted upon by the U.S. Supreme Court and on May 20, 1968, the Court vacated the judgment and remanded the case to the district court of appeals for consideration in the light of the *Gault* decision.

In re Winship. In 1970 the U.S. Supreme Court considered another case dealing with the law of juvenile delinquency. Samuel Winship, age 12, had stolen $112.00 from a woman's purse. This crime, if committed by an adult, constitutes larceny in New York state. Samuel was found delinquent and placed in a training school where he could be kept for six years or until his eighteenth birthday. The judge in the case rejected the contention that due process required proof beyond a reasonable doubt and he based his findings of delinquency on a preponderance of the evidence. Therefore, the U.S. Supreme Court held that when the juvenile court sets out to prove that a youngster is delinquent for having committed a criminal act "the same considerations which demand extreme caution in factfinding to protect the innocent adult apply as well to the innocent child." Thus, the Court applied proof beyond a reasonable doubt to juveniles.

The importance of the *Winship* decision is its stand that the rehabilitative capacity of the juvenile justice system need not be unleashed upon a child until it has been determined that he has done something wrong. In the past, we have attempted to rehabilitate innocent youngsters.

McKeiver* v. *Pennsylvania. The decision in the fifth and final case was delivered by Justice Harry A. Blackmun in 1971. The Court upheld a practice followed in a majority of the juvenile courts in the nation, that the right to a trial by jury is not constitutionally mandated in state juvenile delinquency hearings. Justice Blackmun added, "If, in its wisdom, any state feels the jury trial is desirable in all cases, or in certain kinds, there appears to be no impediment to its installing a system embracing that feature. That, however, is the state's privilege and not its obligation." This case involved separate juvenile court hearings for two boys, ages 15 and 16, in Philadelphia, Pennsylvania. The delinquent act of one constituted a felony if committed by an adult, and the behavior of the other a misdemeanor. Each boy requested a jury trial; the judge, denying both requests, ruled them juvenile delinquents. One received probation, while the other was committed to a juvenile institution. Therefore, in this decision the high court has said that, in juvenile proceedings the formalities from the adult court need not include the jury trial since the *parens patriae* and the due process model are compatible.

The Golden Years, in which the U.S. Supreme Court afforded Bill of Rights protections to many juvenile defendants, had ended. The rights of due process have been granted the juvenile while at the same time the informality and flexibility of the juvenile court process has been retained. Justice Blackmun states, "If the formalities of the criminal adjudicative process be superimposed upon the juvenile court system, [then] there is little need for its separate existence. Perhaps, the ultimate disillusionment will come one day, but for the moment we are disinclined to give impetus to it."[20] Some are content with the actions of the U.S. Supreme Court, while others, more reform oriented, will push for additional changes. Literature dealing with this important period, 1966–71, is listed in Appendix D, General Bibliography, Children's Rights.

This same period saw the passage of federal laws establishing guidelines and standards for delinquency prevention and control. Little concern was shown before 1961.

FEDERAL LAWS FOR DELINQUENCY PREVENTION AND CONTROL

Congress did establish the Children's Bureau of the Justice Department in 1912. This act directed the bureau:

> . . . . to investigate and report . . . on all matters pertaining to the welfare of children and child life among all classes of our people and . . . especially investigate the questions of infant mortality, the birth rate, orphanages, juvenile courts, desertion, dangerous occupations, accidents, and diseases of children, employment, legislation affecting children in the several States and territories.[21]

The Children's Bureau set up its separate Division of Juvenile Delinquency Service in 1936. The staff specialists provided consultation to the states until 1970 when the bureau was terminated and the staff transferred to the Youth Development and Delinquency Prevention Administration. This abrupt action created severe morale problems for the small group of specialists who had set the standards for delinquency prevention and control during a period of more than 30 years. The Office of Child Development, established in 1969, is the "new" Children's Bureau.

The Juvenile Delinquency and Youth Offenses Control Act of 1961 (Public Law 87-274), signed by John F. Kennedy, created the machinery for a federally coordinated program against juvenile delinquency. This act, administered by the Office of Juvenile Delinquency and Youth Development within the U.S. Department of Health, Education, and Welfare, was initially conceived as a three-year effort. It was extended, and passage of the Juvenile Delinquency Prevention and Control Act of 1968 (Public Law 90-445) revealed an enduring concern with delinquency. Interest was high but appropriations remained low.

The Great Society

In the 1960s programs for resolving social ills were administered by various federal bureaucracies dealing with health, education, welfare, and labor. John F. Kennedy and Lyndon B. Johnson endeavored to eliminate poverty and reduce delinquency through such programs as: the Job Corps; the Neighborhood Youth Corps; Operation Headstart and Follow Through; VISTA (Volunteers in Service to America); community action agencies; legal services for the poor; neighborhood health centers; and programs for native Americans and for migrant and seasonal farmworkers. The Office of Economic Opportunity, formed in 1965 as part of the executive office of the president, administered many of the programs.

From the birth of the Great Society programs in the 1960s until their dismantling in the 1970s, there was mounting criticism of their effectiveness. Those who built the programs say that many people were helped. But the social scientist should ponder why it is that the original conception of a program is lost or drastically altered as it passes through the bureaucracy. Day care centers, to cite one example, were closed without calculating the risk to working mothers. The pro and con of the Great Society argument is futile; attention would be better focused on evaluating the effectiveness of its programs.

The New Federalism

In any event, these programs were dismantled by Richard M. Nixon in the final years of his presidency. The former president felt that poverty could be better attacked at the local level. His philosophy, known to many as the New Federalism, recommended revenue sharing as the means for financing services to the nation's poor and disenfranchised. Supporters argue that this method permits the continuation of public services which have proven effective at the local level.

Revenue sharing is a rather basic principle, which guarantees that state and local governments should have access, albeit limited, to federal personal income tax monies. The system is designed to provide general budgetary support to state and local government from the federal revenue system. One-third of the general revenue sharing funds are distributed to the states and two-thirds to cities, counties, and other units of local government. These funds are disbursed to local governments on the basis of formulas subject only to changes in the demographic characteristics of the locality such as population size, local and state tax efforts, and personal income. Under the formula the amount of revenue-sharing funds is reduced when local taxes are reduced. Funds are disbursed through the Office of Revenue Sharing within the U.S. Treasury Department. The general revenue-sharing concept is embodied within the State and Local Fiscal Assistance Act of 1972 (Public Law 92-512).[22] This legislation calls for the disbursement of $30 billion during the five year period, 1972 to 1976. General revenue sharing provides nearly unrestricted funds that states and communities can use as they wish.

Response to revenue sharing has been mixed and vocal. The initial infusion of general revenue-sharing funds into the local community occurred at the same time that federal funds supporting many social services programs were drastically curtailed. Revenue sharing did not supplement ongoing federal funding. This complaint was made by many city mayors during the initial years of the revenue-sharing plan. General revenue sharing has been criticized because many communities have used funds for services which do not continue aid to the ill, the poor, and the elderly. One large urban community received an $8 million general revenue-sharing check from the Department of the Treasury but a simultaneous $22 million reduction of federal aid. Unfortunately, this community (through its elected officials) used 75 percent of the award for the construction of city and county office buildings. A state-by-state review of general revenue-sharing funds and their use for the first year revealed that 39 percent of the money was allotted to capital expenditures (i.e., construction and land acquisition).

The amount of revenue-sharing funds spent on delinquency prevention is not hard to determine. Enabling legislation required each locality to make public disclosure of its use of these monies. Priority trends can be charted easily at the community level.

In late 1974, federal agency responsibilities related to juvenile delinquency were revised. The Juvenile Justice and Delinquency Prevention Act (Public Law 93-415), signed by President Gerald R. Ford, placed all federal juvenile justice and delinquency prevention programs under the guidance of the Law Enforcement Assistance Administration, which is becoming more influential in providing standards and goals for delinquency prevention and control. It is unfortunate that President Ford refused to allow any funds to be used to implement the Act; his refusal may severely limit the

132,670

College of St. Francis Library
Joliet, Illinois

effectiveness of the Act. The legislation created the Office of Juvenile Justice and Delinquency Prevention within the U.S. Department of Justice. The U.S. Department of Health, Education, and Welfare continues to deal with the growing problem of young people who run away from home. Funds are provided to establish temporary shelters and counseling services for an estimated million young people annually.

The new role of the state planner in criminal justice is promising. The state agency is responsible for developing and coordinating a comprehensive plan for crime and delinquency prevention and control, based upon information supplied by each state region. This is a good way to assess whether we have been effective in combatting delinquency. Comprehensive state planning for delinquency prevention and control is essential if necessary services are to reach vulnerable youth.

A study of delinquency affords the reader an opportunity to respond to the following challenge by Karl Menninger:

> Public education and involvement are the first steps in any permanent, constructive change in our wretchedly inadequate, self-destroying, self-injuring, crime-encouraging system. Not that the public will straightaway rise up and ask for the radical changes that ought to be made. But once it knows, once it really perceives that the present pretentious procedure is falling on its face and endangering us all, once the public becomes informed, it will become correspondingly aroused. It will let its demands be known to legislatures and officials, and the situation will change.[23]

STUDY QUESTIONS

---

1. Identify and describe an imaginative delinquency prevention program in your community.
2. Has your community utilized general revenue-sharing funds for local delinquency prevention or control programs?

3. Is juvenile delinquency a serious social problem in your community?
4. Does your local police department utilize diversion in the disposition of juvenile cases?
5. Has a juvenile record hampered any of your acquaintances in acquiring employment? If so, how?
6. What does recognition, power, and respect mean to you? Would these concepts be perceived differently by a juvenile delinquent? Explain.
7. Identify the provocations, aggravations, and pressures you face in your school situation. Are similar pressures present in the life situation of the juvenile delinquent? Explain.
8. Differentiate between delinquency prevention and delinquency control.
9. How many of the minimum services required for an adequate delinquency prevention and control program have you found in your community?
10. How many bills, introduced in your state legislature this year, deal with the rights of children? How many passed? Were vetoed? Does your state have a Children's Lobby?
11. How might youth be used to achieve some stated program goal which you consider important in delinquency prevention and control?
12. Do the youngsters in your neighborhood understand their constitutional rights?
13. Do you feel the U.S. Supreme Court decisions (1966–1971) should have offered more procedural safeguards to the child? Why?
14. Does your state permit trial by jury in state juvenile delinquency hearings?
15. Assess the Great Society programs which endeavored to eliminate poverty. Determine whether your community has attempted to meet the needs of its citizens through general revenue-sharing funds.

NOTES

1. Only one article in the field of delinquency control assumes that a police record does not stigmatize a youth: James Vandiver, "Juvenile Records Are Justifiable," *Police*, 15 (November-December 1970): 41–42. Those interested in the problem, see Appendix D, General Bibliography, Employment of Ex-Offenders.

2. A promising form of diversion is the Youth Services Bureau, see Chapter 3.

3. *Report to the President, 1970 White House Conference on Children* (Washington, D.C.: U.S. Government Printing Office, 1971), p. 373.

4. George Edwards, "In Defense of the Juvenile Court," *Juvenile Justice*, 23, no. 2 (August 1972): 5.

5. *Report to the President, 1970 White House Conference on Children* (Washington, D.C.: U.S. Government Printing Office, 1971), p. 369.

6. Personal communication in the author's files.

7. Alfred J. Kahn, Sheila B. Kamerman, and Brenda G. McGowan, *Child Advocacy: Report of a National Baseline Study*, U.S. Department of Health, Education, and Welfare, Office of Child Development (Washington, D.C.: U.S. Government Printing Office, 1973), p. 37.

8. Ibid., pp. 15 and 45.

9. Further information is available from the Office of Children's Services, 270 Broadway, New York City, New York.

10. For a history of the youth involvement concept see J. Robert Weber and Carson Custer, *Youth Involvement*, U.S. Dept. of Health, Education, and Welfare, Social and Rehabilitation Service, Youth Development and Delinquency Prevention Administration (Washington, D.C.: U.S. Government Printing Office, 1970).

11. Fred Cohen, "A Lawyer Looks at Juvenile Justice," *Criminal Law Bulletin*, 7 (July-August 1971): 518. Copyright © 1971 by Warren, Gorham & Lamont, Inc., Boston, Massachusetts. All rights reserved. Reprinted with permission.

12. *Commonwealth* v. *Fisher*, 213 Pa. 48, 62 Atl. 198 (1905).

13. *Kent* v. *United States*, 383 U.S. 541, 16 L.Ed.2d 84, 86 S.Ct. 1045 (1966).

14. See sources in Appendix D, General Bibliography, under Children's Rights.

15. National Council on Crime and Delinquency, *Standard Juvenile Court Act* 6th ed. (New York: National Council on Crime and Delinquency, 1959.)

16. Nicholas N. Kittrie, *The Right to be Different: Deviance and Enforced Therapy* (Baltimore: Johns Hopkins Press, 1971), p. 122. Copyright The Johns Hopkins University.

17. State of California, *Welfare and Institutions Code*, Section 625. (Amended by Stats. 1971, Ch. 1748).

18. *Miranda* v. *Arizona*, 384 U.S. 436, 86 S.Ct. 1602 (1966).

19. A. Bruce Ferguson and Alan C. Douglas, "A Study of Juvenile Waiver," *San Diego Law Review*, 7 (1970): 39–54.

20. *McKeiver* v. *Pennsylvania*, 403 U.S. 528, 29 L.Ed.2d 647, 91 S.Ct. 1976 (June, 1971).

21. Dorothy E. Bradbury, *The Children's Bureau and Juvenile Delinquency*, U.S. Department of Health, Education, and Welfare, Welfare Administration, Children's Bureau (Washington, D.C.: U.S. Government Printing Office, 1960), p. 1.

22. See David C. Coleman III, "The State and Local Fiscal Assistance Act of 1972: General Revenue Sharing," *Clearinghouse Review*, 6, no. 9 (January 1973): 529–533, a publication of National Clearinghouse for Legal Services, Northwestern University School of Law. See also Appendix D, General Bibliography, under Revenue Sharing.

23. Karl Menninger, *The Crime of Punishment* (New York: The Viking Press, 1968), pp. 278–279. From THE CRIME OF PUNISHMENT by Karl Menninger, M.D. Copyright © 1966, 1968 by Jeannetta Lyle Menninger. All rights reserved. Reprinted by permission of The Viking Press, Inc.

DEFINING DELINQUENCY

2

Juvenile delinquency refers to the misbehavior of youth. Public fear of crime and violence tends to impose the delinquency label on youth indiscriminately. Fritz Redl said that communities exhibit "love of kids, neglect of children, and hatred of youth."[1] His observation applies to the legal definition of delinquency which makes the justice system clamp down on children and youth.

We are still a long way from being able to define delinquency satisfactorily. We have come far enough to know that a useful definition can be arrived at only when we are familiar with the issues surrounding (1) the legal definition of delinquency; (2) the methods of measuring delinquency; and (3) a nonlegal definition of delinquency.

The delinquency label tends to make youngsters delinquent. Marvin Wolfgang suggests

> . . . the *pivotal point of social cost reduction* appears to be when juveniles have committed their *first* offense. To produce delinquency desisting at this stage in the biography of the child might thus be considered the most efficient procedure.[2]

In a recent study Wolfgang, Figlio, and Sellin emphasized that the first offense can lead to a continued delinquency pattern.[3] In *Delinquency in a Birth Cohort,* they systematically studied 9,945 Philadelphia boys born in 1945, through the ages of 10 to 18; a majority were born and attended schools there from the first grade. In this cohort analysis—the study over an extended period of time of a number of individuals with some common characteristic—it was possible to follow the careers of all the youngsters including those having one or more contacts with the police.

An analysis of the total birth cohort reveals the following:

1. 35 percent of the boys (N=3,475) experienced at least one contact with the police and were labeled delinquent.
2. Police contacts were recorded for 29 percent of the white males and 50 percent of the nonwhite males in the birth cohort.
3. Among the delinquents, 46 percent were single, one-time offenders and 54 percent were recidivists.
4. The boys who were known to the police on one or more occasions committed a total of 10,214 delinquent acts between the ages of 7 and 17. However, the 1,862 recidivists were responsible for 8,601 of these offenses.
5. Nearly three-fourths of the offenses committed by the one-time only offenders were status offenses such as running away from home, incorrigibility, and truancy. This pattern is the same for both whites and nonwhites.
6. Recidivists committing five or more offenses were classified as chronic offenders. The 627 chronic offenders comprised 18 percent of the delinquent cohort and 6.3 percent of the total birth cohort. However, the chronic offenders were responsible for 5,305 delinquencies, or 52 percent of the delinquencies committed by the delinquency cohort.
7. The chronic offenders committed 71 percent of the robberies, 62 percent of the property offenses (i.e., auto theft, burglary, and larceny), and 53 percent of the personal attacks (i.e., homicide, simple or aggravated assault, and rape).
8. The chronic offender committed most of the offenses involving bodily injury to others. Chronic offenders carried out 45 percent of the violent crimes committed by white males in the delinquent cohort while the chronic offender committed 70 percent of the violent crimes carried out by the nonwhite males in the study.[4]

The Pennsylvania study emphasizes the need to create alternatives to the ingrained punishment response. Services to youngsters seem to promise most for public safety. Wolfgang concludes:

> It is clear that *preventing the group of nonwhite lower SES* [socio-economic status] *boys from continuing delinquency*

after their first offense would indeed produce the maximum delinquency reduction. By focusing resources and attention on the lower SES nonwhite subset of a birth cohort who have a first delinquency, not only would the general rate of delinquency be affected; the most serious acts, those involving physical violence or assault on others, would be most *drastically decreased.*[5]

THE LEGAL DEFINITION

A juvenile becomes eligible for processing by police, courts, and corrections when his misbehavior coincides with conduct legally defined as delinquent. The legal definitions vary from state to state, and include a wide variety of behavior ranging from criminal (i.e., robbery, auto theft, or burglary) through forms of conduct not illegal when committed by adults (i.e., refusal to obey the reasonable orders of parents or guardians, habitual truancy).

Committing Adult Crimes

All the states agree that a juvenile is delinquent if he is found guilty of an act considered a crime if committed by an adult. Crime refers to conduct prohibited by law, for which legislative bodies specify prescribed punishments upon conviction in court. Certain crimes—murder, rape, robbery, assault, forgery, and burglary—have received universal disapproval; these offenses are felonies and the sanctions are severe. Misdemeanors involve behavior considered less dangerous to the public. Severity of punishment usually serves as the guide to the separation of crimes into felonies and misdemeanors. The recommendation for incarceration in felony cases is one year or more, and for misdemeanors less than one year. The penal code for each state provides legal definitions for criminal behavior and the nature of the sanctions imposed. The classification of crimes used by the Federal Bureau of Investigation in its national crime reporting system is helpful for those who desire a uniform set of definitions for the most frequently reported crimes.[6]

Status (Non-adult) Offenses

Specific juvenile delinquency statutes vary from state to state. In an attempt to protect juveniles from possible adult criminal careers the juvenile court movement has designated various forms of noncriminal conduct as potential trouble areas for youth. The runaway, the truant, and the curfew violator represent forms of juvenile behavior designated as status offenses in order to differentiate them from adult crimes (see Appendix D, General Bibliography, Status Offenses).

Sussmann and Baum identify over 30 status offenses which appear in the delinquency statutes of the various states.[7] No state has adopted all of the acts enumerated in the Sussmann and Baum listing; the number of juvenile offenses called delinquent by any one state's delinquency laws ranges from one item to nearly one-half the acts on the list. States are cutting down on the type of offense legally defined as delinquent and so the total number is being reduced. Evidence does not support the continued use of such noncriminal legislation.[8]

Status offenses comprise the bulk of referrals to juvenile court, and a review of them reveals a tremendous range of items, some designated as non-adult crimes by Sussmann and Baum and others similar to the state misdemeanant statutes. Many states put status offenses under a general category such as "children in need of supervision" (Colorado); "minor otherwise in need of supervision" (Illinois); or "person in need of supervision" (New York). California has not adopted this form of legislation but gives the child a safeguard under Section 601—namely, he may not be committed to the California Youth Authority until his second appearance before the juvenile court. Unfortunately, such a child is in need of immediate treatment and, if it is not forthcoming a second appearance before the juvenile court is likely. In 1975, the California Youth Authority declared it would no longer accept young people who have committed status offenses. The decision grew out of concern about the effect of their association with more difficult wards, who comprise most of the institution's population. One probation department, moved by the failure of its juvenile court to provide services for these children at the time of their first court appearance, instituted immediate short-term counseling in lieu of long-term open-ended services available through the traditional procedures of the court.

Early success in the program is noted; fewer than 3 percent of the cases required court processing, and a smaller number of juveniles were rebooked on new offenses within the next seven months.[9]

Status offense legislation is often ambiguously worded; the following is an illustration from the California Welfare and Institutions Code (Section 601):

> Any person under the age of 18 years who persistently or habitually refuses to obey the reasonable and proper orders or directions of his parents, guardian, custodian or school authorities, or who is beyond the control of such person, or any person who is a habitual truant from school within the meaning of any law of this state, or who from any cause is in danger of leading an idle, dissolute, lewd, or immoral life, is within the jurisdiction of the juvenile court which may adjudge such person to be a ward of the court.[10]

The most ambiguous item here refers to an idle, dissolute, lewd or immoral life. How does a youngster prove he is none of these things? A vague charge which defies treatment is an additional problem for probation officers. Fortunately, the courts have declared unconstitutional that portion of the California Welfare and Institutions Code (Section 601) which reads "or who from any cause is in danger of leading an idle, dissolute, lewd or immoral life." Courts declared the wording too vague to serve as a standard for the arrest or adjudication of a juvenile as a ward of the juvenile court.[11] Hopefully, other states will reassess their laws for constitutionality and precise meaning.

Efforts to repeal status offense legislation have met resistance in various states. Opponents of repeal offer the following arguments: (1) such offenses, which may be committed only by those of juvenile court age, indicate to adults the future criminals; (2) delinquency cannot be prevented unless such juveniles are discovered; and (3) non-adult offenses like truancy may shield adult offenses. The abolition of status offenses would not resolve the need for services to children whose problems bring them to the attention of the juvenile court or the labeling of delinquency. Juveniles need not be processed in the juvenile justice system in order to receive services. Therefore, we should redefine delinquency and exclude the status offenses. Of course, the diversion of potential delinquents from the system requires that intensive services be available.

A redefinition of the law, which designates some conduct as delinquent, would help prevent delinquency; it would reduce the stigma of arrest for a large number of juveniles whose misbehavior is presently included in the delinquency statutes. Arrest can remove the dangerous juvenile from the community but it is less successful in deterring future delinquent and criminal behavior. The success of courts and corrections has been hampered by lack of manpower; many cases have received impersonal handling. Glaser says, "The younger a prisoner is when first arrested, convicted, or confined for any crime, the more likely he is to continue in crime."[12] Thus, a dual problem is present: (1) the legal definition of delinquency is characterized by gross imprecision, and (2) the processing of juveniles in the formal authoritarian agencies is likely to reinforce the pattern of delinquency which the system proposes to eradicate.

Remember that a juvenile is an official delinquent only after the following conditions are met:

1. the behavior is defined as delinquency in the specific statutes of the state or jurisdiction in which the misbehavior or crime occurred;
2. the youngster is processed through the juvenile court where the delinquency label may or may not be applied.

A New Legal Definition?

Perhaps the most obvious way to prevent delinquency is to redefine it by statute—and to include as delinquent only that conduct defined as criminal when engaged in by an adult. We, therefore, remove all those forms of youthful behavior clearly outside the definition of criminality (as defined in the penal codes). The term *misbehavior* might be substituted for *status offense*. When the community defines the actions of the youngster as misbehavior, we can be certain that the child is in conflict with the neighborhood. Then, the community can immediately use its services for the youth in trouble. The availability of services, not the imposition of the status offense label, is more likely to assure the community that alleviation is possible. Of course, you may prefer the use of the term *person in need of supervision* rather than *misbehavior*. A new concept, *family in need of service*,[13] provides the court with jurisdiction over the family unit rather than the individual child. This approach permits the refocusing of individualized services, formerly directed toward the child, to the whole family of the neglected or unruly child.

Age Limits for Delinquency

Not only do we need new concepts for defining delinquency; we also need to set uniform age limits in the definition. Presently, statutes from state to state differ in the following categories: (1) the lower age limit; (2) upper age limit; (3) upper age limits for boys and girls; and, (4) age limits for transferring a juvenile to the adult court.

A lower age limit is seldom found in the laws of juvenile delinquency although six states have minimum ages under which a child cannot be charged with delinquent acts. The minimum age is seven in Massachusetts and New York, and ten in Colorado, Mississippi, Texas, and Vermont. For those who fear that the juvenile court might violate the rights of a child in the absence of a specified lower age limit in the juvenile delinquency statute, Sanford Fox says, "It may be significant to note that even in the absence of a minimum age in the statutes, there are no reported cases involving an attempt to charge delinquency against a child under the common law immunity age of seven. Administrative common sense appears to supplement legislative drafting."[14] However, the same writer warns that "under the great majority of laws it appears possible for a child to be found delinquent at any time from the day it is born, *unless* there is some continued vitality to the common law rule of immunity below the age of seven. Having the law incorporate such an immunity would clearly be preferable . . ."[15]

The absence of a specific lower age limit in the statutes can be traced to: (1) a body of common law which holds that a child under the age of seven is granted immunity from prosecution for a crime; and (2) the juvenile court philosophy of assisting children who violate adult criminal statutes, who need supervision because their behavior is defined as delinquent in the statute, and children who are defined as neglected or dependent.

The absence of a lower age limit in the legal definition of juvenile delinquency would not appear to endanger juveniles entering the system of juvenile justice. Common law offers protection to the child since special attention is given to immunity below age seven and particular consideration is granted to juveniles until the age of 14. Some writers, such as Ted Rubin, suggest that the lower age limit be raised to 10, 11, or 12. A community then could accept the premise that children under a specific age should be handled by agencies other than the juvenile court.[16]

The upper age limit for juvenile court jurisdiction is always stated in the legal definition of delinquency. Most states follow the recommendation found in the Standard Juvenile Court Act which sets "less than 18" as the upper age limit. Other states designate the sixteenth or seventeenth birthday as the upper limit.

Some states designate different upper age limits for girls and boys. The jurisdiction of the juvenile court is extended an additional year or two for girls in such instances. Different upper age limits for boys and girls are found in the juvenile delinquency statutes of Illinois, Oklahoma, and Texas. These distinctions have been declared unconstitutional in the courts. The New York Family Court Act designates that the court has exclusive jurisdiction over a "juvenile delinquent" or a "person in need of supervision." "Juvenile delinquent" means a person over 7 and less than 16 years of age, who commits any act which, if committed by an adult, would constitute a crime. The latter term refers to males less than age 16 and females under age 18 who are habitually truant, incorrigible, ungovernable, or habitually disobedient and beyond the lawful control of parent or other lawful authority. However, in 1972 the New York Court of Appeals ruled unconstitutional that portion of the state's "person in need of supervision" statute which discriminates against women on the basis of age.[17] The state supreme court has ruled that it is unfair to subject a girl of 16 or 17 to a loss of liberty for conduct which is entirely acceptable for a boy of the same age. Consult current issues of *Juvenile Court Digest*, published by the National Council of Juvenile Court Judges, for recent changes in juvenile delinquency legislation.[18]

The presence of an upper age limit for juvenile delinquency is accompanied by provisions for the transfer of serious cases from the juvenile court to the adult court in many states. The Advisory

Council of Judges of the National Council on Crime and Delinquency has issued the following policy statement dealing with the transfer of such cases:

> If the petition in the case of a child sixteen years of age or older is based on an act which would be a felony if committed by an adult, and if the court after full investigation and a hearing deems it contrary to the best interest of the child or the public to retain jurisdiction, it may in its discretion certify him to the criminal court having jurisdiction of such felonies committed by adults. No child under sixteen years of age at the time of commission of the act shall be so certified.[19]

And, later, the advisory council added:

> In brief, the criteria to be considered by the court . . . are (1) the prior record and character of the minor, his physical and mental maturity, and his pattern of living; (2) the type of offense —whether it demonstrated viciousness or involved force or violence; and (3) the comparable adequacy and suitability of facilities available to the juvenile and criminal courts.[20]

States differ in their power to transfer certain juvenile cases to the adult court for criminal prosecution. Such statutes are likely to include a minimum age under which a youngster may not be transferred to criminal court. It varies from age 13 to 18, but the most frequently cited minimum is 14 or 16. There is no lower age limit in Alaska, New Hampshire, and South Dakota, and two states, Kentucky and Maryland, may disregard their minimum when the juvenile is charged with certain serious offenses. A majority of states are divided on whether to restrict waiver of jurisdiction on the basis of the offense. Therefore, each state may decide whether to place a youngster under adult jurisdiction for all offenses which would be a felony if committed by an adult; it may specify a list of felonies that apply to juveniles; or, it may claim that a violation of any criminal statute is sufficient cause for a juvenile to face adult prosecution. A few states offer additional guidelines for use by juvenile court judges considering case transfers. And, a number of states are introducing legislation seeking mandatory transfer of juvenile cases to criminal courts when the offense is one of violence and there is a history of previous juvenile court appearances.

There is little controversy associated with the age categories set in delinquency legislation. However, all juvenile delinquency statutes throughout the country should reflect: (1) a uniform upper age limit and (2) a specified lower age limit. Some authorities recommend that concurrent jurisdiction of juvenile and adult courts be omitted from juvenile court law. This position reflects the view that the juvenile court should have absolute jurisdiction over certain ages. The student can find the "age under which the juvenile court has original jurisdiction" listed by state and county in the appendix to *Juvenile Court Statistics* (see Appendix D, General Bibliography, Statistics).

MEASURING DELINQUENCY

We are ready now to examine the second approach to defining delinquency; when we know how delinquency is measured, we have a far better idea of what it means. Control agencies deal with the juvenile offender after they learn that a delinquent act has been committed; thus, the two major sources of information on the volume of delinquency in this country are arrests and juvenile court cases.

Arrests

To be able to interpret crime statistics, we must know the processes involved. The decision to arrest is crucial, and is usually determined by the police officer. The concern of the police for youth is documented in the statistics on the disposition of juveniles taken into custody. The sensitivity of police to the unnecessary labeling of youth as delinquents deserves much more recognition than is noted in the literature. In fact, the police are as likely to dispose of a juvenile arrest by handling the case within the department as they are to refer the case to the juvenile court. In other words, the police department diverts the case rather than permit it to proceed further along within the system. In the 1970s, approximately 95 percent of juvenile offenders taken into custody (arrested) by the police have been handled within the department and released, or referred to juvenile court. Statistics show that 50 percent are referred to juvenile court jurisdiction while 45 percent are handled by the police and released. Thus, only 5 percent of juvenile arrests are referred to welfare agencies, other police agencies, or to the adult criminal court. As youth service bureaus are introduced, the juvenile court referrals will decrease.

The most important source of arrest information is the annual *Uniform Crime Reports for the United States,* published each August by the FBI since 1930 (see Appendix D, General Bibliography, Statistics). This compilation, based on voluntary information submitted by local law enforcement agencies, is a statistical source for offenses known and cleared by arrest. It includes the following information (see the appropriate table in a current issue):

1. Police disposition of juvenile offenders taken into custody
    a. Handled within the department and released
    b. Referred to juvenile court jurisdiction
    c. Referred to welfare agency
    d. Referred to other police agency
    e. Referred to criminal or adult court
2. Total arrests by age category and offense
    a. Under age 18: city, suburban, and rural arrests
    b. Under age 15: city, suburban, and rural arrests
3. Number of full-time police department employees in cities with a population of 25,000 or more. This listing gives the number of sworn officers and civilians in each department according to state and city. It is very helpful in selecting cities for in-depth analysis of the delinquency problem.

Of course, because the *Uniform Crime Reports* deal only with crimes known to the police, it is impossible to determine the amount of unreported crime and delinquency. Studies of undetected delinquency suggest that many juveniles and adults commit offenses never known to the police (see Appendix D, General Bibliography, Undetected Delinquency). The development of the self-reporting technique has permitted further study of delinquencies unknown to the police. In this research method, an academician usually directly questions juveniles or adults about one or more forms of behavior found in the criminal code or the juvenile delinquency laws.

When information from official and unofficial sources is brought together, we can get an idea of how much crime is committed in a community. This amount is determined by factors outside the control of national agencies whose task is gathering statistics. Such a study requires an intimate knowledge of how social-planning and policy decisions are made in the local juvenile justice system (i.e., the police, courts, non-authoritarian agencies) and how the local system implements state and federal guidelines on delinquency prevention and control. A wealth of unanalyzed data is available in the local juvenile court, probation department, and correctional institution.

From the *Uniform Crime Reports* we can find trends that emphasize the importance of juvenile arrests. Table 2-1 reveals the

TABLE 2-1

Recent Arrest Rates
for Persons under Age 18 for Crime Index Offenses

Offense charged	*Percentage of persons under age 18 arrested in 1973**	*Increase 1960-1973** (percent)*
Auto theft	57	51
Burglary	54	104
Larceny-theft	48	124
Robbery	34	299
Forcible rape	20	132
Aggravated assault	17	206
Murder and nonnegligent manslaughter	10	255

SOURCE: *Federal Bureau of Investigation, U.S. Department of Justice, *Uniform Crime Reports for the United States, 1973* (Washington, D.C.: U.S. Government Printing Office, 1974), p. 130. Arrests are based upon reports from 6,004 agencies with estimated 1973 population of 154,995,000.

**Ibid., p. 124. Percentage change in total arrest trends based upon reports from 2,378 agencies with estimated 1973 population of 94,251,000.

percentage of Crime Index offenses committed by juveniles under age 18 who were arrested during the 13-year period, 1960–73. Crime Index offenses are murder, forcible rape, robbery, aggravated assault, burglary, larceny-theft, and auto theft.[21] Persons under age 18 account for over 50 percent of the arrests for property crimes (i.e., auto theft, burglary, and larceny); arrests for crimes against the person are increasing substantially, although these crimes are still committed more frequently by adults. However, the arrest of juveniles for all Crime Index offenses increased 116 percent between 1960 and 1973.[22] The number of juveniles under age 18 arrested for all offenses (not only the Crime Index crimes) increased 144 percent from 1960 through 1973.[23] Also, 31 percent of all arrests reported to the Federal Bureau of Investigation in 1973 involved juveniles under 18.[24] Juveniles, 10 to 17 years of age, comprise approximately 16 percent of the United States population.

Juvenile Court Cases

The second major source of information for juvenile delinquency statistics is *Juvenile Court Statistics,* issued yearly by the Office of Youth Development (see Appendix D, General Bibliography, Statistics). This publication is useful in showing:

1. How frequently the juvenile court is utilized by the community in handling known delinquencies.
2. The tendency of the police to handle juvenile offenders within the police department and then release them rather than refer them all to the juvenile court.

The report also provides data on:

1. Types of juvenile courts—urban, semiurban, rural—determined by the percentage of the population in each area.
2. Cases, according to
   (a) delinquency;
   (b) dependency and neglect;
   (c) traffic; and

(d) special proceedings, which include cases involving adoption, institutional commitment for special purposes, application for consent to marry or to enlist in the armed forces, determination of custody or guardianship of a child, or permission (to hospitals) to operate on a child. Many juvenile courts do not handle special proceedings.

3. Methods of case handling, i.e.,
   (a) judicial or official where the court has acted on the basis of a petition or motion; or
   (b) nonjudicial or unofficial where the cases have been adjusted by the judge, referee, probation officer, or officer of the court without the invocation of the court's jurisdiction through petition or motion.
4. Cases according to sex.

The national juvenile court statistical reporting program does not identify the types of offenses as does the Federal Bureau of Investigation. It has been estimated that 1,143,700 juvenile delinquency cases (excluding traffic offenses) were handled by all juvenile courts in 1973. The estimated number of children involved in these cases was about 986,000 since some were referred to the court more than once during the year; they represent almost 3 percent of all children in the country between 10 and 17.[25] Since 1949, the number of cases referred to juvenile court has continued to rise each year, except for slight decreases in 1961 and 1972.[26] Delinquency is primarily a problem for boys, but the traditional pattern, four boys for every girl, is being reduced. By 1973, one girl for every three boys was being referred to the juvenile court.

In a recent projection, the Office of Youth Development in the U.S. Department of Health, Education, and Welfare has conservatively stated that an increasing number of children will be handled by juvenile courts in the future. Table 2-2 suggests that over 1,410,000 juvenile delinquency cases will be referred to the juvenile courts by 1977.

Most frequently, the courts do not file a petition in juvenile delinquency cases; 54 percent in 1973 were nonjudicial.[27] When a case is handled unofficially or nonjudicially, the juvenile court is using diversion; thus, there can be diversion even after the case is referred to juvenile court. This method permits a child to avoid further involvement with the judicial system. Greater use of

TABLE 2-2

Rate of Referrals to Juvenile Court, 1974–77
—A Projection

Year	*Child population 10-17*	*Rate (%)*	*Court delinquency cases*
1974	33,136,000	3.7	1,226,000
1975	33,311,000	3.9	1,299,000
1976	33,049,000	4.1	1,355,000
1977	32,787,000	4.3	1,410,000

SOURCE: Robert J. Gemignani, "Youth Services Systems: Diverting Youth from the Juvenile Justice System," *Delinquency Prevention Reporter*, July-August 1972, p. 2.

diversion could save more than $1.3 billion dollars in official court costs between 1974 and 1977. Table 2-3 reveals the projected cost savings if our communities considered services to youth outside of the justice system. The actual costs within the system include the following: intake for 100 percent of the cases, probation service for 25 percent, training schools for 10 percent, and community services to 10 percent of the court referrals. It is estimated that the

TABLE 2-3

Cost Savings of a Suggested Plan of Diversion

Year	*Actual costs in juvenile justice system*	*Diversion rate*	*Revised costs in juvenile justice system*	*Savings*
1974	$1,042,000,000	6%	$873,000,000	$ 169,000,000
1975	1,104,000,000	12%	821,000,000	283,000,000
1976	1,152,000,000	18%	758,000,000	394,000,000
1977	1,199,000,000	25%	694,000,000	505,000,000
		Cumulative Savings		$1,351,000,000

SOURCE: Robert J. Gemignani, "Youth Services Systems: Diverting Youth from the Juvenile Justice System," *Delinquency Prevention Reporter*, July-August 1972, p. 2.

annual cost per youth processed through the juvenile justice system is: referral and intake, $100.00; probation services, $500.00; training schools, $5,700.00; other residential commitments (i.e., foster care, group homes, or halfway houses), $1,500.00.[28] Some caution is required in assessing the cumulative savings that diversion accomplishes. The figures do not take into account the cost of the programs—services paid for outside the justice system obviously cut court costs.

Summary

Measuring official delinquency is limited to the voluntary reporting of police and the juvenile court. The reports of academicians inform us about undetected delinquency, not known to the official delinquency processing agencies. Police discretion and community attitudes influence the imposition of the delinquency label. Hopefully, more accurate information will become available in the future. Perhaps comprehensive state plans, which chart the direction of delinquency prevention and control programs, will provide an atmosphere for more accurate measurement. More important, however, is that the community provide a youth service bureau which permits a youngster to seek help without fear of arrest. Services without stigma give the most accurate measurement of detected and undetected delinquency.

The volume of juvenile delinquency is determined by many factors much too elusive to be captured by the statistics of national agencies. These agencies do provide useful guidelines which permit us to determine the magnitude of the problem. They have served us well if our community makes delinquency prevention and control an item of high priority. But it is up to the student to determine the size of the problem in his community. He will want to explore several areas in order to determine the extent of official delinquency:

1. The number of status offenses present in the juvenile statutes of his state. The number of juveniles processed by the police and the juvenile court on status and nonstatus offenses in his community.

2. The disposition of juvenile cases by the police (handled within the department or by referral to juvenile court) and the juvenile court (judicial or nonjudicial handling) in the jurisdiction under study.
3. The use of probation, the youth service bureau, and the statewide corrections agency (i.e., the correctional institution) by the juvenile court.
4. The availability of alternate methods of treating juvenile offenders in the community (e.g., resources *outside* of the police, the juvenile court, and corrections).

Through these methods, the student can determine whether the community is aware of its delinquency problems.

THE NONLEGAL DEFINITION

The legal definition of delinquency is important because it determines who can be sanctioned for conduct which is disapproved by the community. A juvenile encounters the formal justice system only after he violates delinquency statutes and his behavior is known and acted upon by the police or the juvenile court. Thus, the legal definition of delinquency determines entrance into the system of juvenile justice.

A nonlegal definition of delinquency affords a framework for understanding the misbehavior of youth. It does not presuppose processing through the system of police, courts, and corrections. Nor does it assume discovery of delinquent behavior by others. It serves as an appropriate knowledge base for future programming by agencies, peers, ex-offender self-help organizations, and the juvenile himself. In other words, the legal definition answers the question "Who is eligible for the delinquency label?" and the nonlegal definition endeavors to explore "Why is this youth a delinquent?"

We need an entire chapter to explore what makes young people misbehave. As you read it, remember that people are still crying out for a way to define delinquency. An understanding of the causes brings us closer to satisfying this need.

STUDY QUESTIONS

1. When should intensive services for delinquent youth be introduced?
2. Identify a form of behavior which is delinquency when committed by a juvenile but not criminality when committed by an adult.
3. How many items appear in the status offense category of the juvenile delinquency law in your state?
4. What are the services needed by those classified as persons in need of supervision?
5. Do the juvenile delinquency laws of your state specify a lower age limit? What is the upper age limit? Do the upper age limits differ for boys and girls?
6. Have efforts to repeal status offense legislation met with resistance in your state? If so, why?
7. When is a juvenile an official delinquent?
8. Will recent legislation lowering the age of majority from 21 to 18 have an impact on juvenile court laws?
9. Review the criteria to be considered by the juvenile court when transferring a case to the adult criminal court.
10. What is meant by concurrent jurisdiction?
11. Name two major sources of information on the volume of delinquency in this country.
12. Juveniles, age 10 to 17, comprise what percentage of the United States population at this time?
13. What are the seven Crime Index offenses?
14. What is the most frequent form of court handling?
15. Differentiate between the legal and nonlegal definition of delinquency.

NOTES

1. Fritz Redl, *When We Deal with Children: Selected Writings* (New York: Free Press, 1966), p. 9.

2. Marvin E. Wolfgang, *Youth and Violence,* U.S. Department of Health, Education, and Welfare, Social and Rehabilitation Service, Youth Development and Delinquency Prevention Administration (Washington, D.C.: U.S. Government Printing Office, 1970), p. 42.

3. Marvin E. Wolfgang, Robert M. Figlio, and Thorsten Sellin, *Delinquency in a Birth Cohort* (Chicago: University of Chicago Press, 1972).

4. M. Wolfgang, *Youth and Violence,* pp. 39–48.

5. Ibid., p. 48.

6. Federal Bureau of Investigation, U.S. Department of Justice, *Uniform Crime Reports for the United States, 1973* (Washington, D.C.: U.S. Government Printing Office, 1974), pp. 55–56.

7. See Frederick B. Sussmann and Frederic S. Baum, *Law of Juvenile Delinquency,* 3rd ed. (Dobbs Ferry, New York: Oceana Publications, 1968), pp. 11–14.

8. See Ted Rubin, *Law as an Agent of Delinquency Prevention,* U.S. Department of Health, Education, and Welfare, Social and Rehabilitation Service, Youth Development and Delinquency Prevention Administration (Washington, D.C.: U.S. Government Printing Office, 1971), pp. 1–15.

9. Roger Baron, Floyd Feeney, and Warren Thornton, "Preventing Delinquency Through Diversion: The Sacramento County 601 Diversion Project," *Federal Probation,* 37, no. 1 (March 1973): 13–18.

10. California Welfare and Institutions Code, Section 601 (West Supplement, 1971).

11. See *Gonzalez* v. *Mailliard,* U.S. Northern District of California No. 50424 (February 9, 1971).

12. Daniel Glaser, *The Effectiveness of a Prison and Parole System* Abridged ed. (Indianapolis: Bobbs-Merrill Co., 1969), p. 19.

13. Aidan R. Gough and Mary Ann Grilli, "The Unruly Child and the Law: Toward a Focus on the Family," *Juvenile Justice,* 24, no. 3 (November 1972): 9–12.

14. Sanford F. Fox, *The Law of Juvenile Courts in a Nutshell* (St. Paul: West Publishing Co., 1971), p. 18.

15. Ibid., p. 16.

16. Rubin, *Law as an Agent,* p. 31.

17. *A. v. City of New York,* 286 N.E.2d 432 (1972).

18. *Juvenile Court Digest* is published bimonthly by the National Council of Juvenile Court Judges, P.O. Box 8978, University Station, Reno, Nevada 89507.

19. "Standard Juvenile Court Act—Text and Commentary," *National Probation and Parole Association Journal,* 5 (October 1959): 353.

20. Advisory Council of Judges of the National Council on Crime and Delinquency, "Transfer of Cases Between Juvenile and Criminal Courts: A Policy Statement," *Crime and Delinquency,* 8 (January 1962): 7.

21. *Uniform Crime Reports for the United States, 1973,* p. 55.

22. Ibid., p. 124.

23. Ibid., p. 124.

24. Ibid., p. 30.

25. *Juvenile Court Statistics, 1973,* U.S. Department of Health, Education, and Welfare, Office of Human Development, Office of Youth Development (Washington, D.C.: U.S. Government Printing Office, 1975), p. 1.

26. Ibid., p. 1.

27. Ibid., p. 3.

28. Robert J. Gemignani, "Youth Services Systems: Diverting Youth from the Juvenile Justice System," *Delinquency Prevention Reporter* (July-August 1972): 2.

THE CAUSES OF DELINQUENCY

EARLY VIEWS
BIOLOGICAL EXPLANATIONS
MENTAL HEALTH VIEWS
CONTRIBUTIONS OF SOCIOLOGY
USING THEORY IN PRACTICE

In this chapter, we explore what makes youngsters misbehave and see how people have explained delinquency since the 1700s. Beginning with the early views, we examine biological and then mental-health explanations. I-Level treatment, so successful in California, is fully described. The most space goes to sociology's contribution, which is so specific about the youngster in trouble. The chapter ends by showing how these theories are, and can be, helpful in practice.

EARLY VIEWS

Before 1700 there was confusion in legal matters generally due to vague definitions of what was crime and what was proper punishment. If questions did arise about why people commit crimes they were likely to be referred to religious concepts. About this period, Maestro tells us:

> Contradictions and incongruities in the laws were due to the different influences that through the centuries had altered the old Roman code. Some of the old laws were still in existence, some had been changed, and some new ones had been added. The lack of rational codes and scales of punishments was the cause of unavoidable arbitrariness in the decisions of the judges.[1]

Intellectual sniping directed piecemeal against the criminal justice system culminated in a sweeping attack delivered by a young Italian lawyer, Cesare Beccaria. His essay, *On Crimes and*

Punishments (1764), was the beginning of the end of the old system. Voltaire read the essay and was deeply impressed. He wrote a commentary that appeared in later editions of the work. The essay was widely distributed in Europe and helped create the mood for penal reform.

George Vold has characterized the intellectual climate of the time as follows:

1. An original state of Nature, or of Grace, or of Innocence.
2. Man's emergence from this state involved the application of his reason as a responsible individual:
   a. According to the Doctrine of the Fall (Sin—Garden of Eden), all mankind lives in suffering and pain, because the first human pair chose to disobey Divine injunction.
   b. Under social contract theories individuals come together and contract to form a society; that is, presumably, they survey the pros and cons—what to gain and what to lose—and come to deliberate agreement to live together in a society, each giving up something in order to get other benefits in return.
3. Acceptance of the human "will" as a psychological reality, a faculty or trait of the individual which regulates and controls behavior:
   a. In general, the will was "free"—that is, there were no limitations (except those obvious to common sense such as willing to fly, or to walk on water, and so on) to the choices an individual could make.
   b. "God" and the "Devil" could influence "will"—and so apparently could nature, i.e., impulses or instincts, yet in specific action of the individual the will was "free." Thus:
      w. Montesquieu finds that society is due to four impulses or desires: peace, hunger, sex, and social desires (sociability).
      x. Rousseau made desire for companionship the basis for the formation of society.
      y. Hobbes conceived of "fear" as elemental drive causing men to form societies and accept the necessary restraints. All these, apparently affected the "will," yet in individual action the choice was free.

z. Voltaire recognized that "will" may be strong or weak, thus influencing behavior, but still did not question the basic doctrine of "will," as motive or mainspring of human behavior.

4. Acceptance of idea that the principal instrument for control (affecting the will to behave) of behavior is fear—especially fear of pain.
5. Acceptance of "punishment" (i.e., infliction of pain, humiliation, and disgrace) as principal method of operating to create "fear" necessary to influence the "will" and thus to control behavior.
6. Acceptance of the "right" of society to punish the individual; and, in the pertod preceding Beccaria, transferring this right to the political state exclusively for execution. This follows logically with the state as the strongest practical authority.
7. Acceptance of and experience with some "code of criminal law," or better described as some "system of punishments for forbidden acts." With the growth and development of the national states, replacing the limited controls of the feudal chiefs, centralization in the realm of law, courts, and the police follows.[2]

Against this background, Beccaria outlined his principles about punishment. His contribution is summarized by his biographer:

> Beccaria put the problem of punishments on a new plane, stating that the purpose of penalties is not retribution, but prevention; justice requires a right proportion between crimes and punishments, but the purpose of penalties is to prevent a criminal from doing more harm and to deter others from doing similar damage. . . . Beccaria wanted a society of kind and civilized people and he believed that the abolition of cruel punishments, including the death penalty, would contribute to the formation of such a society.[3]

Beccaria and his followers—the classical school—felt it would be more humane to provide equitable punishments for crime. Beccaria criticized the excessive harshness of his time; believing that pain and pleasure strongly determine the direction of human actions, he conceived the idea of uniform punishment for crime. The work of the sentencing judge was reduced to a legally calculated, administrative act. Punishments consisted of various penalties which were determined in advance by legislative mandate. There was no need for the sentencing judge to concern himself with background conditions. But as time passed, the application of systematic sentences brought additional injustice. It seemed fairer to apply differential sentences based upon an understanding of the individual and his crime. It was the beginning of individualized justice. This philosophy remained virtually unchanged until the nineteenth century and the rise of the positive school.

The founder of the positive school of criminology was an Italian physician, Cesare Lombroso. While serving in the Crimean War he began a careful anatomical observation of known criminals and the mentally ill. Following the war he interviewed Italian prisoners. Impressed with a notorious criminal, Vilella, he interviewed him extensively; soon after his study, Vilella died. Lombroso performed an autopsy; his findings appear in the introduction to the English edition of his work, *Crime: Its Causes and Remedies.* Here he develops his theory of atavism or the born criminal:

> At last I found in the skull of a brigand a very long series of atavistic anomalies, above all an enormous middle occipital fossa and a hypertrophy of the vermis analogous to those that are found in inferior vertebrates. At the sight of these strange anomalies the problem of the nature and of the origin of the criminal seemed to me resolved; the characteristics of primitive men and of inferior animals must be reproduced in our times.[4]

With this evidence, Lombroso decided that Vilella and a number of other criminals represented a return to the viciousness of animals. This reversion to an earlier, less civilized state he termed atavism. Therefore, he claimed, some individuals were born criminals. The theory was refuted, but it did lead to a new way of looking at crime—that is, the scientific study of the individual offender. The emphasis shifted to the offender and away from the sentence. The impact of Lombroso on criminological thought can be seen in the popularity of his book, *Criminal Man,* published in 1876 and revised or reprinted five times in the next 20 years. However, in his last book *Crime: Its Causes and Remedies,* 1911, his attention was centered upon social and cultural factors, not heredity. In fairness to him, we should note his conclusion at that time, "The fundamental proposition undoubtedly is that we ought to study not so much the abstract crime as the criminal."[5]

The scientific study of criminals was the important goal of the positive school. Later controversies raged among the adherents of this approach. However, it paved the way for many new explanations. They stressed the role of biology, psychology, psychiatry, and sociology in understanding those who violate the established laws. If the criminal was influenced by conditions within himself and his environment, then reformation was possible. Thus, the twentieth century became the age of criminal reform or "treatment to fit the offender." Later, the mood changed from treating the offender to adjusting the inequalities within American society.

BIOLOGICAL EXPLANATIONS

In a recent study workers in the field of delinquency control were questioned about which theory of delinquency "best explained" the delinquent act; respondents indicated that biological explanations were wholly inadequate.[6] Lombroso, the earliest proponent of this viewpoint, himself finally rejected the idea of the born criminal. Further refutation is found in Goring's study, *The English Convict*, published in 1913. This systematic study of 12,000 criminal recidivists, as well as a carefully selected sample of noncriminals, revealed no physical or criminal type.[7]

However, the idea of a born criminal type has an easy attraction. At the beginning of World War II an anthropologist from Harvard named Earnest Hooton sought to relate social behavior to individual physical characteristics. For 12 years he studied a (highly criticized) sample population composed of the following: prison and reformatory inmates, county jail prisoners, defective delinquents, insane civilians and the criminally insane, and sane civilians. He used elaborate body measurements to differentiate criminals from noncriminals and even attempted to relate body type to offense pattern. The results of his work were contained in the volume entitled *Crime and the Man*, which may be summarized in his own words:

> . . . I think that inherently inferior organisms are, for the most part, those who succumb to the adversities or temptations of their social environment and fall into antisocial behavior, and that it is impossible to improve and correct environment to a point at which these flawed and degenerate human beings will be able to succeed in honest social competition. The bad organism sullies a good environment and transforms it into one which is evil.[8]

Hooton's work was quickly rejected by a majority of those involved in criminological research.

In 1949, William Sheldon completed the last American study emphasizing a relationship between physique and the constitutional propensity toward crime and delinquency. He took photographs of 200 boys referred to a Boston social agency known as Hayden Goodwill Inn, and used these to relate physique and delinquent behavior. He defined this activity as somatotyping. Sheldon's basic body types were the endomorph who tends to put on fat easily and is characterized as an extrovert; the mesomorph who is athletic and aggressive; and the ectomorph who is thin (almost fragile) and tends to be introverted.[9] Sheldon hoped that his classification of delinquents would be used by others and refined more fully. However, his emphasis on constitutional inferiority and temperament was unpopular; he supported Hooton's premise that superiority and inferiority in individuals is predetermined by biological makeup. These values were unacceptable to criminologists.

In 1965, researchers decided that the elusive cause of crime and delinquency might be traced to genetics. Genetic factors are known to affect not only the sex of the infant and physical traits such as skin and eye color but also such factors as intelligence. The imbalance that results from an extra number 21 chromosome, for instance, produces mongolism, a syndrome associated with severe mental retardation. Chromosome imbalances also occur in XYY males who have an extra Y chromosome and in XXY males who have an extra X chromosome. Since the mid-1960s, the effects of these extra chromosomes upon behavior have been of particular interest, because reports appeared that XYY and XXY males were overrepresented among the mentally disordered or retarded who have committed some crime. As many as 3 percent of all such individuals have been reported to have an XXY or XYY genotype. However, there are also a great many socially well-adjusted, normally intelligent XYY and XXY males. It appears that an XYY or XXY infant is more likely (than a XY male) to eventually manifest deviant behavior; just how much greater his risk is, or why, is still unknown. And it is very probable that environmental factors also affect the likelihood of XYY or XXY individuals becoming delinquent.[10]

MENTAL HEALTH VIEWS

The mental health profession, composed of psychiatrists, psychoanalysts, psychologists, and social workers, contributes valuable diverse input to an understanding of juvenile delinquency. Realizing the importance of this study, they made it possible to specialize in counseling, and in practical ways to deal with problem situations. The few early psychiatrists who became interested in delinquency managed to imbue the entire mental health profession with their personal prestige. The contributions of August Aichhorn, Bruno Bettelheim, and Fritz Redl are paramount (see Appendix D, Referred Texts). These men treated juveniles through acted-out, palpable portrayals of antagonisms and hostilities. The key to the success of this child-saving venture was undoubtedly the compelling personality of August Aichhorn.

The main contribution of the child-saving movement was the creation, in 1899, of the juvenile court. Platt declares:

> Contemporary programs of delinquency control can be traced to the enterprising reforms of the child savers who, at the end of the nineteenth century, helped to create special judicial and correctional institutions for the labeling, processing, and management of "troublesome" youth. . . . The child savers viewed themselves as altruists and humanitarians dedicated to rescuing those who were less fortunately placed in the social order.[11]

The movement was accompanied by a fervent belief that delinquent children and adolescents could be rehabilitated and redirected. The aspirations of Aichhorn and the child savers went unrealized. The sheer mass of delinquents, which precluded developing one-to-one relationships, rendered their altruistic ideas unworkable. The problems arose from (1) insufficient funds for programs; (2) continuing conflict between control and treatment ideologies; (3) shortage of manpower to treat delinquents; and (4) the absence of rewards for upgrading personnel. In addition, it is well to keep in mind a further handicap—juveniles treated away from home sometimes return to an aggravating environment.

The rehabilitative ideal assumes that (1) the individual is uncomfortable about the behavior which has labeled him a delinquent; and (2) he views himself as abnormal and wants to be thought normal. The public defines the normal person as highly rational, completely responsible for his acts, and fully able to control himself. In addition, the normal person is expected to be reasonable, act appropriately in all circumstances, and be intelligible to others. The public sees the opposite of this behavior as unusual or abnormal. A more accurate view of normality is given by Cameron:

> The normal person in our society is one who first of all gains a basic confidence or trust through his interactions with a mother figure early in life. This leaves him free to take a great deal for granted in his relationship to the world around him, to feel reasonably secure about himself and others. He is one who, in growing from infancy to adulthood, has managed to weather the . . . emotional crises which all maturing normally entails. . . . He has learned to give and to get love and loyalty, at each phase of his development, in ways that are appropriate for each level. . . . He has learned to control his aggressions without becoming passive, without losing enterprise and initiative, and without missing the enjoyment of competition and cooperation. He takes pleasure in mutual interdependence, in needing others and in being needed by them. He is a person who experiences a reasonable degree of self-fulfillment in his major social roles, feels warmth toward other human beings, and is able to communicate his feelings acceptably in such a way that they are reciprocated by other persons in his daily life.[12]

Mental health techniques have been used successfully with normal people in situations where the client (1) sees his problem; (2) accepts the therapy; and (3) does so without coercion. But the juvenile delinquent does not respond as the more normal adult does. It is felt that somehow the counselor's rationality will rub off and change the delinquent's behavior, yet this seldom happens. We discover that certain delinquents, described as impulsive and dangerous by the community, are model prisoners.

Nonetheless, the mental health profession understands why delinquents act as they do, because delinquents seek approval from a peer group prescribing delinquent behavior for acceptance, they are willing to violate the law. They may also have internalized deviant values from parents. Still others are acting out family crises, identity struggles, and internal conflicts.

I-Level Treatment

The most systematic classification of delinquents was developed by Marguerite Warren (formerly Marguerite Grant) and associates in 1957.[13] The development of interpersonal maturity levels has been followed by the application of this typology to a community treatment program which has operated continuously since 1961.[14] The seven stages of interpersonal maturity focus upon how the delinquent sees himself and the world. There is an effort to assess the juvenile's understanding of what is happening between himself and others—his interpersonal relationships. Although there are seven categories, the majority of delinquents are found in maturity levels 2, 3, and 4. Individuals are assigned the classification level which identifies their current level of functioning and adaptation to their environment. The levels represent a continuum; an individual must pass through each level to achieve full maturity. Progress to the next level requires the solution of an important interpersonal problem. Warren describes the most frequent recurring levels among delinquent populations:

> Maturity Level 2 (I_2): The individual whose interpersonal understanding and behavior are integrated at this level is primarily involved with demands that the world take care of him. He sees others primarily as "givers" or "withholders" and has no concept of interpersonal refinement beyond the behavior or reactions of others. He is not interested in things outside himself except as a source of supply. He behaves impulsively, unaware of the effects of his behavior on others.

> Maturity Level 3 (I_3): The individual who operates at this level is attempting to manipulate his environment in order to get what he wants. In contrast to Level 2 he is at least aware that his own behavior has something to do with whether or not he gets what he wants. He still does not differentiate, however, among people except to the extent that they can or cannot be useful to him. He sees people only as objects to be manipulated in order to get what he wants. His manipulations may take the forms either of conforming to the rules of whoever seems to have the power at the moment . . . or of the type of maneuvering characteristic of a confidence man. . . . He tends to deny having any disturbing feelings or strong emotional involvement in his relationships with others.
>
> Maturity Level 4 (I_4): An individual whose understanding and behavior are integrated at this level has internalized a set of standards by which he judges his and others' behavior. He is aware of the influence of others on him and their expectations of him. To a certain extent, he is aware of the effects of his own behavior on others. He wants to be like the people he admires. He may feel guilty about not measuring up to his internalized standards. If so, conflict produced by the feelings of inadequacy and guilt may be internalized with consequent neurotic symptoms or acted out in antisocial behavior. Instead of guilt over self worth, he may feel conflict over values. Or, without conflict, he may admire and identify with delinquent models, internalizing their delinquent values.[15]

The interpersonal (I) maturity levels provide a means for classifying adolescent delinquents according to their interpretation of themselves and others. Also, a number of I-Level subtypes have been established. Each subtype identifies the mode of adaptation used by the adolescent in relating to his environment.

There are two subtypes for Maturity Level 2 (I_2):

1. *Asocial, Aggressive* (Aa) often responds with active demands, open resistance, "malicious mischief," or verbal and physical aggression when frustrated by others.
2. *Asocial, Passive* (Ap) often responds with passive resistance, complaining, pouting, or marked withdrawal when frustrated by others.[16]

There are three subtypes for Maturity Level 3 (I_3):

1. *Immature Conformist* (Cfm) usually fears and responds with strong compliance and occasional passive resistance to peers and adults whom he thinks have "the power" at the moment. He sees himself as deficient in social "know how," and usually expects rejection.
2. *Cultural Conformist* (Cfc) likes to think of himself as delinquent and tough. He typically responds with conformity to delinquent peers or to a specific reference group.
3. *Manipulator* (Mp) often attempts to undermine or circumvent the power of authority figures, and/or usurp the power role for himself. He typically does not wish to conform to peers or adults.[17]

There are four subtypes for Maturity Level 4 (I_4):

1. *Neurotic, Acting-out* (Na) often makes active attempts to deny—and distract himself as well as others from—his conscious feelings of inadequacy, rejection, or self-condemnation. He sometimes does this by verbally attacking others, or by "gaming" and conning.
2. *Neurotic, Anxious* (Nx) frequently manifests various symptoms of emotional disturbance—psychosomatic complaints, etc.—which result from conflicts produced by feelings of failure, inadequacy, or conscious guilt.
3. *Situational-Emotional Reaction* (Se) responds to immediate family, social, or personal crisis by acting-out—although his childhood and preadolescent development seem fairly normal in most respects.
4. *Cultural Identifier* (Ci) expresses his identification with an anti-middle class *or* with a non-middle-class value system by occasionally acting-out his delinquent beliefs and/or by "living-out" in commonly unacceptable ways. Often sees himself as competent and, sometimes, as a leader among peers.[18]

The I-Level diagnoses were initially assigned to a number of juveniles committed to a statewide juvenile corrections agency, the California Youth Authority (CYA). The information was used in an experimental program, set up in 1961, known as the Community Treatment Project (CTP). It was divided into two parts for more careful analysis: 1961–69 and 1969–74.

During 1961–69, the program sought to determine the effectiveness of community corrections in lieu of training school; the decision to commit a juvenile to a correctional facility is usually an action taken as a last resort by the local juvenile court. The offenders, between 13 and 19 years old, were typical recidivists with an average prior offense frequency of 5.8, and had usually committed property crimes such as burglary or auto theft. All were known to the courts prior to Youth Authority commitment; violent juveniles charged with forcible rape, armed robbery, or assault with a deadly weapon were excluded. The 1,014 youth assigned to the program were divided into an experimental (N=686) and a control (N=328) group. The experimental group moved directly into the Community Treatment Project, thus avoiding the traditional institutional setting. The control group were sent to a training school for several months before being returned to their home communities where they received routine parole supervision as members of a regular size caseload.

Juveniles in the experimental group were assigned to CYA parole agents whose caseload was light; these agents had no more than 12 youths who were allowed to remain in their home communities (Sacramento, Stockton, or San Francisco). An intensive individualized treatment was developed from detailed interviews between the parole agent and the delinquent, and from a conference with numerous members of the CTP staff. It was known as a differential treatment plan, and attempted to consider such items as (1) the capacities and interests of the youth; (2) his interpersonal maturity level; and (3) specific conditions in the social situation (i.e., family, peer group, and relationships with community members). A variety of treatment programs, selected on the basis of I-Level and subtype classification, were used: individual and/or group treatment; varied living situations (i.e., group home, individual foster home, or out-of-home placements), enrollment in an accredited school program, individual tutoring, and recreation or cultural activities.

The conclusions reached during the first part of the project are summarized below.[19] Success was determined by the recidivism rate two years after being paroled; recidivism was defined as revocation of parole, recommitment by a juvenile or adult court, or unfavorable discharge from Youth Authority supervision.

1. The neurotics (Na's and Nx's) performed much better in the CTP program than in the traditional program. After two years on parole the recidivism rate for the experimental group was 45 percent and for the control group 66 percent. Five years later, following discharge from CYA control, the unfavorable discharge rate was 17 percent for the experimentals and 40 percent for the controls. The neurotic group comprised 53 percent of those under study.
2. Power oriented youth (the Cfc's and Mp's) who were assigned to the CTP program performed substantially worse than those within the traditional program. After two years on parole the recidivism rate for the experimental group was only 40 percent and for the control group 66 percent. However, the five year follow-up shows 23 percent of the experimental group receiving an unfavorable discharge compared to 15 percent in the control group. The second largest category of offenders in the study (21 percent) was the power group. The power individual sees himself as a confirmed delinquent who does not care to conform to adult expectations.
3. Passive conformists (Cfm's) comprised only 14 percent of the study population. This group is usually found on probation caseloads at the city and county level. In the present study the Cfm's who participated in the CTP program performed somewhat better than those in the traditional program. An extended period of supervision is recommended because many return to delinquency. A favorable discharge from the Youth Authority does not seem to obviate the need for supervision.

The first phase of the project ended in 1969 on a disheartening note. At least 33 percent of the individuals placed in the CTP program since 1961 were once more involved in acts of delinquency. This paved the way for the second phase, 1969–74. Failure was related to residence, so the Youth Authority introduced another setting that offered more controls than the CTP. The question was asked, Within *which* type of setting should the treatment and control of the youth commence? Two choices were available: (1) residential dormitory on the grounds of a minimum security correctional facility, followed by release to the intensive program of the CTP or (2) direct release to the CTP as was done in 1961–69.

Individuals requiring the residential program were identified as Status 1 youth while those recommended for the old style CTP were Status 2's. When staff recommendations were followed, the decision was called an appropriate placement. An inappropriate placement was one which ignored the staff opinion. For this portion of the project a new sample was selected. It consisted of males, age 13 to 21 at the time of Youth Authority commitment. All were new to the state corrections agency. Status 1 youth were characterized as difficult to handle and the staff felt they had serious problems. Status 2 delinquents were defined by the staff as those who were less difficult to handle, less resistive to programs, and less likely to have problems. Palmer offers the following conclusions from the final phase of the study:

> (1) Status 1 youths who were inappropriately placed are performing *considerably* worse than those who were appropriately placed. However, in the case of Status 2 youths *no substantial differences* are observed between individuals who were inappropriately placed and those who were appropriately placed. . . .
>
> (2) *Inappropriately* placed *Status 1* youths . . . are performing substantially worse on parole than inappropriately placed *Status* 2 youths. . . . However, appropriately placed youths . . . are performing about equally well . . . regardless of status.[20]

A number of earlier studies attempted to classify juvenile offenders by offense or personality traits (see Appendix D, General Bibliography, Personality Traits). The importance of the CTP Project lies in its ability to classify offenders and then utilize the classification in an actual juvenile correctional setting. This kind of information is needed for progressive program planning in delinquency control. The study suggests that careful diagnosis and a proper placement reduces delinquent behavior. Hopefully, a trained staff would assure a correct diagnosis, placement, and program. Therefore, manpower development is critical. Warren and associates understand the practical difficulties involved in assigning interpersonal maturity level and subtype ratings. The Center for Training in Differential Treatment was established in 1967 to correct this situation. It offered I-Level training for use in classifying offenders and setting up differential treatment programs. The California Youth Authority now classifies all juvenile offenders according to interpersonal maturity subtypes, but there have been some major difficulties with this plan, known as Project SEQUIL (sequential system for the classification of juvenile offenders). A major difficulty is the need for lengthy interviews with each new offender; another is providing the staff with a working knowledge of I-Level concepts. This has taxed the training capacity of the CYA. Furthermore, classification decisions at various reception centers have proved inaccurate and inconsistent. These problems are being corrected.

CONTRIBUTIONS OF SOCIOLOGY

Since the turn of the century, courses in social problems, criminology, delinquency, and corrections have been offered in sociology departments. Sociologists traditionally evinced a sensitive concern for the individual tied to a ghetto environment, but sociology gradually became a scientific, theory-building discipline. The detached viewpoint of the natural scientist replaced the personal involvement of the social reformer; sociologists became less involved with police, probation, and parole departments, and juvenile institutions. The student, preparing for employment in the juvenile justice system, had to select a department which stressed criminological theory but did not ignore practical agency skills like interviewing and field study. Frequently, the individual had to supplement his sociology courses with undergraduate programs in social welfare or graduate social work.

A number of sociology departments pioneered in the development of criminology or juvenile delinquency as an area of specialization. Among them were the University of Washington with faculty members like Norman Hayner and Clarence Schrag; the University of Pennsylvania with Thorsten Sellin and Marvin Wolfgang; and the University of California campuses with Donald Cressey and Edwin Lemert. Schools of social work seldom considered the skills needed to work with correctional clients a high priority specialization. However, there were some notable exceptions. Walter Reckless held a joint appointment in sociology and social work at Ohio State University for many years. Vernon Fox established a Department of Criminology and Corrections within the School of Social Welfare at Florida State University in 1955. Because these men combined sociology and social work in their own teaching, they were effective guides for students. The growth of criminal justice departments has reduced the dilemma of practice versus theory.

The first sociology department in America was established in 1892 at the University of Chicago. The earliest writings about the causes of delinquency appeared in theses and dissertations there. A number of dedicated graduate students trained at Chicago influenced the study of crime and delinquency; they were fascinated by the observations of Lincoln Steffens in his study *The Shame of the Cities* (1904). Steffens was a muckraker who used his reportorial skills to expose the misconduct of prominent politicians in a number of cities. These included Chicago, Minneapolis, New York, Philadelphia, Pittsburgh, and St. Louis. He was pleased with the reform attempts in Chicago, praising its citizens and officials for their efforts to obtain ethical government. The search for political reform in a city familiar with the problem of organized crime provided graduate students with an environment for observing the administration of justice. Thereafter, the study of crime and delinquency became a legitimate concern for sociology. Those neighborhoods identified as high delinquency areas attracted attention. The juvenile gang became the unit for study because the majority of delinquencies were committed by one or more juveniles working together.

Frederic Thrasher

The first sociological study of the gang was written by Frederic Thrasher and entitled *The Gang: A Study of 1,313 Gangs in Chicago*. This monumental work, published in 1927, remains a major classic. Thrasher was greatly influenced by his major professor, the respected sociologist Robert Park, who urged his students to explore the city seeking answers to numerous urban problems including juvenile delinquency. Thrasher, an industrious student, followed this advice. He spent seven years collecting information about the 1,313 gangs with approximately 25,000 members. It was obtained by means of personal observation and interviews with gang members and their acquaintances. Juvenile court records and census data were used to supplement this information. Until the more sophisticated research techniques of the 1960s, no one has gathered so much information on the male gang.

Thrasher found support for his earlier assumption that juvenile gangs were most prevalent in the ghetto or what he called interstitial (crime-producing) areas. He described the gang as a natural small group of youth congregating rather spontaneously to seek out exciting activities. In itself there is nothing psychologically abnormal or deviant about such memberships; it is just one aspect of childhood and adolescence. However, he noted that gangs go through different stages of evolution: diffuse peer grouping; solidified conflict grouping; and finally conventionalized group-typing as in an athletic club. If the conflict gang does not develop into a conventional club, it may become a criminal gang. Membership in a gang is a source of delinquent values for juveniles residing in high crime areas, although such membership is not in itself the cause of delinquency. A crime-breeding area does not control its lawlessness. Therefore, this breakdown in social control can create a tradition of delinquency easily transmitted to others. Thrasher writes:

> Gangs represent the spontaneous effort of boys to create a society for themselves where none adequate to their needs exists. . . . The failure of the normally directing and controlling customs and institutions to function effectively in the boys' experience is indicated by disintegration of family life, inefficiency of schools, formalism and externality of religion, corruption and indifference in local politics, low wages and monotony in occupational activities, unemployment, and lack of opportunity for wholesome recreation.[21]

If ghetto areas are natural breeding grounds for delinquency it follows that Thrasher, through his study, would conclude that a local community ought to organize programs which would prevent gangs from becoming delinquent. Thrasher concludes with a recommendation that such prevention programs be comprehensive and extend to all children living in a delinquency area. The following elements should be present in such programs:

1. Concentration of responsibility for crime prevention for the local delinquency area in question. . . .
2. Research to procure essential facts and keep them up to date as a basis for an initial and a progressively developing crime prevention program (child accounting).
3. Utilization of services of, and cooperation among, all preventive agencies existing in the given community. . . .
4. Application of the preventive program *systematically* to all children in the delinquency area of the local community.
5. Creation of new agencies, if necessary, to supplement existing social organization when and at what points definite needs are discovered which cannot be met by existing facilities. . . .
6. Continuing educational program to enlist and maintain public interest and support.[22]

Thrasher was interested in reorganizing communities that failed to provide for the basic needs of youth. He was a child advocate before the concept was fashionable. What he sought is now being implemented in communities where the youth population is a primary target.

Clifford Shaw and Henry McKay

Thrasher found support for his viewpoint that a poverty culture and its accompanying problems produces a neighborhood that sustains delinquent behavior. He was helped by the work of two other men, closely identified with the Chicago school of sociology, Clifford Shaw and Henry McKay. They were codirectors of the Institute for Juvenile Research, a state agency located in Chicago, which worked closely with the university and its department of sociology. The institute traced the incidence of officially recorded delinquency in various city neighborhoods. The groups were divided in the following manner: (1) alleged delinquents brought before the Cook County Juvenile Court; (2) delinquents committed to correctional institutions by the court; and (3) alleged delinquent males handled formally and informally by police probation officers. Three time periods—1900–1906, 1917–23, and 1927–33—and three specific years, 1926, 1927, 1931, were used in studying the juveniles known to the police probation officers. Shaw and McKay identified delinquency areas by comparing variations in delinquency rates throughout the city by means of spot maps (i.e., census tracts) on which the home addresses of the 60,000 juveniles had been highlighted. Police departments often use the same kind of maps to identify areas of specific crime.

Shaw and McKay, like Thrasher, held to the premise that delinquency is transmitted by means of the culture or traditions prevalent in the community. The delinquency rates were found to vary according to the economic well-being of the neighborhood. In their words:

> . . . The variations in rates of officially recorded delinquents in communities of the city correspond very closely with variations in economic status. The communities with the highest rates of delinquents are occupied by those segments of the population whose position is most disadvantageous in relation to the distribution of economic, social, and cultural values. Of all the communities in the city, these have the fewest facilities for acquiring the economic goods indicative of status and success in our conventional culture. Residence in the community is in itself an indication of inferior status, from the standpoint of persons residing in the more prosperous areas. It is a handicap in securing employment and in making satisfactory advancement in industry and the professions. Fewer opportunities are provided for securing and training, education, and contacts which facilitate advancement in the fields of business, industry, and the professions.[23]

Shaw and McKay revealed that official delinquency is highest in areas where social rewards and economic advantages are limited. Delinquency rates remained high in certain areas regardless of ethnic or racial composition. Population shifts did not change this trend. The investigators were careful to observe that every neighborhood included families not involved in crime and delinquency. Conformity is a dominant trend among people, not delinquency. There is no area of a city which is free from juvenile misbehavior. For this reason, Shaw and McKay argued that the stable population should be mobilized to reduce the pressure on youth to accept delinquency as a way of life.

The work of Shaw and McKay gained in popularity with the publication of *Social Factors in Juvenile Delinquency* (1931), one of

14 reports prepared for the National Commission on Law Observance and Enforcement. It was the first national crime survey in the United States, remembered by the name Wickersham Commission, after the name of the chairman. In 1942 the two researchers published *Juvenile Delinquency and Urban Areas* in which they expanded their information on delinquency areas in Chicago and included material about other American cities. A later revision, 1969, included Chicago data through 1966. Their study traces neighborhood delinquency over a continuous period of 65 years. The commitment of the Chicago school of sociology to the study of delinquency and its causes is both noteworthy and unique.

Clifford Shaw edited a number of case histories of individual male delinquents residing in the high delinquency areas. He believed in listening to what the juvenile had to say. This sometimes helped to clarify how the delinquent tradition had been transmitted. Shaw thought that his case histories might make available material which would produce a better understanding of the dynamics of community treatment. These studies were entitled: *The Jack-Roller: A Delinquent Boy's Own Story* (1930); *The Natural History of a Delinquent Career* (1931); and *Brothers in Crime* (1938). With these, Shaw and McKay provided a statistical analysis of delinquency rates and in-depth autobiographies of delinquents. This sociological concern for the individual and his environment held great promise. The Chicago Area Project, founded by Shaw and McKay, attempted to reduce apathy in high delinquency neighborhoods. The prevention program sought to involve the community in the interests of its children; critical attention was focused on the tendency to offer services without regard to the child's environment. The project did call attention to the child and his world. By so doing it also mobilized existing resources in his behalf. Later, the program was continued as a unit of the Illinois Department of Corrections.

Frank Tannenbaum

A professor of history at Columbia University published *Crime and the Community* in 1938. In it, he attempted an interdisciplinary approach to the study of crime and delinquency, but it was premature. His work received little attention. Tannenbaum strengthened the cultural transmission theory:

> Conduct is learned in the sense that it is a response to a situation made by other people. The smile, the frown, approval and disapproval, praise and condemnation, companionship, affection, dislike, instruments, opportunities, denial of opportunities, are all elements at hand for the individual and are the source of his behavior. It is not essential that the whole world approve; it is essential that the limited world to which the individual is attached approve. . . . It is here that we must look for the origin of criminal behavior.[24]

Edwin Sutherland

Another sociologist was studying professional theft and white collar crime; Edwin Sutherland was a product of the Chicago school and supported the premise that the acquisition of criminal behavior patterns is a social process. He introduced the theory of differential association in 1939; it remains the most popular sociological theory of causation. Clarence Schrag has elaborated on the ideas contained in differential association:

1. Criminal behavior is learned. In this respect crime is similar to all other forms of social behavior. Crime is neither inherited nor is it invented by unsophisticated persons. . . .
2. Criminal behavior is learned as a result of the communication that occurs in social interaction, and this communication is most effective in primary groups that are characterized by intimacy, consensus, and shared understandings. Impersonal communications, in general, are less effective.
3. When criminal behavior is learned, the learning includes both the techniques that are necessary in order to commit the crime and the motives, rationalizations, and social definitions that enable an individual to utilize his criminal skills. In some situations (societies, neighborhoods, families, groups, etc.) an individual is surrounded by people who almost invariably define the laws as rules to be observed, while in other situations he encounters many persons whose definitions are favorable to law violations. . . .

4. More specifically, criminal behavior is learned when an individual encounters an excess of definitions favoring law violations over those that support conformity. This is the basic principle of differential association. . . .
5. Differential association with criminal and noncriminal behavior patterns may vary in frequency, duration, priority, and intensity. Frequency refers to the number of contacts during a given interval of time. Duration indicates the length during which a pattern of contacts is maintained. Priority designates an individual's age at the time he establishes contact with distinctive behavior patterns or develops certain modes of response. Intensity is not precisely defined but deals with things such as the prestige of the carriers of social norms or the affective attachments that may be generated among individuals involved in certain contact patterns.[25]

Clifford Shaw said that he never met a juvenile offender who had committed his first delinquency alone. The misbehavior was always the result of some activity carried out in a group. This was observed by Sutherland who found a process of communication operating among individuals as they weighed the impact of legal and illegal behavior.

Many individuals select an occupation or profession because of the influence of a respected person. The same learning pattern may apply to delinquency or crime as a way of life. Rehabilitation is a difficult concept to understand for the same reason. A probation officer often feels powerless when a probationer returns to crime even though his potential had seemed positive. But one should recall that the techniques for the commission of a crime are learned just as carefully as the methods for counseling delinquents. Few counselors change their profession. Yet crime specialists are expected to change merely because they have been to juvenile hall! It is doubtful whether control agencies see the need to correct career objectives for delinquents.

William Whyte

An economist with training in sociology completed the first study of delinquency in a working class neighborhood using the participant observation approach. William Whyte's *Street Corner*

Society, gives the reader an intimate understanding of an Italian neighborhood in Boston. He lived among the people and participated in their activities. Whyte studied the social relationships of "Cornerville" residents. He found they had no immediate access to power even though upward social mobility was their goal. In order to analyze the problems of the younger generation, Whyte focused on one corner group known as the Norton gang. He compared this group with the college boys who were members of the Italian Community Club. It was discovered that communication and interaction with those in power was the most satisfactory way to advance in both organizations.

Whyte points out the difficulties when a community remains isolated from the larger city. Among them is the failure to provide the young adult with options for conformity and recognition. Because of this, the path to social success is incompatible with the reality of the environment. The easier path leads to the rackets. People who live in the community should work in the social agencies; Whyte hoped this would happen. However, he found most agencies staffed by outsiders (i.e., nonresidents of Cornerville). Even after the completion of his research there was no move on the part of agencies to hire future leaders from Cornerville. Whyte concluded that future students majoring in juvenile corrections should read his book and develop empathy and concern for their clients. *Street Corner Society* reveals the necessity for examining the day-to-day lives of the indigenous population. Effective service is not possible if an agency fails to understand the community subgroups which are interacting and striving toward goals of their own definition.

Albert Cohen

In his work *Delinquent Boys,* Albert Cohen emphasizes the importance of a delinquent subculture, and describes it as a set of reactive attitudes obtained from the gang. These attitudes are characterized by nonutilitarianism, maliciousness, and negativism. It is impossible to explain delinquency through altogether rational means. Shoplifting, a case in point, may have status as its only purpose. Security personnel in department stores often find that juveniles take clothing which does not fit. Sometimes the stolen articles are discarded soon after leaving the store. These are examples of nonutilitarianism. Maliciousness motivated the group of youngsters who poured gasoline on a pet turtle and burned it. There was an unexpected explosion injuring everyone involved. Negativism also often characterizes the mode of life and attitudes of delinquents. Their values are antithetic to the adult community; correct behavior is whatever affords trouble and anxiety to the general population. There is much versatility in the forms of meanness employed by the delinquent subculture. Respectable middle class society is the enemy. On the surface the delinquent does not seem to want rewards or recognition from the middle class, but this reaction comes of his knowing, subconsciously, that they are beyond his grasp. He achieves status where he can—from his peers in the delinquent subculture. Cohen revealed that middle class values are a vehicle to success and respectability for some but not for others; when the door to status is closed, the individual joins the delinquent subculture. Cohen, unlike Thrasher and Whyte, did not test his assumptions empirically.

Richard Cloward and Lloyd Ohlin

In 1960, five years after the appearance of the Cohen theoretical statement, Richard Cloward and Lloyd Ohlin wrote *Delinquency and Opportunity*, probably the most important contribution to the study of causation which has appeared since Sutherland's differential association. In place of middle class values, Cloward and Ohlin stressed the uniformity of conventional success goals. In our culture the emphasis is upon financial success and the acquisition of material goods. Since mass advertising campaigns reach everyone, most youngsters and young adults want the same things; they are sensitive to artificial barriers against achievement. Therefore, they look for alternatives when the legitimate occupations are closed. Schrag tells us:

> Opportunity theory maintains that legitimate and illegitimate methods of achieving social objectives are differentially distributed among the various groups and classes of a society so that some young people have access primarily to legitimate means, others to illegitimate means, and still others to both methods of attaining their goals.[26]

Cloward and Ohlin point out that the delinquent gang or subculture arises when there is a conflict in the search for goals. The lower income youngster is unable or unwilling to obtain these goals normally. One solution to this dilemma is to revise priorities and to lower expectations. The individual who cannot achieve the goals he has set for himself will be frustrated. He may seek to obtain material possessions in other ways. Illegitimate, delinquent, or criminal alternatives are reviewed and sometimes elected. Therefore, the gap between aspiration and opportunity is reduced. The greatest barrier to success, according to Cloward and Ohlin, is the handicap of being uneducated.

They discuss three delinquent subcultures which arise in response to blocked opportunities. There is the criminal subculture, which thrives on such activities as extortion and theft. This group is active in neighborhoods where illegitimate opportunity structures exist, where contacts with the criminal element are readily available. Second, there is the conflict subculture, characterized by violence. Since both legitimate and illegitimate opportunity structures are closed in this environment, the individual proves himself through gang fights and personal attacks. Frustration is released in hostility toward others; this, in turn, becomes a subcultural value and binds the group together in loyalty and shared pride. The third subculture identified by Cloward and Ohlin is that of the retreatist, for whom drugs become a way of life; it closely resembles isolation. It marks an attempt to avoid inevitable failure by retreating from the struggle.

Unfortunately, Cloward and Ohlin could suggest only one solution to the problem of delinquent subcultures. They recommended the reorganization of ghetto communities. New York City's Mobilization for Youth attempted to use this theory as the theoretical framework for their delinquency prevention program. That it was unsuccessful, the reader will discover in a later chapter dealing with diversion and the youth service bureau concept. Cloward and Ohlin failed to provide the policy suggestions which would have made it possible to implement their ideas.

When the illegitimate opportunity structure can be minimized, the benefits of crime should be reduced. This can be done through increasing the penalties for certain crimes, reducing the use of probation for recidivists, or expanding diversion programs to include all juveniles known to the police even when the disposition "warn and release" is used. These controversial policies have a negative outlook. Crime may be less attractive but no catalyst exists to expand legitimate opportunity. Although Cloward and Ohlin significantly probe the inevitable conflict of curtailed opportunity, they fail to supply empirical information useful in formulating a delinquency prevention program. However, we do know that every youngster either views himself as responsible, respected, and of considerable potential, or he perceives himself in some negative way. It is important to build a realistic perception of self, thereby acquiring a self-concept immune to the vicissitudes of life. The youth service bureaus have shown, through their analysis of referrals, that many youngsters and young adults feel blocked out and desperate. Education and employment are their major concerns.

Richard Quinney

A recent movement in sociology seeks to identify the juvenile justice system and the structure of American society as the source of delinquency. Richard Quinney is one of the critics of the existing juvenile justice establishment.[27] He finds the current system resistive of real alteration; in his opinion, it supports both political and economic repression. He considers diversion programs like the youth service bureau basically ineffective. Along with a few sociologists, he proposes some radical changes; because they call for dismantling the juvenile justice system, they will probably not be adopted. Calls for eliminating existing programs are seldom accompanied by alternatives. Quinney's criticism assumes that as the people control programs more, sensitivity to the needs of youth in trouble will be enhanced. This radical approach alienates sociology from the operational agencies and inhibits reasonable, planned change.

Some authorities suggest that changing society will reduce social inequality and therefore lessen the delinquency problem, an ideal hardly to be achieved soon. In the meantime, child advocacy is a reasonable alternative and can serve as a viable agent for change. Massive legislation on a larger scale is unrealistic until we apply our knowledge of delinquency causation to policy issues. The Great Society programs foundered because they were assembled in haste and without proper research into their effectiveness. We must look for the conditions that breed misbehavior—it is simplistic to conclude that poverty and racism create crime. No doubt they do, but they are difficult to completely eradicate. Sociological theories of causation cannot, in themselves, create a world free of delinquency, poverty, racism, and sexism. But they provide guidelines for salvaging people who have been damaged by these conditions. In delinquency prevention programs it is important to apply the findings of sociology to the analysis of peer relations before the eruption of misbehavior.

USING THEORY IN PRACTICE

If the worker is familiar with theoretical explanations for delinquency, he can identify and explore leads which may have been overlooked in the processing of delinquents. Good theory makes visible what might otherwise pass unnoticed in the daily routine. Theory may not always seem to agree with practical experience, but it may be helpful in understanding the offender and his problems.

Only when the juvenile delinquent finds a stake in American life will he be able to conform. The patrolman, the probation officer, the institutions worker, and the parole agent must seek new directions in order to meet these expectations. The challenge for tomorrow is evident in the following remark by Matthew Dumont, a community psychiatrist:

> A wholly new urban professional is being spawned from the universities. Social policy planners rather than brick and mortar city planners are being developed. These are people whose training is in sociology, anthropology, criminology, political science, and mental health as well as in architecture and urban design. Systems analysts from large and sophisticated organizations capable of developing elaborate defense systems or sending missiles into space are turning their attention to air pollution, traffic patterns, solid waste disposal and the delivery of social services.[28]

A new study, entitled Project STAR, reduces the historical conflict between practice and theory. The goal of this project, known more fully as Systems and Training Analysis of Requirements for Criminal Justice Participants, is to upgrade personnel. It explores various working roles: police officer, prosecuting attorney, defense attorney, judge, probation officer, correctional officer, and parole officer. The behavior for satisfactory performance in each of these roles is identified. Then this information influences the selection of training materials, including theoretical explanations for delinquency causation, which help people in their work.[29] Projects like this help overcome the terrible gap in this field between carefully formulated theoretical information and specific suggestions about reducing delinquency.

Causation theories are most useful for understanding the delinquent in relation to his offense and to the situation in which the act occurred. It is important to know how the youth's misbehavior is looked at by (1) the agency preparing information on the case; (2) the youth himself; and (3) the various members of the community (i.e., family, friends, neighbors, school authorities, etc.). A useful approach, which permits careful compilation of this information, is the sociogenic case study technique. Advanced by Martin, Fitzpatrick, and Gould, the case history begins with a "description of the complete official version of the delinquent act" and is followed with data gathered under seven different topics. These topics are (1) the subject of the history, the youth himself; (2) peer group relationships; (3) the family; (4) local institutional ties (i.e., churches, police, schools, etc.); (5) the neighborhood; (6) cultural variables, (which permit us to identify general differences between our own life-style and that of various ethnic groups); and (7) clinical evaluation, which includes the examination by psychiatrist or psychologist.[30]

This approach overcomes the serious limitation in this field of placing everyone in a profile. Workers assign individuals to the profile syndrome they seem to fit; there is the welfare syndrome, the probation syndrome, the institution, and the "sick" syndrome. The profile syndrome does not give proper weight to the community's responsibility for providing services nor does it allow for the fact that no single explanation for delinquency is adequate. A chain of causes is responsible for the delinquent act; a search for the why of delinquency is best undertaken by looking at a delinquent act in the light of some future program that will prevent or control such acts. This enlightenment comes to some individuals when they are involved in a volunteer or in an agency program with delinquents. For others it takes place because a son, daughter, or close friend becomes delinquent. Then there is a genuine attempt to understand the cause. Chapter 11 offers a list of selected journals, which give current explanations for delinquent behavior. New studies on this matter appear in recent issues of the *Document Retrieval Index.*[31] The criminal justice agencies in the various states prepare studies dealing with the delinquent and his misbehavior. For the individual names and addresses of all criminal justice agencies and institutions, consult the *National Criminal Justice Directory;* a separate volume is published for each region.[32]

This body of knowledge should be used by agency personnel and informed citizens. Its value depends on the priority given to delinquency by the local community, the state, and the executive branch of the federal government. Public expenditures for the administration of justice, the treatment of offenders, and the diversionary services to juveniles in trouble will depend upon the skilled manner in which we unite theory and practice in seeking solutions to specific causation questions. But there is something just as important as familiarity with delinquency causation—the worker in the juvenile justice system. Vernon Fox has said:

> In the practical situation, the most successful worker is the one who can constructively relate to the most delinquents, both emotionally and intellectually, with the purpose of promoting within the delinquent positive social attitudes, self-sufficiency in interpersonal relations, and a cooperative relationship with authority. The identification of these relating people for recruiting workers and the elimination of nonrelating workers who are doing more damage than good to disturbed youth is a practical application of our knowledge. The right man may be trained to work with delinquents better. The wrong man trained is still the wrong man.[33]

STUDY QUESTIONS

1. Why should the delinquency worker be familiar with theoretical explanations for delinquency?
2. What is Project STAR?
3. Discuss the impact of the Community Treatment Project on the institutional handling of juveniles committed to a state correctional agency. Has this program influenced juvenile corrections in your state? If so, explain.
4. Who was the founder of the classical school of criminology? The positive school?
5. Define atavism.
6. Why do many find the biological explanations for delinquency to be inadequate?
7. Summarize the contribution of genetics to the study of delinquency.
8. Define normality.
9. Identify the subtypes within each interpersonal maturity level.
10. Why is the study of delinquency a legitimate concern for sociology?
11. Define differential association.
12. How might the opportunity theory of Cloward and Ohlin be utilized in establishing a delinquency prevention program in a low-income area?
13. Summarize the contribution of Thrasher, Shaw and McKay, and Whyte to your knowledge of juvenile gangs.
14. Why is Quinney critical of the existing juvenile justice system?

NOTES

1. Marcello Maestro, *Cesare Beccaria and the Origins of Penal Reform* (Philadelphia: Temple University Press, 1973), p. 12.

2. George B. Vold, *Theoretical Criminology* (New York: Oxford University Press, 1958), pp. 16–17.

3. Marcello Maestro, *Cesare Beccaria and the Origins of Penal Reform* pp. 158–159.

4. Cesare Lombroso, *Crime, Its Causes and Remedies,* trans. Henry P. Horton, 1911; reprinted as Publication No. 14, Patterson Smith Series in Criminology, Law Enforcement and Social Problems, (Montclair, N.J.: Patterson Smith, 1968), p. xiv.

5. Ibid., p. 364.

6. Doug Knight, *Delinquency Causes and Remedies: The Working Assumptions of California Youth Authority Staff,* Research Report No. 61 (Sacramento: California Youth Authority, Division of Research and Development, 1972), p. 21.

7. Charles Goring, *The English Convict: A Statistical Study* (London: His Majesty's Stationery Office, 1913).

8. Earnest A. Hooton, *Crime and the Man* (Cambridge: Harvard University Press, 1939), p. 388.

9. William H. Sheldon, *Varieties of Delinquent Youth* (New York: Harper & Brothers, 1949).

10. This summary is based upon information provided by Ernest B. Hook, M.D., in a letter to the author dated September 1974. Dr. Hook is on the staff of the New York State Birth Defects Institute, Albany Medical College, Albany, New York. For a review of existing studies, see Ernest B. Hook, "Behavioral Implications of the Human XYY Genotype," *Science,* 179, no. 4069 (12 January 1973): 139–150.

11. Anthony M. Platt, *The Child Savers: The Invention of Delinquency* (Chicago: University of Chicago Press, 1969), p. 3.

12. Norman Cameron, *Personality Development and Psychopathology: A Dynamic Approach* (Boston: Houghton Mifflin Co., 1963), pp. 13–14.

13. Clyde Sullivan, Marguerite Q. Grant, and J. Douglas Grant, "The Development of Interpersonal Maturity: Applications to Delinquency," *Psychiatry,* 20 (November 1957): 373–385.

14. Marguerite Q. Warren, "Action Research as a Change Model for Corrections," in *New Approaches to Diversion and Treatment of Juvenile Offenders,* U.S. Department of Justice, Law Enforcement

Assistance Administration, National Institute of Law Enforcement and Criminal Justice (Washington, D.C.: U.S. Government Printing Office, 1973), pp. 125–146.

15. Marguerite Q. Warren, "What Is I-Level?" *California Youth Authority Quarterly*, 22, no. 3 (Fall 1969): 4–5.

16. Ted B. Palmer and Guy W. Grenny, *Stance and Techniques of Matched NX, NA, MP-CFC, CFM and I_2 Workers: A Self-Description of the Treatment Methods Used as Well as Rejected by Five Groups of Low Caseload Parole Agents at California's Community Treatment Project,* Community Treatment Project Report Series: 1971, No. 2, Fall, 1971 (Sacramento: California Youth Authority, 1971), p. 29.

17. Ibid., p. 30.

18. Ibid., pp. 30–31.

19. See Ted Palmer, "The Community Treatment Project in Perspective: 1961–1973," *California Youth Authority Quarterly*, 26, no. 3 (Fall 1973), pp. 29–43.

20. Ibid., pp. 40–41.

21. Reprinted from *The Gang: A Study of 1,313 Gangs in Chicago* by Frederic M. Thrasher by permission of the University of Chicago Press. Copyright 1927 by The University of Chicago. Abridged Edition © 1963 by The University of Chicago, pp. 32–33.

22. Ibid., p. 363.

23. Reprinted from *Juvenile Delinquency and Urban Areas* by Clifford R. Shaw and Henry D. McKay by permission of The University of Chicago Press. Copyright 1942, 1969 by The University of Chicago. Revised edition published 1969, pp. 317–18.

24. Frank Tannenbaum, *Crime and the Community,* (New York: Columbia University Press, 1938), p. 11.

25. Clarence Schrag, *Crime and Justice: American Style,* National Institute of Mental Health, Center for Studies of Crime and Delinquency, U.S. Department of Health, Education, and Welfare (Washington, D.C.: U.S. Government Printing Office, 1971), pp. 46–47. For an extended discussion of differential association see Edwin H. Sutherland and Donald R. Cressey, *Criminology,* 9th ed. (Philadelphia: J. B. Lippincott, 1974).

26. Clarence Schrag, *Crime and Justice,* p. 67.

27. Richard Quinney, *Critique of Legal Order: Crime Control in Capitalist Society* (Boston: Little, Brown and Company, 1974); idem, *Criminology: An Analysis and Critique of Crime in America* (Boston: Little, Brown and Company, 1975); Richard Quinney, ed., *Criminal Justice in America: A Critical Understanding* (Boston: Little, Brown and Company, 1974).

28. Matthew P. Dumont, *The Absurd Healer: Perspectives of a Community Psychiatrist* (New York: Jason Aronson, 1968), p. 69.

29. The American Justice Institute, *Project STAR: Systems and Training Analysis of Requirements for Criminal Justice Participants—Project Summary* (Sacramento: The American Justice Institute, 1971).

30. John M. Martin, Joseph P. Fitzpatrick, and Robert E. Gould, *The Analysis of Delinquent Behavior: A Structural Approach* (New York: Random House, 1970), pp. 25–64.

31. See *Document Retrieval Index*, United States Department of Justice, Law Enforcement Assistance Administration, National Criminal Justice Reference Service, Washington, D.C., 20530. This publication is issued intermittently commencing with 1, no. 1 (July 1972).

32. *The National Criminal Justice Directory* is periodically updated and published in separate regional editions. For example, *Criminal Justice Agencies in Region 9*, U.S. Department of Justice, Law Enforcement Assistance Administration (Washington, D.C.: U.S. Government Printing Office, 1974). There are 10 LEAA administrative regions, each with a similar directory. Region 9 includes the following states: Arizona, California, Hawaii, and Nevada.

33. Vernon Fox, "Clinical Classifications and Delinquency Labels" (paper delivered at the Ninetieth Annual Meeting of the National Conference on Social Welfare, Cleveland, Ohio, 19–24 May 1963), pp. 12–13.

YOUTH SERVICE BUREAUS

DEFINITIONS
HISTORY
ESTABLISHING A YOUTH SERVICE BUREAU
TYPES OF YOUTH SERVICE BUREAUS
REFERRALS TO THE YOUTH SERVICE BUREAU
SERVICES OF THE BUREAUS
THE FUTURE OF THE YOUTH SERVICE BUREAU

Many juveniles engage in delinquent behavior too serious for a mere warning and release by the police, and too trivial for the judicial restraints of the juvenile court. In 1967, the President's Commission on Law Enforcement and Administration of Justice recognized the need to deal with these delinquent activities in a new way. The commission recommended the establishment of the youth service bureau (see Appendix D, General Bibliography). The 1970 White House Conference on Children and the 1971 White House Conference on Youth have suggested immediate implementation of the youth service bureau concept to ensure that justice is rendered in behalf of children and youth (see Appendix D, General Bibliography, under *Report*.)

The youth service bureau coordinates and expands services to young people in their own community. The services are local, voluntary, and are dispensed to the juvenile without the restraints that the control agencies impose. More important, the youth service bureau sees those juveniles who can benefit from social services *before*, rather than after, the police and courts have had to label them official delinquents. Some people assume that services to youth are available upon request; unfortunately, agencies reserve the highest priority for those juveniles and adults who create a crisis which endangers the community. Too often, justice is tenuously served by quieting the behavior of the adjudicated delinquent or criminal while overlooking the potential miscreant.

This often-repeated story is documented in one mental health clinic. According to a much-worn file, a youngster and his parents sought community mental health services on many occasions. The agency did not act upon the request because of a lengthy waiting list. Later, the youngster murdered a young woman, unknown to him before the attack, in her motel room; he cut her body into many parts and twirled her intestines around the room as though he had a lariat. Following this offense the young man was incarcerated and clinical services were provided. Social services must be made available to those whose potential for danger lies documented in musty clinical files. Delinquency prevention means action *before* a community is traumatized. The President's Commission states, "The most significant feature of the Bureau's function would be its mandatory responsibility to develop and monitor a plan of service for a group now handled, for the most part, either inappropriately or not at all except in time of crisis."[1]

DEFINITIONS

The late Sherwood Norman pioneered in the development of the youth service bureau. His definition is commonly used:

> The Youth Service Bureau is a noncoercive, independent public agency established to divert children and youth from the justice system by (1) mobilizing community resources to solve youth problems, (2) strengthening existing youth resources and developing new ones, and (3) promoting positive programs to remedy delinquency-breeding conditions.[2]

A second definition describes it in the following manner:

> The Youth Service Bureau is a place in the community to which delinquent-prone youths can be referred by parents, law enforcement agencies, the schools, etc. It should have a wide range of services reflecting the coordination and integration of important public and private prevention resources existing in the community. . . . The Youth Service Bureau concept asks those agencies, organizations, and individuals in a community who are involved in delinquency prevention to inventory, organize, and coordinate their resources in an exploration of new avenues of referral, education, and treatment adapted to meet the unique problems represented by delinquency in their community.[3]

FIGURE 4-1

The Youth Service Bureau Referral Services

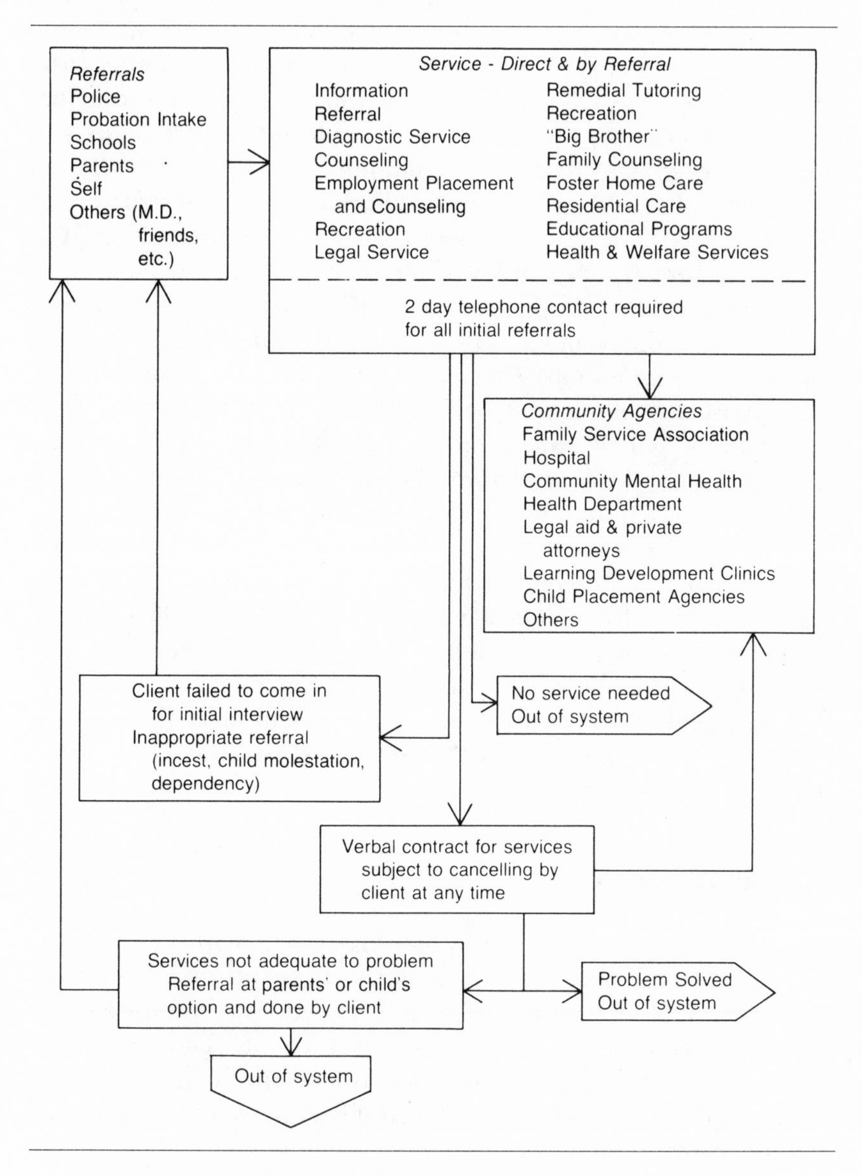

SOURCE: Prepared by Mrs. Elizabeth Clark and reproduced by permission of Kenneth F. Fare of the San Diego County Probation Department, San Diego, California.

The organization of a youth service bureau, revealing the wide range of services and the various sources of referrals from the community, is shown in figure 4-1. This referral flow chart was prepared by Elizabeth Clark, founder and former coordinator of the highly successful San Diego Youth Service Bureaus. By definition the youth service bureau is disarmingly simple and logical; it shows that a community can identify its troubled youth and provide them with appropriate services. It allows a community to facilitate the flow of unmanageable children from the authoritarian agency structure to the non-authoritarian social service agency, and vice versa. The process utilizes the principles of cooperation and diversion.

Matching the proper services to a particular youth means focusing upon different kinds of programs for different forms of misconduct. The community agencies are not being used enough. The community does not learn that a youth is in trouble until *after* he is known to the police, courts, or the training school. Nonetheless, a child in trouble does make himself known to us in various ways: (1) he engages in conduct which might lead to delinquency; (2) he is known to social agencies for various problems not related to delinquency as yet; (3) his conduct has created a negative response from the community although no agency has been asked to offer services to the youth; (4) he has been defined as a potential delinquent; or (5) he has been formally adjudicated in juvenile court.

The goal of the youth service bureau is to meet the needs of youth through applying coordination and diversion. These questions are complex and need analysis.

Coordination

The task of matching troublesome youth with available resources requires agency coordination. The youth service bureau is an appropriate means for meeting this need. The literature warns that coordination efforts must take into account: (1) definitions of delinquency; (2) the incidence of delinquency in the neighborhood or community; and (3) the availability of resources in the public and private sector.

Agency cooperation means the coordination of all services for maximum effectiveness. Agencies have a tendency to blame youth for failures rather than to question their own programs. If they cannot help, they have the option of referring the case to private, public, or self-help organizations. This is what interagency cooperation means.

There should be, but often are not, open channels of communication between citizens and their agencies. The police are qualified to fill this gap and may even serve as advocates where there is a breakdown in agency-community relations. In one community where the streets were dark, the housing authority had decreed that no lights would be replaced before three consecutive lamps burned out. However, the police asked them to bend that rule, and the lighting was installed as a necessary protection.

Why have community agencies failed to deliver services to children in danger of becoming delinquent? Alfred J. Kahn has made the following observations:

1. Cases are found but opportunities are lost.
2. Resources are allocated to cases through competition and uneconomical "shopping."
3. Dispositions are often arrived at through inadequate case evaluation.
4. Police and plans of diverse agencies are uncoordinated and services offered are, therefore, inadequate or in conflict.
5. Services of diverse agencies, which concurrently affect a given case or family or which affect a given case sequentially, are not meshed.[4]

In turn, Kahn suggests that services to children must be organized in a manner permitting a community to overcome the limitations mentioned above. Services can be organized so that:

1. Agencies will cease to be so "hard to reach";
2. The rights of clients will be served in the right places;
3. Cases will not be "lost" in the gaps between agencies or in the inadequacies of agencies;
4. Agencies will work together more efficiently, putting people before functions;
5. Necessary knowledge will be developed and taught to adequate numbers of personnel;

6. Sufficient resources will be available and, as a result, our community patterns of service will yield more effective and lasting results.[5]

Although the youth service bureau concept was introduced in 1967, the problem of coordination continued to reduce the efficiency of agencies until 1969. Norman, in his survey of agencies involved in delinquency prevention, found fewer than 12 that operated within the youth service bureau definition. Only these few agencies:

1. were strictly noncoercive,
2. were planned on a jurisdiction-wide basis,
3. were neighborhood-based,
4. received referrals from law-enforcing agencies, schools, and other sources, and
5. coordinated appropriate resources on behalf of the child and followed through to see that he received the appropriate service.[6]

Diversion

Diversion screens out of the justice system those juveniles who do not require the formal restraints and compulsory services of a juvenile court or a probation department. It tailors services to meet the needs of the youngster. The goal is to enhance his desire for conformity rather than delinquency. In other words, we endeavor to provide services through a network of agencies not identified with delinquency processing procedures. We have succeeded in the field of drug abuse; many agencies and services are equipped to assist the juvenile with drug-related problems. Youngsters receive these services without fear of being arrested. In other words, the cost of the cure does not include arrest and the delinquency label.

The police have been using diversion for many years. Many children and youth known to them are not referred to the juvenile court for further processing, but it is difficult for the police departments to find appropriate agencies for children in trouble. The police agency cannot be asked to serve as the coordinator for community youth-serving agencies because this action might be considered coercive. Thus, the local community must designate an agency which receives referrals from police, parents, schools, and the juveniles themselves. This issue must be met before diversion becomes an operating principle.

There are limits in using diversion for delinquent and predelinquent youth. Some authorities point out that there may be pressures to accept the services even though the treatment is unwanted. This pressure is similar to a procedure used too frequently in the past: namely, a youngster was told that "voluntary" enlistment in the armed forces could substitute for a juvenile court hearing. Although such "diversion" has been used in the past, the military has been successful in requesting that the armed forces not be used as a substitute for community social services. A second limit of diversion occurs in the overanxious community, which may endeavor to "treat" all misbehavior. Is all delinquent behavior actually unacceptable behavior? The tolerance of each community must be assessed. A recent publication states:

> . . . as long as mainstream America continues to view all deviations from a narrowly defined acceptable norm as evidence of pathology requiring some kind of control response (whether punitive or rehabilitative), diversion is likely to remain largely a technique of enforcing conformity by alternate means.[7]

Perhaps diversion includes two obligations: (1) identifying youth who want and can benefit from available social services; and (2) redefining the juvenile delinquency statutes in order to expand the varieties of conforming behavior. Identification can be determined only by establishing explicit procedures for selection; the criteria should be developed in cooperation with the police, the juvenile court, private and public agencies serving youth, and neighborhood citizen groups. Redefining delinquency requires community support in removing specific forms of behavior from the legal category of delinquency. This process is difficult, and requires sensitivity to the level of tolerance in the community for various kinds of misbehavior. A moralistic viewpoint must be tempered by an awareness that some forms of misbehavior are more serious than others. Conversely, there might be a tendency to eliminate the delinquent label entirely—on the basis that all delinquent behavior found in the statutes is a form of weakness on the part of youth.

The desire to redefine delinquent behavior is evident today in any discussion about legalizing marijuana or removing curfew violations as forms of juvenile misconduct. Much controversy surrounds the marijuana issue but less is directed at curfew violations. A recent policy statement by the National Council on Crime and Delinquency lists two important priorities: (1) promoting the youth service bureau concept and (2) opposing the new curfew ordinances and statutes while at the same time urging the repeal of existing curfew laws for juveniles.[8] Curfew ordinances have not been useful in preventing or controlling delinquency; most youth crime occurs before 10:00 P.M. when the law usually goes into effect. Many communities may prefer to repeal curfew ordinances and increase recreation programs for juveniles; if so, the youth activity centers should be open longer hours and volunteer adult supervisors should be used. As we redefine existing youth misconduct so that it is not officially "criminal"—possible when delinquency is viewed as other forms of behavior—we must be sure that there is a tolerance scale of acceptability in the community. It is an open question just where marijuana use should be placed on the continuum of behavior. Hopefully, communities can reach a compromise more easily on the question of curfew ordinance repeal.

An increasing emphasis on services outside of the juvenile justice system suggests criticism of the entire juvenile court movement.[9] It is not. The Joint Commission on Correctional Manpower and Training cites the need for more diversion in order to meet the growing needs of youth. The commission views the youth service bureau as an ally of the juvenile court. It further recognizes the need for diversion and informal adjustment as a means of reducing the heavy caseloads which burden juvenile courts.[10]

The progressive juvenile court has fought to include mental health services in its program. Sometimes the mental health professional forgets what these services cost the child. The stigma of court referral often precedes the granting of services by a highly professional and concerned staff. The juvenile court staff, therefore, has little reason to consider the importance of the stigma to the individual undergoing well-intentioned treatment programs. Referral may come because the juvenile is charged with a serious adult crime, truancy, incorrigibility, or being a runaway. The non-adult offenses may be the result of disordered family life or some other condition which cannot be controlled by the juvenile himself. Stigma attaches to the youngster and he experiences isolation and disapproval in his peer group, the school, the family, or the community; this process demands attention because it is the price of obtaining mental health services in the juvenile court (see Appendix D, General Bibliography, Employment of Ex-Offenders).

We should not forget that stigma remains long after the completion of court services, and interferes with the achievement of educational and occupational goals. Mental health services ought to be a source of strength. However, it is doubtful that a well-meaning mental health program can remove the anxiety associated with community experiences which attack the self-worth, esteem, or newly found conformity of the former delinquent. Rehabilitation services which give undue emphasis to the earlier juvenile court record make things worse. This is why the White House Conference on Children suggests: (1) "offender" stigma can be reduced by treating children outside the justice system when possible; and (2) agencies, educational institutions, private business, and the armed services should be prohibited from inquiring into juvenile records when considering applicants for employment, school admittance, or military service.[11]

It seems as if the juvenile court or institutional setting imposes stigma as the price of its services. The situation is akin to that of an accident victim in a hospital emergency room who receives the services of skilled doctors; the patient remains grateful to the physician but it is unlikely that he will return to express his appreciation. Ex-offenders are not thankful for what has been done. Occasionally, one who has achieved a successful life remembers a dedicated court worker; visits may be brief and infrequent. Both the concerned court worker and the physician operate in crisis environments; their skills may save emergency cases. Keep in mind the differing reactions of those who give and those who receive. The offender who remembers can understand stigma and can appreciate the alternative, diversionary services.

HISTORY

The involvement of local communities in the coordination of services to the delinquent and potentially delinquent began in 1919. It was in Berkeley, California. A renowned police chief and the director of a citywide public school guidance bureau met to discuss the problems of children. The police chief was August Vollmer, whose contributions to the professionalization of law enforcement are recognized today. The chief of the guidance bureau was Dr. Virgil E. Dickson, who later became the superintendent of schools in Berkeley. These two men were joined by other professionals from the fields of psychiatry, psychology, health, and welfare. This voluntary committee, which called itself the Berkeley Coordinating Council,[12] met weekly for ten years; they identified children in need of the services of one or more social service agencies, and they mobilized community agencies. Efficiency and cooperation characterized the provision of services to children in danger of becoming delinquent.

The Berkeley model was successful, and the coordinating council concept became very popular in the United States. By 1939, there were more than 700, characterized by: (1) an alliance of professionals and concerned citizens who were united in an effort to identify those conditions in the community which tend to reduce the effective functioning of children and youth; (2) an awareness that delinquency prevention requires specific knowledge of private and public resources in the community; (3) a concern for the coordination of these available agency resources; and (4) the immediate application of specific services as required to protect vulnerable youth from delinquent conduct.

Local coordinating councils have been most successful in states that pioneered in establishing statewide, highly professionalized juvenile corrections systems (e.g., California and Wisconsin). The important contribution of the early coordinating council movement was the alliance of concerned laymen and dedicated law enforcement and corrections personnel who mobilized grass-roots support for delinquency prevention and control.[13]

Community Welfare Planning Councils

Community welfare planning councils are composed of representatives from most or all agencies identified with health, welfare, and recreation. Known as social planning councils, community welfare councils, community planning councils, or health and welfare councils, they endeavor to provide a conciliatory atmosphere of coordination and cooperation among the autonomous agencies. Some years ago the United States Children's Bureau, which operated from 1912 through 1969, sent questionnaires to 258 community welfare councils and inquired about their involvement in delinquency prevention activities. The bureau found that only 74 out of 258 councils were active in work directed toward the prevention of juvenile delinquency.[14]

While the community welfare planning council does not provide specific services to delinquent children, it has contributed much to the effective police-community relations programs in our cities. The council provides a continuing dialogue among member agencies who have assembled in order to assume some responsibility for services which are not being provided in the community. This dialogue is necessary for the exchange of information about programs and services. A limitation: sometimes there is a tendency for a representative to overemphasize his own agency when coordinating new programs.

Joan Ecklein and Armand Lauffer cite a case study in which the organizational changes in three cooperating member agencies and one nonmember made it possible to offer new services to delinquent girls. Unfortunately, although the additional services were made available, no one remembered to ask whether these services were really helpful, or whether more beneficial programs were available.[15] Excessive concern for coordinating agency services may decrease the development of new, innovative forms of assistance.

The community welfare planning councils and their fund-raising groups are represented by the national organization United Way of America. Through its Institute of Community Studies, United Way is attempting to overcome the criticisms aimed at the community health and welfare council approach to urban problems. In a three-year project, Voluntarism and Urban Life, the institute endeavored to identify the needs of urban dwellers; list the obstacles that prevent the community from dealing constructively with the problems of people; enumerate programs and policies used as solutions; and recommend priorities for service by calling attention to the degree of disablement the specific problem brings to the person as well as by citing the effectiveness of the programs suggested for overcoming the obstacles. The problems of people are categorized as follows: income and employment; physical and material situation; health; knowledge and skills needed for personal achievement and social usefulness; and personal and social development. The project emphasizes the role of the volunteer leader in finding useful information about urban issues. Juvenile delinquency is identified as an obstacle to personal and social development in social relationships. Eleven programs in delinquency prevention and control are discussed and all are considered important responsibilities of the volunteer leader.[16]

The initiative of the local coordinating council and the community welfare planning movement in meeting the urban crisis was supplemented by massive federal legislation during the 1960s. The social reform programs, begun during the presidential terms of John F. Kennedy and Lyndon B. Johnson, provided a new focus on issues which could not be solved by local communities operating alone. Some of the important legislation includes the following: Juvenile Delinquency and Youth Offenses Control Act of 1961, Economic Opportunity Act of 1964, Community Services Act of 1966, Juvenile Delinquency Prevention and Control Act of 1968, and Juvenile Delinquency Prevention Act of 1972.

The War on Poverty became a battle against delinquency. For the first time, the politicization of a sociological theory occurred. The theory of delinquency introduced by Richard Cloward and Lloyd Ohlin became the basis for a program of action. Their theory states that delinquency is associated with the overt denial of opportunity to youth, and it argues that the absence of legitimate educational and employment opportunities necessitates the use of alternate routes to competency by disenfranchised youngsters. These alternate routes involve the use of illegitimate means to achieve fulfillment of the expectations which signify success in our culture (see Appendix D, General Bibliography). There is general agreement that delinquency cannot be reduced until our children receive the services which are the right of every child: health, housing, education, necessary welfare and social services, and employment. Some opponents of opportunity theory contend that delinquent and predelinquent youth may reject programs designed to assist them. Supporters reply that it is difficult to determine rejection of services until we actually provide legitimate opportunities to *all* who desire them.

Neighborhood Service Centers

An early attempt to provide services to the delinquent in his own locality is found in the proposals to establish neighborhood service centers. Robert Perlman and David Jones offer the following working definition of a neighborhood service center:

1. It provides information and referral services to assist people to use established agencies. In some instances, a reaching-out operation brings "information and referral" to the neighborhood resident in his home or on the street.
2. The center acts as advocate to protect a client's interests and rights with respect to another agency. It may also seek a change in another agency's procedure or policy that will become a precedent for similar situations.
3. Concrete services are provided directly to individuals and families. The list varies from project to project and may include one or more of these: legal aid, day care for children, employment counseling, training and job placement, casework, assistance in homemaking, recreation and group work, health services, and help with housing problems.
4. The center organizes and mobilizes groups for collective action on behalf of the residents of the neighborhood. This ranges from facilitating two-way communication between residents and local institutions to assisting groups to confront and challenge those who make decisions affecting conditions and services in their neighborhood.[17]

The initial experience with programs designed to serve the neighborhood was characterized by difficulties. An idea, no matter how noble, is not easily implemented without guidelines. In addition, the massive War on Poverty overwhelmed the community action programs.[18]

The problems associated with innovation are found in the activities of Mobilization for Youth. This program originated in 1962 on the lower east side of New York City, an area of limited opportunities. Based on the opportunity theory of Cloward and Ohlin, it unfortunately focused on the causes of delinquency in the neighborhood but did not dwell on delivering services to the individual delinquent. Weissman, in his careful four volume history of this demonstration project, indicates:

> . . . opportunity theory, as developed in the agency's original proposal, was not fully operationalized. What is the relation between an educational opportunity and a job opportunity? Is the way an opportunity is provided as significant as the presence of the opportunity itself? Is one opportunity more important than another? Mobilization was hampered by the incomplete development of its theoretical base. As such, it suffered from all the problems attendant on invention and innovation—false starts, mistakes, unanticipated events, and the like.[19]

A limitation of the preceding program lies in its mass provision of blanket services. It offers no tailored programs for individual youngsters, and does not tell us about the youth who accepted or rejected services. Perhaps it is more important to provide services individualized for the specific client, while remembering also that social conditions breed delinquency.

Further, in the early neighborhood service center a good deal of suspicion existed. Sometimes the mental health professional seemed suspicious of the indigenous poor who were recruited as neighborhood service center workers; at other times, the paraprofessional bias against the formal treatment agencies surfaced.[20] Such suspicion blocked the neighborhood staff members who were motivated to serve their clients and eager to increase their working skills. At the same time, the formal agencies and their professional workers were aware of their own limitations in meeting community problems. How necessary it is for the traditional agency and the indigenous worker to coordinate their individual skills!

No agency, whether it be a public service social agency or a private voluntary agency, can remain isolated. Cooperation requires a climate of trust. Optimum use of private and public services in the prevention and control of delinquency has the support of the legislative and executive branches of federal and state governments. A recent study of United Fund executives and their agencies (i.e., the health and welfare agency membership in the United Way of America organization) indicates that a majority of these executives express favorable attitudes toward federal programs like urban renewal, the antipoverty program, and the comprehensive mental health program. These supplement their existing health, character-building, family and child welfare services.[21] In the 1970s the time is ripe for introducing community-based programs which recognize that the adolescent is torn between legitimate and delinquent solutions. The youth service bureau will strengthen those resources that help youth acquire status. Perhaps the advocacy role of the youth service bureau is best summed up by a 15-year-old ghetto youngster, "I don't want out; I want in."

ESTABLISHING A YOUTH SERVICE BUREAU

The youth service bureau is considered most effective when it is organized as an independent public agency. Both Gorlich and Norman suggest the advantages of this form: (1) the accompanying authority, status, and prestige of the autonomous agency permits greater cooperation with existing agencies; and (2) the legislation required for the establishment of a public agency provides the community with an organization which is as accountable to the people as any traditional agency in the field of juvenile justice.[22]

In turn, Martin advises that the bureau might well be a private agency operated by the indigenous population whose children would be the recipients of the diversionary services.[23] This approach gained support from the private welfare programs which dominated the American scene at the turn of the century when immigrants and religious groups assisted their members in achieving the skills necessary for upward mobility, conformity, and success. In the 1970s it is agreed that the low-income child has been overrepresented in the formal processing of the long-established control agencies and he has the most to gain from this new service delivery format. However, the private agency controlled by the indigenous population faces several limitations: (1) inner city populations tend to be apathetic; (2) the agency does not have political power (although it sometimes tenuously achieves such power amid bitter battles, the agency still cannot coordinate needed social services); and (3) the continuous search for state and federal funds so necessary for agency survival displaces the energy required for successful operation of the bureau.

The advocates of the independent public agency have offered important guidelines which answer the critics of this recommended agency structure plan: (1) the bureau should never be within existing agencies of the local or state correctional system; (2) widespread community support and citizen involvement in the program is necessary; (3) the youth population to be served should be defined carefully (e.g., age groups), and the target group limited to a specific geographical area identified by its high juvenile arrest rates; (4) services should be tailored to specific youth and the voluntary acceptance of services stressed; and (5) the bureau concept, responding to the limits of traditional agencies, should endeavor to serve as the conscience of the community and diminish the impersonality which has characterized many earlier forms of agency assistance.

New legislation will be necessary in those states interested in establishing youth service bureaus. While the President's Commission on Law Enforcement and the Administration of Justice enunciated the purpose of the bureaus in its recommendation, it was not specific about the operation of the new youth serving agency. The commission made the following recommendation while deferring to the states the details for implementing the proposal:

> Communities should establish neighborhood youth-serving agencies—Youth Service Bureaus—located if possible in comprehensive neighborhood community centers and receiving juveniles (delinquent and nondelinquent) referred by the police, the juvenile court, parents, schools, and other sources.[24]

Pilot Youth Service Bureaus in California

California has pioneered in legislation for the establishment and funding of these bureaus. The Youth Service Bureaus Act was passed in 1968. This legislation provided an appropriation of $100,000 for the establishment of pilot youth service bureaus in four communities. The California Youth Authority was responsible for the administration of the funds set aside for the four programs. Twenty-five communities submitted proposals for the bureaus. The legislation put responsibility for the development of bureau standards and guidelines on the California Delinquency Prevention and the County Delinquency Prevention commissions. The County Delinquency Prevention Commission is composed of laymen rather than representatives of community agencies. The participation of lay board members in the establishment of these bureaus in California is unique. That flexibility was permitted will be noted in the following excerpt from the guidelines:

> The number and types of services which can be provided through a Youth Service Bureau are limited only by the imagination of local individuals who are responsible for the program and/or by the willingness of various public agencies and private organizations to commit themselves to a cooperative effort. The Youth Service Bureau concept asks those agencies, organizations, and individuals in a community who are involved in delinquency prevention to inventory, organize, and coordinate their resources in an exploration of new avenues of referral, education, and treatment adapted to meet the unique problems represented by delinquency in their community.[25]

By early 1969 representatives of the California Delinquency Prevention Commission and staff of the California Youth Authority reviewed the proposals from the 25 communities. The selection committee made its choices allowing representation to different kinds of communities: a rural agricultural community (Yuba-Sutter Youth Service Bureau); a middle-class, metropolitan, suburban community (San Diego Youth Service Bureau); an industrial suburb located between Oakland and Vallejo with an increasing minority population and a decreasing white, middle-class population (Richmond Youth Service Bureau); and an ethnically mixed community (Bassett Youth Service Bureau in Los Angeles County). At the time of the initial selection of proposals a federal grant was obtained from the Law Enforcement Assistance Administration through the California Council on Criminal Justice for the funding of five additional youth service bureaus.[26] Nine bureaus were established: four were financed by state funds provided by the new legislation and five by federal funds. Thus, we find sponsorship can include state, local, and the federal government. The rural Yuba-Sutter pilot project is regional, involving two contiguous counties.

Fortunately, a small sum of money was allocated for evaluation of the new projects. The importance of the evaluative component in the California Youth Service Bureau legislation should be stressed. Norman, in his endeavor to identify earlier delinquency prevention programs which might be operating in the manner of the youth service bureau, found two serious limitations: (1) none of the programs were aware of the existence of the others and an exchange of information never seemed to occur; and (2) none of the programs assessed the effectiveness of their operations because data collection and evaluative research had never been accorded high priority.[27]

The pilot youth service bureaus were evaluated annually by the California Youth Authority as required by the legislation passed in 1968. Progress reports were submitted to the state legislature annually for three years. The final report, completed in late 1973, recommended continuation and expansion of the youth service bureau concept. The California Legislature concurred and passed the following legislation which is incorporated into the California Welfare and Institutions Code (Sections 1900–1904). The law, which became effective on July 1, 1975, reads:

ARTICLE 10. YOUTH SERVICE BUREAUS [NEW]

Sec.
1900. Legislative findings.
1901. Public or private organizations; application for funds for youth service bureaus; purpose of programs.
1902. Minimum standards; duties of department of youth authority.
1903. Manner of application for funds.
1904. Payment of costs by state funds; limitations.

Article 10 was added by Stats.1974, c. 1488, p. —, § 2, operative July 1, 1975.

§ 1900. Legislative findings

The Legislature hereby finds that the most significant trend in the development of delinquency prevention programs has been in the direction of multipurpose youth service bureau projects implemented at the neighborhood level, receiving delinquent and predelinquent youth referred by parents, schools, police, probation, and other agencies, as well as self-referral. Designed especially for less seriously delinquent youth, programmatic aspects often include group and individual counseling, work and recreation programs, employment

counseling, special education, utilization of paraprofessionals and volunteers, outreach services, and youth participation in the decisionmaking process. Often activities encouraging youths' families, local community citizens, and representatives of established agencies are included in project activities. While youth service bureau programs have been effective in diverting youth out of the justice system, it has also been the case that these programs have been hampered in their operations due to lack of consistent and stable funding. Therefore, it is proposed that a significant number of youth service bureaus be established throughout the state and be located in areas with a high concentration of vulnerable youth, by means of a cost-sharing plan between local communities and the state.
(Added by Stats.1974, c. 1488, p. —, § 2, operative July 1, 1975.)

§ 1901. Public or private organizations; application for funds for youth service bureaus; purpose of programs

Pursuant to the provisions of this article, any public or private organization may make application to the Department of the Youth Authority for the purpose of receiving funding from the department of the Youth Authority for the establishment or operation or both of one or more youth service bureaus. Such youth service bureaus shall develop and operate direct and indirect service programs designed to:

(a) Divert young people from the justice system;

(b) Prevent delinquent behavior by young people;

(c) Provide opportunities for young people to function as responsible members of their communities.
(Added by Stats.1974, c. 1488, p. —, § 2, operative July 1, 1975.)

§ 1902. Minimum standards; duties of department of youth authority

(a) The Department of the Youth Authority shall develop, adopt, prescribe, monitor and enforce minimum standards for youth service bureaus funded under the provisions of this article. Such standards shall be for the purposes of carrying out, and not inconsistent with, the provisions of this article.

(b) The Department of the Youth Authority shall seek advice from knowledgeable individuals, groups and agencies in the development of such standards.

(Added by Stats.1974, c. 1488, p. —, § 2, operative July 1, 1975.)

§ 1903. Manner of application for funds

Application for funding of youth service bureaus under the provisions of this article shall be made in the manner prescribed by the Department of the Youth Authority.
(Added by Stats.1974, c. 1488, p. —, § 2, operative July 1, 1975.)

§ 1904. Payment of costs by state funds; limitations

From any state moneys made available to it for such purpose, the Department of the Youth Authority may, in accordance with this article, share in the cost of each youth service bureau meeting the standards prescribed for youth service bureaus by the department at the rate of 50 percent of the actual fiscal year costs of each youth service bureau, or eighty thousand dollars ($80,000) per fiscal year for each youth service bureau, whichever amount is the lesser.
(Added by Stats.1974, c. 1488, p. —, § 2, operative July 1, 1975.)[28]

TYPES OF YOUTH SERVICE BUREAUS

The establishment of a youth service bureau in the community requires much sensitivity. The neighborhood selected should have a high incidence of officially reported delinquency. The citizens in the neighborhood must view this situation as serious; gaps in existing services to youth must be recognized and inventoried; better cooperation and coordination of agency activities should be viewed as one solution to the high delinquency problem. Citizens must express concern because the youth are not meeting their potential to conform. The agency personnel must recognize the necessity for active participation in the bureau. Citizens, agencies, and youth must seek to sustain a dialogue in order to create a bureau.

There is no ideal model which can be imitated in all communities. Flexibility and innovation are required if gaps in services are to be reduced. The vitality of the bureau can be sustained only if citizens, youth, and formal agencies (especially the police) refer youngsters to the bureau. Not only must referrals come from the community itself, but agencies must volunteer services and skills too. The bureau is a new kind of agency equipped to offer short-term (less than six months) service to youth who voluntarily accept assistance for problems that might lead to arrest if not resolved.

Norman has observed five youth service bureau models which have met the needs of various communities. The five models are the following:

> *A cooperating agencies model,* in which several community agencies each donate the full-time paid services of one worker to the Youth Service Bureau. Working as a team with a coordinator, these workers accept individual referrals and involve citizens, youth, and professionals in solving problems related to acting-out behavior in youngsters.
>
> *A community organization model,* in which neighborhood citizens, under the direction of a coordinator, mobilize to form a board, develop services, and meet crises as circumstances in the neighborhood indicate urgency.
>
> *A citizen action model,* in which the YSB citizen committee has many subcommittees active in developing a great variety of youth services, while staff receive direct referrals and use case conference techniques and community resources to resolve individual problems. (This program originated in Pontiac, Michigan, where it has been in operation over 10 years.)
>
> *A street outreach model,* which grew out of the New York City Youth Board and uses storefront neighborhood service centers as bases for therapeutic group activities including administration of the neighborhood youth corps.
>
> *A systems modification model,* which focuses on helping schools, institutions, programs, agencies, etc., become more sensitive and responsive to the needs of young people and thus contribute less to their behavior problems. Demonstration projects encourage new approaches to old problems, diverting offenders into positive, community-based efforts.[29]

In addition, Norman identifies three possible functions which can be performed within the framework of the agency models. Ideally, all the functions will receive attention, although it is doubtful whether this will happen until a bureau has been in operation for five years or more. Inadequate funding and inattention to evaluating operations by competent researchers can limit the introduction of one or more of these functions:

1. *Service Brokerage.* The Youth Service Bureau bridges the gap between available services and youth in need of them by referral and follow-up. It acts as an advocate of the child to see that he gets the service he needs, and it strives to avoid any suggestions of stigma so that those in need of assistance will not be reluctant to seek it. However, it does not intervene in the lives of children and their families if its services are not wanted. By receiving voluntary referrals and making referrals to other agencies, with the consent of the child or his parents, the YSB can free court intake departments and probation officers to deal with more serious offenders. It can prevent minor behavior problems from reaching serious proportions and can keep within the community the responsibility for—and the solution to—behavior problems. Furthermore, it avoids associating the minor offender with sophisticated delinquent youth. All this is possible, however, only if law-enforcing agencies, parents, the general public, and youth itself have confidence in the quality of service delivered.

2. *Resource Development.* It is of little value merely to divert a youngster from the justice system unless the resources he requires to stay clear of it are identified and supplied. Therefore the Youth Service Bureau works with citizens in developing new resources where they are lacking. It also contracts for urgently needed services that would otherwise be unavailable. When such services cannot be purchased, the bureau encourages existing agencies to expand their programs or develop specialized services for disadvantaged youth. The bureau works to strengthen these agencies rather than attempting itself to fill the gaps; it obtains data on gaps in youth services but passes the information on to whatever authority has responsibility for establishing priorities.

3. *Systems Modification.* There is little sense in helping a young person adjust to home, school, and community difficulties without also intervening to change the conditions that create them. Therefore the Youth Service Bureau seeks to modify,

> in established institutions, those attitudes and practices that discriminate against troublesome children and youth and thereby contribute to their antisocial behavior. It constructively challenges public school and agency procedures that affect youth adversely, and it guides citizens and groups in fact-finding and fact-dissemination. It is the bureau's job to educate, to consult, to demonstrate, and to resort when necessary to political pressure to see that resources and institutions are responsive to needs.[30]

Some successful programs, which fulfill one or more of the above functions, need mention. The San Diego Youth Service Bureau is a cooperating agencies model with participation by three departments: probation, law enforcement, and county welfare. The cooperation of agencies permits systems modification through service brokerage and resource development. The Bassett Youth Service Bureau in La Puente, a section of Los Angeles, is a community organization model stressing resource development. The Bassett program is operating in an area characterized by limited agency resources.

One successful program of citizen action is the Oakland County (Michigan) Youth Assistance Program. In operation since 1958 and formerly known as the Protective Services Program, it began in a suburb of Detroit when Probate-Juvenile Judge Arthur E. Moore and a number of concerned citizens determined that delinquency prevention was the responsibility of the local community. Oakland County, with a metropolitan population of nearly a million, has approximately 25 programs in the same number of county municipalities. The program is sponsored by the local municipality, the local board of education, and the Oakland County Juvenile Court. A central planning and coordinating committee within each jurisdiction is selected to carry out the program. This committee, known as the General Citizens Committee, includes volunteer representatives from community agencies, churches, local government, service clubs, YMCA-YWCA, PTA, Scouts, and recreation programs. A subcommittee, the Case Study Committee, accepts referrals from schools, private citizens, or the police.

Most of the youngsters have been referred because of home incorrigibility, school truancy, shoplifting, or drinking. Some 20,000 predelinquent and preneglect cases have been processed on an individual basis since 1958. Over 85 percent of these youngsters, it has been claimed, have made an adequate community adjustment. A carefully structured research component is not part of this program. The Youth Assistance Program is a viable partnership involving the municipal government, the school board, the juvenile court, and some 4,000 volunteers. The cost to taxpayers for this program is only $50 per year per case referred to the program (see Appendix D, General Bibliography, Youth Service Systems).

REFERRALS TO THE YOUTH SERVICE BUREAU

A successful youth services agency must receive the approval of the community in which it operates. Its reception can be measured, in part, by the frequency of its use by other agencies and individuals.

The support of local law enforcement is crucial. The police officer, familiar with official delinquency in his neighborhood, is the individual most likely to make a decision about the disposition of a juvenile in trouble. An officer understands the need for services to youngsters who do not require arrest, probation, or institutionalization. The organizers of the youth service bureau will find their closest ally in the law enforcement community. Cooperation and assistance should be sought *before* the bureau is in operation; otherwise, suspicion will be aroused. Close police cooperation during the planning period will help define their responsibilities and insure their cooperation. The police have strongly criticized the agency that accepts the delinquent, expresses a desire to help him, and then fails to deliver services. In fact, when caseloads are too heavy it is possible that services are not being provided. We need to know who is responding and who is not responding to services and why.

Police have long grappled with the problem of appropriate programs for juveniles referred to their own youth divisions. A well organized youth service bureau can offer much assistance to a police department. It is prepared to provide services for children whose cases have been terminated by the police department. The alliance between the youth service bureau and the police youth bureau is a good one. We noted, in our earlier discussion, that delinquency prevention programs cannot serve all children. Maybe we should spend less time determining how to reach all youngsters and devote more attention to the question of who is seeking our services. The source of referrals to the youth service bureaus will help cast some light on the question. A well functioning youth serving agency is a source of help to police, neighborhood social institutions, and youth. An agency which has the support of only one of these potential referral sources is not serving its community.

A review of the referrals for all new cases served by the original California youth service bureau reveals high participation by local citizens (Table 4-1). A little over 54 percent of the referrals were received from individual youngsters and young adults, their parents, or other individuals (usually personal friends). Approximately 46 percent of the cases were referred by local agencies such as the schools, police, and probation intake departments.

TABLE 4-1

Referral Sources to California Youth Service Bureaus: July 1970 to June 1972

	Number	*Percent*
Total new clients served	*7,875*	*100.0*
Referred by:		
Agency	*3,610*	*45.9*
Law Enforcement	1,181	15.0
Probation	793	10.1
School	1,213	15.4
Other agency	423	5.4
Individual	*4,264*	*54.1*
Parent	770	9.8
Self	2,002	25.4
Other individual	1,492	18.9
Not specific	*1*	*

*Less than .1%.

SOURCE: Elaine Duxbury, *Evaluation of Youth Service Bureaus* (Sacramento: State of California Department of the Youth Authority, 1973), p. 43.

Why do individuals use the youth service bureau more than agencies? In each community, the number of direct services available, the quality and adequacy of staffing, the successful outcome of cases help answer this question. The effectiveness of a bureau is seriously limited if immediate services are not available at the time of the referral from the outside agency.

Criteria used by agencies when referring youth to the bureaus were generally the following: (1) the youth was not on probation at the time of the referral; (2) he was considered troublesome in the community as noted in the commission of offenses in the "delinquent tendencies" category (i.e., incorrigibility, truancy, or runaway); (3) if he committed a specific adult crime it was likely to be a drug violation or theft (excluding auto theft); (4) he or she was in a personal crisis such as unemployment, pregnancy, poor health, or an emotional problem; and (5) the youngster and his parents appeared willing to participate in a voluntary program of services.[31]

The problems of the youth referred to the bureaus in California may be grouped into three areas: juvenile offenses, personal problems, and specific adult crimes committed by juveniles. A personal problem was the most frequently mentioned reason for referral. The largest category of personal problems relates to health and income maintenance (36.3 percent). Many youth need employment and are poorly equipped to enter the labor force. Poor health, pregnancy, emotional problems, and difficulties in school (i.e., with language and grades) rank high among the troubles experienced by the youngsters and young adults. Continuing emphasis on the youth who have not committed serious adult offenses is noted in the referral pattern. Approximately 36 percent of all new clients were referred for juvenile offenses such as incorrigibility, truancy, and runaway. Less than 18 percent of the referrals gave a specific adult offense as a reason for service.[32]

The demographic characteristics of the youth served by the bureaus is next reviewed briefly with special attention to age-sex groupings and ethnic composition. These bureaus should help youth between the ages of seven and 18. The California bureau serves this age range. It is surprising to find that young adults, 18 and over, are receiving 21 percent, an increasing proportion of services. Most new clients of the bureaus are attending school or have graduated by the time they come in contact with the service. Hardly any, i.e., less than 5 percent had quit or dropped out of school. The median age for youth referred to all bureaus dropped from 16.1 to 15.3 years during the second year of operation. The median grade in school, recorded at time of the referral, shifted from 9.2 to 9.7 as those over age 18 received more attention. The dramatic need for acquiring work skills to obtain employment supports the increasing demand to accept the young adult as a case referral.

Although delinquency is traditionally a male activity, these bureaus are accepting an increasing number of girls and young women. This trend supports the long-held viewpoint that the female delinquent should be officially processed only when absolutely necessary. Girls often become delinquent because they are exploited by others and diversionary services remain the appropriate form of assistance. Emphasis on medical treatment at Bassett (and earlier at Ventura) has increased the number of girls and young women referred there.

The breakdown of cases by ethnic groups reveals the importance of the locally operated bureau to the target area. In each situation, the dominant ethnic group is being served. Duxbury states:

> Reflecting the ethnic composition of the target areas in which they are located, the Richmond Youth Service Bureau has chiefly served black youth; the East San Jose, San Fernando and Bassett bureaus have all served a sizable proportion of Mexican-American youth; and the remaining bureaus have provided service mainly to white youth.[33]

Placement of bureaus in communities with a predominantly white youth population has been criticized. The initial funding called for the selection of counties presenting different types of bureaus, problems, and services. Hopefully, the expansion of the bureau concept into more neighborhoods will overcome this limitation.

Some of the bureaus made the decision to focus their activities upon a younger age group (14 and under), others chose the more traditional delinquency years (ages 14 through 16), and several selected the young adult group (age 18 and over). No individual was denied service regardless of the age group selected for special attention.

SERVICES OF THE BUREAUS

You will recall that the bureaus are asked to tailor services to the individual. Bureau services are provided under a time limit pattern. The family has the option to request a juvenile court referral rather than accept it. The bureau may provide the service or it may refer youngsters to another agency outside the juvenile justice system. Once a program is formulated participation by the youth and his family is voluntary. When a case is closed by the agency it is common practice to state the reason. It can include any of the following: refused further service; dropped out of the program; moved from the area; or, no further services needed.

Gemignani, in his discussion calling for the establishment of a nationwide system of youth services systems, provides a useful summary of services which are remedial in nature:[34]

1. Direct services to youth
   - A. Counseling
     1. individual counseling
     2. group counseling
     3. utilizing the individual as a counsel aide
     4. family counseling
     5. independent housing placement if parent-youth conflict cannot be resolved
   - B. Educational problems
     1. individual tutoring
     2. preparation for the General Education Development test
     3. admittance to the community college following completion of the GED test
   - C. Employment issues
     1. pre-vocational training
     2. vocational training provided through the Manpower Development and Training Act
     3. job development and placement
     4. job upgrading
   - D. Health services
     1. tattoo removal

        2. eye examination
        3. dental examination
        4. plastic surgery
        5. psychiatric and psychological services
2. Youth involvement
    A. Social, cultural and recreational activities
    B. Issue oriented concerns: ecology, aging, delinquency, poverty, etc.
3. Developmental program planning operation and evaluation
    A. The problem of runaways and the provision of emergency shelter care facilities
    B. Hotlines
    C. Youth to youth advocacy
    D. Drug abuse
        1. school drug information program
        2. crisis center

The California bureaus have emphasized direct services rather than referral to other agencies. Family counseling is the most frequent form of service; individual counseling, employment services (job placement and preparation), and medical treatment are next. Medical treatment is now provided only at Bassett through its volunteer-staffed free clinic. Other direct services to youth include summer camp recreation programs, school tutoring, and serving as an advocate for clients.

The emphasis on counseling as the primary form of service has been criticized by Rosenheim, who states:

> . . . a Youth Service Bureau would be misconceived, in my judgment, if thought of primarily as a counseling establishment. On the contrary, it ought to be a first-aid station, a place where patching up occurs, where immediate crisis aid is freely given, where one can find a broker of benefits for youth.[35]

Rosenheim has described the youth service bureau as a "device for applying middle-class strategies of intervention to lower-class deviant youth."[36] She suggests that the bureau will be offering the same services to youth that middle-class parents provide their own children when it appears that official intervention by the police or the juvenile court is pending. She supports the youth service bureau concept but feels we should be aware of the middle-class bias. Her concern is whether a community will provide the financial resources necessary to support these same services for low-income youth.

In the early youth service bureaus short-term counseling was emphasized. The youngster and young adult defined as troublesome, then and now, is in need of such supportive services. Employment and educational referrals are useful when the youth perceives value in these specific activities. The labor force has failed to find a place for the high school dropout or the untrained. The school has always provided a more comfortable environment for the college-bound student as opposed to the disruptive and the truant. However, troublesome youth see themselves as "left out"; it is not easy to find a solution unless the youth is forced to deal with the environmental pressures that produced the problem. This process can occur only in the community with the help of counselors who know and understand the youth and the pressures operating there. The counselor attempts to assist the youth or young adult to resume his role in the community. The same counseling in a correctional institution has limitations: the counselor would probably be unfamiliar with the pressures in the community from which the individual was committed; the problems of the past are easily forgotten when daily living pressures and face-to-face contact with local inhabitants is not possible; and the goal of an incarcerated offender is release from the institution rather than successful reentry into the community. Counseling in the community where the individual resides, usually also the scene of his trouble, has an additional benefit because bureaus can make use of ex-offenders and the peer population.

State and local governments sometimes find it impossible to fund viable youth-serving programs. However, citizens who have been the victims of delinquent acts are likely to blame the attitudes of delinquent youths for their misbehavior. Only when local communities themselves become accountable for services to youth will the political power structure respond with the funds essential for delinquency prevention and control.

THE FUTURE OF THE YOUTH SERVICE BUREAU

The bureau concept can revolutionize remedial assistance to the youth population in any community. Youngsters in trouble can find services without getting lost in the existing bureaucratic structure. A recent national census has identified approximately 170 programs which appear to be youth service bureaus.[37] These programs are breaking the connection between getting community services and being an official delinquent. Norman indicates:

> For the court, the YSB provides a relief from many "nuisance cases" and a source of follow-up services for nonadjudicated children.
>
> For probation officers, the YSB provides a reduction in time-consuming "informal adjustment" cases, which are more effectively worked with outside an authoritative framework.
>
> For police officers, the YSB provides an alternative to detention and court referral when, in the officer's judgment, release with warning is insufficient but filing a petition is not imperative.
>
> For the public schools, the YSB provides a link with the social work community so that truancy and other school behavior difficulties may be handled through cooperative problem-solving with other agencies.
>
> For citizen volunteers, the YSB provides a chance to turn from frustration over juvenile delinquency to constructive efforts on behalf of youth and youth-serving agencies.
>
> For private social agencies, the YSB provides an extension of youth services through citizen action.
>
> For the Welfare Department, the YSB provides an advocate for troubled youth and support for protective services available to young children.
>
> For youth, the YSB provides the listening ear of someone who can cut establishment "red tape" in an effort to solve their problems.
>
> For the community as a whole, the YSB provides an opportunity to accept responsibility for assisting its troubled and troubling youth by coordinating services on their behalf rather than relying on court authority.[38]

The contribution of the youth services bureau to delinquency prevention and control awaits further assessment. Its effectiveness will be determined by such factors as the following:

1. Will the recipients of such services in diversionary programs, such as the youth service bureau, later acquire a negative community label in the same way as juveniles who have experienced arrest and juvenile court referral?
2. How do progressive, well-staffed police youth bureaus differ from the youth service bureau in methods of operation when *both* accept diversion and remedial services as priority goals in delinquency prevention and control?
3. Are remedial services actually available to youth in every community? If not, then the emphasis on coordination and cooperation among agencies is unlikely to reduce the delinquency problem.
4. When services are available in a community, will referral agencies maintain an interest in developing new kinds to meet the liabilities of its youth population? Several years ago there was a noticeable trend toward changing the name of local youth centers to drug abuse centers. Those requesting funds for the drug counseling centers knew very little about drugs. These proposals revealed a great deal about adult anxiety regarding adolescent drug use, but nothing about new services for their youth population. One would not expect these organizers to be especially knowledgeable about drugs but they could have asked their children about the drug problem. That way service priorities would have been easy to establish.
5. A careful accounting of youth service bureau activities is very important. The evaluation of the agency is crucial. Very few proposals provide a research component permitting the kind of evaluation prepared by Elaine Duxbury and other members of the California Youth Authority.
6. The introduction of a youth service bureau ought to result in a reduction of juvenile arrests. This should be a long-term goal although the California bureaus noted an immediate reduction in juvenile arrests in some of the target areas as early as the first year of operation.

In conclusion, the youth service bureau is one way a community can provide the adolescent and young adult with:

a. a chance to "be somebody," i.e., they must move into economically rewarding positions;

b. a chance to become competent and to experience the feeling of competence;

c. opportunities to participate in roles which yield a sense of contribution, i.e., that out of what they do, they obtain a feeling of meaningful participation and contribution;

d. experiences which yield a sense of belonging, i.e., that they are part of the institutions and communities where they study, work and live; and

e. supportive counseling services: (1) to overcome psychological residues of earlier failure and delinquency experiences and (2) to provide supports necessary to deal with the strains imposed by new experiences.[39]

Continued support for the youth service bureau concept is contained in the recommendations of the National Advisory Commission on Criminal Justice Standards and Goals (see Appendix D, General Bibliography). Most important, though, is that the agencies in the community become aware of these needs of youth and of using the youth service bureau to help youngsters meet them. The police are crucial in this process; we look next at how the police deal with juveniles.

STUDY QUESTIONS

1. What is a youth service bureau?
2. When is the youth service bureau a delinquency prevention agency?
3. Why is the youth service bureau considered a noncoercive agency?
4. Identify the various ways in which a child in trouble comes to the attention of the community.
5. How will cooperation and coordination facilitate the delivery of services to children in trouble?

6. What is diversion? Are there limitations in using diversion when providing direct services to youth?
7. Summarize the major contribution of the early coordinating council movement to the field of delinquency prevention and control.
8. What is a neighborhood service center?
9. Describe the Mobilization for Youth program and identify the sociological theory upon which the program is based.
10. What is the advocacy role of the youth service bureau?
11. Should the youth service bureau be organized as a newly created independent agency? If so, list appropriate guidelines for such an agency.
12. Identify the state that pioneered in introducing legislation for the establishment and funding of youth service bureaus. Identify the year in which the legislation was passed.
13. Why must agency evaluation procedures accompany plans for the organization of a youth service bureau?
14. Describe the youth service models identified in this chapter. What functions are performed within the framework of the agency models?
15. Which community agencies are most likely to refer juveniles to a youth service bureau?
16. What contributes to the uniqueness of the individual youth service bureau? Why do these bureaus differ in the type of services offered?
17. List the criteria used by various agencies when referring youth to a youth service bureau.
18. What are some of the direct services provided?
19. Has your statewide criminal justice planning agency funded any youth service bureau projects?
20. Has your state passed legislation supporting the establishment of youth service bureaus?

NOTES

1. The President's Commission on Law Enforcement and Administration of Justice, *The Challenge of Crime in a Free Society* (Washington, D.C.: U.S. Government Printing Office, 1967), p. 83.

2. Reprinted with permission of the National Council on Crime and Delinquency, from Sherwood Norman, *The Youth Service Bureau: A Key to Delinquency Prevention* (Paramus, N.J.: National Council on Crime and Delinquency, 1972), p. 8.

3. California Delinquency Prevention Commission, *Youth Service Bureaus: Standards and Guidelines* (Sacramento: Department of the Youth Authority, 1968), p. 1.

4. Alfred J. Kahn, *Theory and Practice of Social Planning* (New York: Russell Sage Foundation, 1969), p. 6. © 1969 Russell Sage Foundation.

5. Alfred J. Kahn, *Planning Community Services for Children in Trouble* (New York: Columbia University Press, 1963), pp. 24–25.

6. Sherwood Norman, *The Youth Service Bureau: A Key to Prevention*, p. 3.

7. Eleanor Harlow, *Diversion from the Criminal Justice System*, Crime and Delinquency Topics series, National Institute of Mental Health, Center for Studies of Crime and Delinquency (Washington, D.C.: U.S. Government Printing Office, 1971), p. 26.

8. Board of Trustees, NCCD, "Juvenile Curfews: A Policy Statement," *Crime and Delinquency*, 18, no. 2 (April 1972): 133.

9. Angelo J. Gagliardo, "Are Youth Bureaus the Answer?" *Juvenile Court Judges Journal*, 22, no. 3 (Fall 1971): 57–59.

10. Ted Rubin and Jack F. Smith, *The Future of the Juvenile Court: Implications for Correctional Manpower and Training*, A Consultants' Paper prepared for the Joint Commission on Correctional Manpower and Training (College Park, Maryland: American Correctional Association, 1968), pp. 32–33.

11. *Report to the President, 1970 White House Conference on Children* (Washington, D.C.: U.S. Government Printing Office, 1971), p. 382.

12. Lowell J. Carr, *Delinquency Control* (New York: Harper & Row, 1940), p. 329.

13. Alfred J. Kahn, *Planning Community Services for Children in Trouble* (New York: Columbia University Press, 1963), p. 466; Herbert A. Bloch and Frank T. Flynn, *Delinquency: The Juvenile Offender in America Today* (New York: Random House, 1956), pp.

525–527; and Roland L. Warren, *Studying Your Community* (New York: Russell Sage Foundation, 1955), pp. 296–299.

14. Mary B. Novick, *Community Programs and Projects for the Prevention of Juvenile Delinquency*, U.S. Department of Health, Education, and Welfare, Welfare Administration, Children's Bureau, Juvenile Delinquency: Facts and Facets, Pamphlet no. 14 (Washington, D.C.: U.S. Government Printing Office, 1960), pp. 1–2.

15. Joan L. Ecklein and Armand A. Lauffer, *Community Organizers and Social Planners* (New York: John Wiley and Sons, and Council on Social Work Education, 1972), pp. 234–262.

16. *Programs Relevant to Urban Problems,* Interim Phase I Report of the Citizens Committee, Voluntarism and Urban Life Project (New York: Institute of Community Studies, 1968). United Way of America is located at 801 N. Fairfax Street, Alexandria, Va. 22314.

17. Robert Perlman and David Jones, *Neighborhood Service Centers,* U.S. Department of Health, Education, and Welfare, Welfare Administration, Office of Juvenile Delinquency and Youth Development, JD Publication no. 1005 (Washington, D.C.: U.S. Government Printing Office, 1967), p. 1.

18. For a careful analysis of community action programs in the 1960s see Peter Marris and Martin Rein, *Dilemmas of Social Reform: Poverty and Community Action in the United States,* 2nd ed. (Chicago: Aldine Publishing Co., 1973).

19. Harold H. Weissman, *Justice and the Law in the Mobilization for Youth Experience,* The New Social Work Series, Vol. 4 (New York: Association Press, 1969), pp. 194–195.

20. John M. Riley and Philip A. Fellin, "Is the War on Poverty Attacking Mental Illness?" *Community Mental Health Journal,* 8 (May 1972): 139–148.

21. Dwight S. Adams, "United Fund Executive Reactions to the Impact of Federal Programs in Their Community Domains," *Community Mental Health Journal,* 8 (May 1972): 130–138.

22. See Elizabeth H. Gorlich, *Guides for Demonstration Projects for Youth Service Bureaus,* U.S. Department of Health, Education, and Welfare, Social and Rehabilitation Service, Children's Bureau (Washington, D.C.: Children's Bureau, 1969), pp. 4–5; and Sherwood Norman, *The Youth Service Bureau: A Key to Prevention,* pp. 19–22.

23. See John M. Martin, *Toward a Political Definition of Juvenile Delinquency,* U.S. Department of Health, Education, and Welfare, Social and Rehabilitation Service, Youth Development and Delinquency Prevention Administration (Washington, D.C.: U.S. Government Printing Office, 1970), pp. 11–15; and John M. Martin, Joseph P. Fitzpatrick and Robert E. Gould, *The Analysis of Delinquent Behavior: A Structural Approach* (New York: Random House, 1968), pp. 177–188.

24. *The Challenge of Crime,* p. 83.

25. California Delinquency Prevention Commission, *Youth Service Bureaus: Standards and Guidelines,* (Sacramento: Department of the Youth Authority, 1968), p. 1.

26. The five federally funded California youth service bureaus were the following: Yolo County Youth Service Bureau; Pacifica Youth Service Bureau; East San Jose Youth Service Bureau; Youth Services Bureau of San Fernando; and Ventura Youth Service Bureau (closed in June 1971).

27. See Sherwood Norman, *The Youth Service Bureau: A Brief Description of Five Programs* (Paramus, N.J.: National Council on Crime and Delinquency, 1970), pp. 1–15.

28. *California Welfare and Institutions Code,* Sections 1900–1904 (West Supplement, 1975).

29. Sherwood Norman, *The Youth Service Bureau: A Brief Description of Five Programs,* pp. 15–16.

30. Sherwood Norman, *Youth Service Bureau: A Key to Prevention,* pp. 12–13.

31. Elaine Duxbury, *Youth Service Bureaus in California,* Progress Report no. 3, January 1972 (Sacramento: Department of the Youth Authority, 1972), p. 41.

32. Elaine Duxbury, *Evaluation of Youth Service Bureaus* (Sacramento: State of California Department of Youth Authority, 1973), p. 46.

33. Elaine Duxbury, *Youth Service Bureaus in California,* p. 35.

34. Robert J. Gemignani, "Youth Services Systems: Diverting Youth from the Juvenile Justice System," *Delinquency Prevention Reporter,* July–August, 1972, pp. 1–7.

35. Margaret K. Rosenheim, "Youth Service Bureaus: A Concept in Search of Definition," *Juvenile Court Judges Journal,* 20, no 2 (Summer 1969): 73.

36. Ibid., p. 70.

37. *The Challenge of Youth Service Bureaus,* U.S. Department of Health, Education, and Welfare, Social and Rehabilitation Service, Youth Development and Delinquency Prevention Administration (Washington, D.C.: U.S. Government Printing Office, 1973).

38. Sherwood Norman, *The Youth Service Bureau: A Key to Prevention,* pp. 11–12.

39. Kenneth Polk, "Delinquency Prevention and the Youth Service Bureau," *Criminal Law Bulletin,* 7, no. 6 (July–August 1971): 510. © Warren, Gorham and Lamont, Inc., Boston. Reprinted with the permission of the publisher.

POLICE, JUVENILES, AND OTHER MINORITIES

THE POLICE DILEMMA
SCHOOLS AND THE POLICE
POLICE AND THE COMMUNITY
THE POLICE OFFICER AND HIS TRAINING
POLICE DISCRETION

The primary functions of the police are to enforce the law and to offer general public service. The authority of the police originates with the law and is limited by it. The fulfillment of the second function, which is community service, does not necessitate the use of this authority or power by the police officer. The involvement of police in both control and prevention creates many of the problems in police-juvenile relations. Everyone recognizes that the police can often resolve noncriminal disputes by simply asserting their authority. But there are those who think the police would like to invoke this authority in all public contacts. This criticism will continue as police agencies become involved in diversionary programs.[1]

THE POLICE DILEMMA

The juvenile generally sees the police officer in a coercive role when he is questioning suspects. When a youngster observes the police officer at work in a coercive situation, he is likely to develop a negative attitude toward all things legal. The mutual suspicion between patrolmen and youngsters is not easily reduced.

The social distance between the police officer and his constituents is a major problem. A recent study indicates that one of the strongest emotions in the young patrolman assigned to the ghetto is fear. In spite of this limitation the new patrolman has good rapport with children, the middle-aged, and the elderly; but he easily generates severe hostility toward teen-agers and young adults.[2]

Robert Coles, in his sensitive portrayal of children in poverty, recalls asking a youngster if he honestly felt the police would harm someone so young. The young boy responded to the question by saying, "To the cops, everyone around here is a little bad boy, no matter how old he is or how many grandchildren he has around."[3] In delinquency prevention and control programs, the policeman and the child must have an opportunity to relate and interact. The patrolman's fear of the inner city and the child's hostility to all law enforcement must be overcome.

School administrators fear delinquents too. Because the delinquent is brought before them for discipline, it is impossible for them to develop a positive relationship.[4] However, there can be no change of behavior unless some kind of communication is established. When the administrators become familiar with youth groups which have an expressed interest in delinquency problems, communication becomes possible. If they allow youth to participate in decisions affecting them, they get a more positive image of youth. When a school administrator dismisses the contribution of youth in decision-making, he spoils the relationship thus made possible.

When law enforcement is at its best, the child might be able to find in these activities an alleviation of the danger and impersonality of the city. On the other hand, when the new patrolman in the ghetto equates his assignment with military warfare, the ghetto youngster will react as if he were an invader.

Wheeler and Cottrell have found that the police and the judges have the most decisive influence on juveniles who have been involved in delinquency. In contrast, for other youth the most important adult outside the family is a teacher.[5] Therefore, the school appears to be a good place for juveniles and police to discover each other. Especially in low income areas, youngsters pattern themselves after successful criminals or hustlers. Opportunities and rewards are known to exist in careers of crime; the juvenile must be aware of openings in noncriminal careers. Respect for the policeman, the crime fighter, can be helpful to youth during career orientation. Unless the police are visible, there is little likelihood that youngsters will consider the law enforcement profession as their model.

The changing and competing values in our society dictate with some urgency that law enforcement agencies be identified with justice and fair play. The growing political cynicism of children, as early as the fourth grade, suggests that the youngster should experience a positive relationship with some representative in an authority position very early.[6] The political cynicism of black youth, as measured in their belief that the government does not care for them, creates damaging feelings of worthlessness. In one community, a parent patrol was formed to search Suicide Park every evening. Within a year, more than eight youngsters between the ages of 12 and 16 committed suicide there. The cynicism and pessimism of youth are destructive forces.

Since 1974 the Law Enforcement Assistance Administration has emphasized an advocacy role in meeting the needs of the criminal justice system. This agency has made special efforts to ensure that effective citizen-oriented programs are a part of each funded project. Its philosophy has been stated as follows:

> . . . the criminal justice system must not be the master of the people. It can only aspire to be the servant of the people. Policemen, judges, corrections officials, and prosecutors cannot be in business for themselves. Their job is not to erect empires and operate outside of the gaze and control of the public.[7]

Such an emphasis can gradually enlist the cooperative goodwill of more and more people.

SCHOOLS AND THE POLICE

The youngster must be allowed to observe the patrolman as a helping agent. Robert Derbyshire, in his study of the elementary school pupil's perception of the police, found that negative feelings were developed from observing policemen at work. Third grade children living in economically depressed areas were more negative about the police than those residing in an area of high social and economic stability.[8] These children need to observe officers working in situations where the policeman has the training and motivation to be in touch with the neighborhood. Derbyshire found that animosity toward the police can be reduced where some form of personal nonpunitive police contact is made directly, as in the elementary school. There, uniformed officers discussed the duties of policemen and the complimentary responsibilities of citizens for controlling criminal behavior. As a result of this study, a large urban police department asked itself, "How do children perceive us?" and then attempted to do something about the negative views held by young children.

The pioneering work of Robert Portune, beginning with his Cincinnati Police–Juvenile Attitude Project in 1965, deserves much credit for reducing social distance between police and youth in city schools. Using a representative sample of one thousand junior-high-school students enrolled in Cincinnati, Ohio schools, Portune concluded:

1. The students who emerged from the ninth grade were found to have attitudes toward the police that were significantly less favorable than those of students entering grade seven.
2. The general population of junior high school students (ages 12–16) displayed an alarming ignorance of law enforcement in a democratic society.
3. The standard junior high school program of studies was almost totally devoid of curriculum materials aimed at improving student knowledge and understanding of law and law enforcement. Curriculum units on these subjects did not exist.
4. A major factor in the formation of adverse attitudes toward police was the police-juvenile contact. This contact brought together a juvenile with little or no knowledge of the nature of law enforcement and a police officer with little or no knowledge of the early adolescent.
5. The standard police training program did not include units or materials on the early adolescent.
6. The attitudes of junior high school students toward the police varied significantly with respect to age, grade in school, sex, race, school achievement, church attendance, and socio-economic level.[9]

The curriculum materials developed by Portune and others are an aid to police departments in their classroom work with juveniles. The course information may be used by police officers or social studies teachers; lesson plans are available for kindergarten through high school (see Appendix D, General Bibliography,

Curriculum Materials). Your state department of education can tell you whether such curriculum resources are available for use in local school districts.

The need for nonpunitive police contacts with all adolescents regardless of social class is well defined in a recent study of police officer contact in the public schools of an upper-middle-class community. The officers of the Davis (California) Police Department introduced the Three R's project in 1967; the program focuses upon regulation, responsibility, and rapport. Regulation refers to the statutes and rules which apply to all citizens. Responsibility is defined as the ability to differentiate between legal and illegal conduct while learning to live within the boundaries of these regulations. Rapport is the development of communication channels among youth, the police, and the community. The effects of the program have been positive:

> The results indicate the Davis Police Department's Three R program is effective in changing student attitudes in a more favorable direction. The changes are uniformly positive, result in significant shifts, and are cumulative over time. . . . The longer the students have been in the program the more likely they are to see police as honest, respectful of citizen's rights, and non-prejudiced toward minority groups.[10]

The study offers the following suggestions for consideration in formulating new programs permitting successful interaction between youth and the police:

1. Extend the Three R program into and through the high school years.
2. Clarify the role of the police relative to the causes and treatment of other social problems.
3. Develop special programs for individuals from different social, cultural, and personality groups.
4. Include more materials and discussion on those topics on which students are uninformed, uncertain or distrustful.
5. Clarify the specific actions that occur in youth-police interactions so that perceptions of arrest and other actions are realistically made by youth.

6. Examine the sources of anti-law, anti-police attitudes in other social institutions, particularly the family.[11]

S.T.O.P. (Student Training on Prevention) in California, a curriculum which involves youth, is an anticrime program sponsored by the state office of the attorney general. Two dozen junior-high-school volunteers are trained for four weeks in a thorough understanding of the juvenile justice system, and then assigned to grade school classrooms armed with puppets, film strips, and class discussion programs. The program, which takes six weeks to complete, focuses on bicycle safety, prevention of bike thefts, vandalism, drug abuse, and the juvenile justice system.

In another most promising school program, youngsters sign up in advance to ride in a police car to find out what a police officer does in his work. Many police departments claim success with the ride-along but the only empirical study has been conducted by Victor Cizanckas and Carleton Purviance. They used an attitude scale to assess the feelings of junior-high-school students toward police both before and after the ride-along. The experiment took twelve weeks, there were four ride-along periods lasting approximately three hours; the participants in the program were black youngsters from the seventh and eighth grades in Menlo Park (California). Chief Cizanckas and his associate concluded that: (1) more positive attitudes toward the police were noted following the ride-along experiment; (2) this shift in attitude continued with the passage of time; and (3) those who did not participate in the program (i.e., the control group) experienced no significant shifts in their attitudes toward the police.[12] Because the youngsters felt their neighbors might think they were being taken to juvenile hall, early in the program they asked if they might ride in the patrol cars with at least one of their peers.

Most students welcome the opportunity to meet law enforcement officers when the problem of authority does not interfere with communication. Youngsters remember officers who show concern for them and who carry out routine police duties fairly. In fact, the following story actually took place in a middle-sized southeastern city. A young policeman assigned to the juvenile division in the town was attending a delinquency control workshop being held over two successive summers on a nearby university campus. He paid for the first summer of instruction out of his own pocket, but hoped the city could subsidize him in the second session; most of the other participants were funded by their agencies. The city manager, however, refused to provide the necessary funds. The officer had a reputation for honesty and fairness among the young people of the community, and they were determined to have him attend the workshop. He was able, through their money-raising efforts, to complete the course in delinquency control, and in addition, the young people mobilized the community to defeat the city manager in the next election.

A number of schools have introduced police–school liaison programs in the past few years. The police officer is assigned to a specific school, his office is located in the building, and he is available each day to counsel students. Critics of the program suggest that these officers are not trained in counseling, that they are trying to carry out delinquency control activities in the school. Such criticisms are much less valid than in the past. Officers in these programs see themselves as preventing delinquency while being trained in the behavioral sciences. Colleges and universities have been placing both in-service and pre-service officers in neighborhood schools for internships as tutors and teachers aides for several years. The experience has been successful because police want greater involvement in the community helping role. The success of the police–school liaison program is dependent upon several important factors: (1) the philosophy of the principal in the school assigned; (2) the support for delinquency prevention offered by the superintendent of schools in the district; (3) the absence of opposition from teachers in the school as well as from the police chief; and (4) the availability of ancillary training in psychology and counseling from a nearby college or university. June Morrison has reviewed the history of police liaison programs in the United States and Great Britain.[13] She found the programs to be encouraging even though resistance is noted when they are introduced.

POLICE AND THE COMMUNITY

A delinquency prevention or control program is more effective when the processing of the delinquent is accomplished by those who care for him. When a community experiences tensions between police and juveniles, it is unlikely that delinquency can be prevented; suspicion and rumors make control weak. David Bayley and Harold Mendelsohn provide a significant observation when they say:

> The burden of improving police-minority relations does not belong exclusively to the police. . . . The police must indeed be malleable and creative; these are new times and policemen are naive if they believe business can be done as usual. . . . At the same time, they are creatures of the society in which they live and work. Unless that society is willing to inaugurate changes in patterns of living that touch everyone—dominants as well as minorities—policemen will remain locked with minorities in a relationship of antagonism which neither created but from which neither can esacpe.[14]

It has been fashionable to assume that more use of foot policemen in the neighborhood reduces the social distance between citizens and police. This dilemma is not resolved by the decision to walk or ride while carrying out policing duties. The patrolman should be trained to recognize the patterns of conformity in his patrol neighborhood, prepared to recognize troublemakers and aid the troubled. During the screening process agencies may avoid sanctioning where there is no prior offense pattern.[15] The police officer should rely on the indigenous leaders as a potent community resource.

In 1931, Shaw and McKay pioneered in mobilizing a neighborhood into community efforts for delinquency prevention and control; the program became known as the Chicago Area Project.[16] Shaw and his associates helped the juvenile overcome his commitment to delinquent values by offering him a visible community of citizens who cared about his welfare; they were not like the caretakers from the outside who processed him as delinquent. Kobrin, an early associate of Shaw, summarized the importance of the Chicago Area Project plan in the field of delinquency prevention as, "a method designed to keep preventional work focused upon its proper object, the delinquent as a person in his milieu."[17]

Patrolmen find it difficult to apply these ideas. For example, when there is a white patrolman in the black ghetto, distrust exists on both sides. The juvenile approaching a pattern of delinquency needs approval from the community. In turn, the patrolman should receive recognition for nonpunitive services given in the course of his daily work. Of course, that recognition is not easily obtained unless the people are visible and accessible. Brodsky has listed five skills which are required in the model of police behavior he has defined as the helping agent:

1. Empathy
2. Interpersonal awareness and sensitivity
3. Ability to listen
4. Nonjudgmental attitude
5. Ability to facilitate others' actions.[18]

All policemen need these attributes. The police department is the only 24-hour community agency offering services to the individual in need.[19] Recent training programs in crisis intervention techniques help the policeman offer maximum assistance to people in conflict situations during those hours when other agencies are closed (see Appendix D, General Bibliography, Crisis). Although the police are associated with the war on crime, the complexity of police work requires the interpersonal sensitivity of the mental health professional. These skills are complementary rather than contradictory. The police community services division is set up to implement the role of helper agent, but it would be unfortunate if these skills were limited to one division of the police department.

To develop empathy between the community and the police is not going to be easy. Some people find it difficult to believe that a policeman in an inner-city neighborhood can become a model for juveniles who hold a negative attitude toward law and its enforcement.[20] Clifford Shaw focused upon the importance of the neighborhood and its members in combatting delinquency. As Kobrin tells us:

> The genius of . . . Clifford Shaw, lay in his sharp perception of delinquency as human behavior and in his sense of the naturalness or inevitability of violative activity in the youngster who, whether singly or in groups, is neglected, despised, or ignored as a person.[21]

Displayed several years ago, at a meeting of the International Congress on Religion, Architecture and the Visual Arts, were a number of cardboard boxes covered with designs, pictures, and quotations. On one, an unknown inner-city youngster had printed a quote which set the tone for the congress: "O God, who can't read or write, who is on welfare, and who is treated like garbage. Help us to know You."[22] As never before the legitimacy of a helping agent role in law enforcement was demonstrated by this plea.

THE POLICE OFFICER AND HIS TRAINING

Greater emphasis on juvenile matters is a new pattern in the training of police officers. Formerly, the traditional police academy curriculum devoted only six to nine hours on issues of juvenile justice administration.[23] Because the urban police role is growing more complex, the technical skills of the academy are scant preparation for work in the field—the officer should possess intimate knowledge of the community he is policing.

The new concept, neighborhood policing, reduces numerous tensions by decentralizing police districts into mini-precincts which combine control and helping services. Frequent face-to-face, nonpunitive contact is emphasized. The training required for the neighborhood officer includes knowledge of the community and its goals, social services referral information, and counseling skills (i.e., crisis intervention, adolescent psychology, and alternate life styles).[24] Neighborhood policing can become the framework for communication with the community. Some people feel that the officer ought to live in the neighborhood where he works, but doing so does not necessarily eliminate the pressures on an officer. More important than place of residence is his commitment to the requirements of successful neighborhood policing. Germann says:

> The police must demonstrate, by attitude, pronouncement, and deed, that the goal "to protect and to serve" applies to every individual and group within the community—young and old, liberal and conservative, rich and poor, black and white, popular and unpopular, believer and non-believer—that crime

> prevention has as high a priority as crime repression, that human rights are as highly regarded as property rights, and that all policies and procedures are implemented with essential fairness always and everywhere.
>
> The citizenry must demonstrate, by attitude, interest, and action, their commitment to ordered liberty, their understanding of criminal justice, their support of, cooperation with, and control of police, and their involvement always and everywhere, so that community policing is the pride of every citizen.[25]

The police establishment is trying to revitalize a traditional curriculum in order to meet current problems, and needs community support. In some cities the police are identified as those who do the dirty work; this creates an image of police repression rather than understanding.[26]

The International Association of Chiefs of Police recently conducted a study of the opinions held by 4,672 experienced police officers on a number of issues. They concluded that training materials should emphasize the role of the community in preventing and controlling delinquency. Sixty-four percent of the officers agreed that the policeman should concern himself with "a juvenile's socio-economic status and home situation in deciding what to do with him."[27]

If knowledge of the community is to be available to the police officer, it should have high priority in training at the academy. This knowledge obviously cannot be acquired when the academy's emphasis is on patrol procedures, investigation, or surveillance. One large police department contracts with a nearby university to offer a 39-hour course in the prevention and control of juvenile delinquency as part of the police academy program. The instructor, a social worker, has found the recruits receptive to this training.[28] Officers in training are denied the use of outside instructors for academy programs dealing with delinquency because of a shortage of funds. But they do have access to pertinent curriculm materials from the International Association of Chiefs of Police, the International Juvenile Officers Association, and the statewide juvenile officers associations. Hopefully, current information from the publications of these professional police organizations will be used to update existing training program information. A number of universities offer short-term institutes dealing with the problems of delinquency. The Delinquency Control Institute, in the School of Public Administration at the University of Southern California, has pioneered in offering specialized academic and practical training. This program, developed under the vigorous leadership of Robert Carter and Dan Pursuit, continues to offer two intensive 8-week programs each year. Recently, the institute has airlifted its faculty to various communities where mini-institutes are held. The National College of Juvenile Justice is the training division of the National Council of Juvenile Court Judges. It is located on the campus of the University of Nevada in Reno and provides highly specialized training to personnel in the juvenile justice system. In-service police officers have been attending the institutes and workshops since 1973.

Academic programs constantly need fresh ideas. Until recently a large urban police agency taught that an illegitimate baby will be mentally retarded. Officers taught this are at a great disadvantage when they meet with people in the neighborhood and at the social service agencies. Harris, in his study of the police academy, says that most recruits want to be fair about enforcing the law; their problem is misinformation rather than special prejudice. He would like to see training in the academy oriented toward:

1. sensitivity to the ambiguities and ambivalences of group and individual interaction, and
2. insight into the recruit's own ideological conflicts and ambivalences.[29]

Many oppose the social-environment material in the police academy curriculum. They say that the beat officer, when reporting a delinquency, does not have time to get to know the youth's situation. Excessive paperwork is given as the reason for an officer's disinterest in the social background of the juvenile offender. The officer is not expected to minimize his traditional duties. Nonetheless, although his paperwork is sometimes heavy, he has closer contact with the juveniles than anyone else. Gary Adams indicates that the law enforcement officer can mobilize and use resources for delinquency prevention and control in the community.[30] This program would mean academy and in-service training, but could only help the officer use his time more constructively. The police department will continue to hear complaints of hostility, suspicion, and harassment until all law enforcement personnel have training in this area. The Joint Commission on Correctional Manpower and Training indicates that in the large inner city by 1985, the minority population will be a majority of 75 percent.[31] We cannot continue to deny the importance of new kinds of training.

Many officers smart under the redefinition of the police role. Their anxiety and discomfort might be reduced if they could release these frustrations in the give and take of classroom discussions. Several years ago the Menlo Park (California) Police Department doffed traditional uniforms in favor of olive blazers with an identifying patch, dark trousers, dress shirt and tie. A name plate replaced the badge; rank was not shown; the nightstick disappeared; guns were carried inconspicuously inside the blazer. During the first six months the new uniforms provoked useful exchanges. Stripped of their usual badges of authority, it was necessary for the officers to develop new styles of communication and new patterns of relating to the community. They report that police efficiency has increased and assaults on police officers have been markedly reduced since the program was initiated. It would seem that the new forms of communication have reduced some of the tensions associated with patrolling.[32]

Human Relations Training

Police power is considered awesome by members of the community and by the officers themselves. The possession of power, alone, does not enhance the success of the patrolman in handling stress situations. The officer needs additional training which permits him to:

1. *Recognize his own attitudes.* To help him pinpoint areas of stress, he must know what angers him, in what way he can be manipulated, and what words affect him negatively.
2. *Recognize the attitudes of others.* As he asks the same questions about others that he has of himself, the officer will come to recognize how the attitudes of others interact with his own. And he will be open to new ways of asserting his authority without at the same time causing undue hostility. Recognition of the forces of interaction is the key to controlling situations and reducing the

antagonism to police. The following areas of study, if included in the police academy curriculum, would hopefully look toward these ends:

1. *Individual behavior*—perception, motivation, attitudes, views and values of man and society, deviant behavior and mental illness;
2. *Inter-personal behavior*—management of conflict, interaction processes, communications;
3. *Group behavior*—group dynamics, influence, cohesion, leadership, problem solving;
4. *Inter-group relations*—prejudice, discrimination, social, religious, economic, and political values;
5. *Community issues*—collective responsibilities, detection and analysis of tensions, environmental influences, community services, unpopular or extremist groups;
6. *Criminal justice administration*—the role of police in a democratic society; police policy and discretionary alternatives; relationships with prosecution, defense, courts, probation, corrections, and parole.[33]

It is sometimes said that citizens support the police because they fear crime. Or, better, that such support is strongest when good policework is combined with respect for the citizen.[34] It seems likely then, that new forms of training at the law enforcement academy will bring support for the police. Good human relations training can ease the major antagonism between the officer and the juvenile, which develops when trust appears to have been abused. Because the juvenile expects the officer to be trustworthy, he is in a favorable position to influence the behavior of the potential delinquent (even though patrol officers regard juveniles as the most difficult citizens to police).

Good human relations training also prepares a police department for successful communication with the social service agencies. The officer trained only in the traditional arrest and control functions is hampered. Many officers pay less attention to conditions which do not involve law violations because they are uncertain about the amount of control they can exercise. There is no reason for this handicap. The officer finds people in distress every day, and should direct them to the proper agencies or community resources; this knowledge is available and waiting to be used.

Establishing rapport among police, citizens, and agencies is the responsibility of all members of the department. In one town the community-relations division of the police department was asked to serve as the intermediary between the district policeman and the citizen. These staff members received complaints from the citizens and then made recommendations to the patrol officers. This program was ineffective because the community relations unit served as an opponent to the patrolman. The Simi Valley (California) Community Safety Agency expects all its officers to be community relations specialists. This city police department focuses on crime prevention, the protection of life and property, and the creation of a community environment that is ordered and stable.

The Simi Valley program is divided into four parts: patrol, investigation, youth, and counseling. The patrol division is comprised of community safety officers (i.e., patrolmen) who are not only patrol specialists proficient in controlling the crime problem, but also capable of investigating their own cases. The investigation program is directed by coordinators who focus their efforts on major crimes and intelligence, as well as maintaining close liaison with other law enforcement agencies; they assist the safety officers when necessary. The youth division is staffed by juvenile crime prevention specialists, who coordinate referral, counseling, and education services with schools, probation, welfare, and other youth-serving agencies throughout the community. Everyone in this program works closely with the school and recreation districts and many meaningful educational programs are developed. The counseling division is directed by an expert who coordinates the work of counselors in the community, particularly the patrol and youth divisions; the town emphasizes this program because of its preventive aspects. The team policing concept familiarizes officers with the various programs of the four divisions.

This police department uses high visibility and participation in the community to good effect without neglecting law and order aspects. Cooperation with agencies is such that each officer sees himself as a human relations specialist. The department has overcome the many limitations of police community relations programs, the most severe being the vastly different view of the law enforcement role held by the police and by the community.[35]

Some police departments recruit officers by first assigning workers to community service. These people perform a variety of police duties, short of law enforcement, with prime emphasis on community service work. After one or two years, they are eligible for promotion to patrolman. Although considered a successful program by many, unfortunately there are problems. The community service officer performs the helping role before he enters law enforcement. Later, as a sworn officer, his status on the police force is determined by his skill in the traditional control functions. Many officers recruited in this way soon deny the importance of the community service aspect of their work. Peer pressure and a desire to obtain permanent patrolman rank may make them change. The community service officer is subject to different values when he becomes a patrolman. This area requires further research.

The helping role in law enforcement is most easily achieved when the officer becomes a source of information about the social services in his community. The delinquent is often the shared client of several agencies. Kahn includes the following activities under the heading of social services:

1. Day-care and similar child development and child-care programs (Head Start, family day care for infants, after-school care, and so on)
2. Homemakers and home helps
3. Personal and family guidance and counseling, including marital counseling
4. Child welfare activities such as foster care, adoption, protective services for neglected and abused children
5. Assessments for courts, schools, camps of parental relationships (are parents neglectful? with which member of a separated couple should a child reside?) or of a child's personality and capacities (is he capable of adjusting to a normal group?)
6. Big Brother, Big Sister, and related volunteer helping and guidance efforts
7. Probation and parole work
8. Family planning services
9. Community centers for the aged, for youth, for families
10. "Meals-on-wheels," "senior citizen" programs, special protective programs for the aged

11. A diversity of group programs such as therapeutic group work with adolescents, organization of tenants in a housing project, organization of parents of retarded children
12. Food stamps and school breakfast and lunch programs or surplus commodity distribution
13. Rural welfare programs and special programs for migrant laborers
14. Special programs to counsel potential migrants or immigrants and to help them adjust in new surroundings
15. Assistance to residents of poverty areas or members of underprivileged population groups, so that they may come together for mutual aid activity
16. Information, advice, referral, complaint, and advocacy services of many kinds
17. Institutional programs for the neglected, dependent, disturbed (state training schools, homes for the aged, residential treatment for children, and so on)[36]

These services should be identified and utilized where they do not conflict with the overall policies of the police department. Police are not expected to do social work but they should be able to refer clients to the proper agency. Police departments should prepare referral brochures for the use of their officers. At the minimum, included for each agency should be: function and purpose, eligibility requirements for service, source of referrals, and addresses where additional information may be obtained. If a youth service bureau exists in the community the booklet could be prepared with their cooperation. Some departments offer community resource field training for police recruits.[37] Others bring together policemen and members of social agencies who sit down informally and discuss the kinds of people they serve and how various problems are handled; these sessions reduce the distance between the two groups.[38] More involvement is needed in all communities, especially since diversion has become more popular.

One of the earliest programs to use social service workers in a police department was the preventive casework service for younger children provided by the Minneapolis Police Department. In 1964, a professional caseworker of the Minneapolis Family and Children's Service was assigned to the Juvenile Division of the Minneapolis Police Department. It was believed that there were many young children, under age 13, who might benefit from social service referrals at the time of their first police contact. The program was discontinued 14 months later when it was learned that most children contacted by the police and referred to the social worker were already well known to welfare agencies and the police. As a result of this experience, the police department initiated a school liaison program in order to reach children earlier.

The police and the public agencies have cooperated through various working agreements in handling delinquent, dependent, and neglected children. These agreements involve the police, school, juvenile court, state and county welfare departments, and the juvenile officers association. One of the first such agreements was the *Dade County Working Agreement for Handling Delinquent, Dependent, and Neglected Children* adopted in Miami, Florida, in 1965. Another is the Wisconsin agreement entitled *A Police Statement of the Working Relationship Between the Dodge County Juvenile Court, Law Enforcement Officers, and Dodge County Welfare Department.*

Haurek and Clark find the police willing to cooperate with private and public agencies.[39] Police training is now emphasizing cooperation with social agencies. Today it is realistic to expect a police recruit to be able to join the community in working for the good of the juvenile. Hopefully, he will be spared the ambivalence which accompanies traditional officer training.

POLICE DISCRETION

When a youngster is apprehended by a police officer, a number of dispositions are possible; the alternatives differ from community to community. Discretion is defined as the selection of a specific disposition by a police officer. The range of possible dispositions available to the officer are as follows:

1. Outright release
2. Release with warning
3. Referral to a youth service bureau

4. Referral to the juvenile court without detention
5. Referral to the juvenile court with request for detention until the court intake process is completed.

A number of studies have tried to determine why some youngsters are accorded outright release while others are referred to the juvenile court or the youth service bureau. These studies are inconclusive and conflicting. A number of police departments do not use all the alternatives listed above. The range of available alternatives depends on the philosophy of the police chief, the sheriff, and the legislation. The background of the individual officer determines which alternatives he uses most frequently when discretion is permitted; our discussion of the police officer and his training suggests that a wide latitude can be expected. At the same time, the availability of referral sources is important. Sometimes these resources exist outside the juvenile justice system (e.g., a youth service bureau) and at other times services to the child are found in the juvenile court or, perhaps, not at all.

A number of these studies are cited in Appendix B. We can conclude from a review of them that:

1. The community tends to stereotype youngsters according to socioeconomic status and/or race, the seriousness of the presenting offense, personal appearance, and attitude.
2. Response to the youngster, as noted in the severity of the sanction employed in selecting a disposition, is often related to the intensity of the feelings invoked in the police officer at the time of the contact.
3. The decision of the police officer to use a specific disposition, when alternatives are available, is often based upon the alleged danger the youth presents to the community.
4. Researchers, concerned with the labeling of youth by the police, do not perform follow-up studies which might help to determine the impact of the officer's decision upon the future conduct of the youngster.
5. These studies are never conducted by the police who make the decision about juveniles in trouble.

The police discretion studies tell us little more than we learn from an analysis of encounters among strangers in public areas. In the last half of the 1970s there will probably be less research on this topic. The new emphasis will be upon decriminalizing the many status offenses and permitting police to use diversion more frequently.[40] These changes require prevention programs with a community focus. The police officer will refer children to agencies for noncoercive assistance when possible. He will no longer be the one who merely opens the gates of the formal juvenile justice system. Perhaps he can redirect those who are brought to the gates. Many police are motivated to work in this area, among them the Sacramento Police Department Youth Services Division, whose brochure states that its officers are

> . . . more concerned with understanding and closely working with young people than in arresting them. It is hoped that through this approach fewer children and youths will ever have first hand contact with detention and other hard core delinquents. Instead, it is believed that a positive interaction between our youth and law enforcement might help to decrease the mutual contempt, distrust, and animosity which has developed over the past decade.[41]

STUDY QUESTIONS

---

1. What are the primary functions of the police?
2. What might we conclude from a review of the police discretion studies?
3. What is one of the strongest emotions present in the young patrolman assigned to the ghetto?
4. Why must the youngster be allowed to observe the patrolman as a helping agent?
5. List the conclusions found in the Cincinnati Police–Juvenile Attitude Project.
6. Does your state department of education have a resource center for curriculum materials dealing with police and the law?

7. What is the ride-along program?
8. Describe the police–school liaison program. Is such a program operating in your community? If so, evaluate it.
9. Identify one or more indigenous leaders in your neighborhood.
10. List the skills required in the helping agent role of police behavior.
11. What is neighborhood policing?
12. How many hours does your police academy devote to matters of juvenile delinquency?
13. Identify some of the areas of study which should be placed in a revised police academy curriculum focusing upon urban issues.
14. How might good human relations training prepare a police department for successful communication with community social service agencies?
15. List five social services which satisfy the high priority needs of children and youth in your community.
16. Does your police department have a referral booklet which might be used by a police officer in assisting a citizen in your community?

NOTES

1. Herbert Kutchins, "Pretrial Diversionary Programs: New Expansion of Law Enforcement Activity Camouflaged as Rehabilitation" (Paper delivered at the Twenty-third Annual Meeting of the Society for the Study of Social Problems, New York City, N.Y., August 25, 1973).

2. Jesse Rubin, "Police Identity and The Police Role," in *The Police and the Community*, ed. Robert F. Steadman (Baltimore: John Hopkins University Press, 1972), pp. 12–50; and Thomas J. Crawford, "Police Overperception of Ghetto Hostility," *Journal of Police Science and Administration*, 1 (June 1973): 168–174.

3. Robert Coles, "Violence in Ghetto Children," *Children*, 14 (May–June 1967): 104.

4. Ernest L. Peters, "Public School Attitudes toward Juvenile Delinquents," *Journal of Research in Crime and Delinquency*, 6 (January 1969): 56–62.

5. Stanton Wheeler and Leonard S. Cottrell, Jr., *Juvenile Delinquency: Its Prevention and Control* (New York: Russell Sage Foundation, 1966), p. 28.

6. Anthony M. Orum and Roberta S. Cohen, "The Development of Political Orientations among Black and White Children," *American Sociological Review*, 38 (February 1973): 62–74.

7. *LEAA Newsletter*, 3, no. 10 (January–February 1974): 1 and 8.

8. See Robert Derbyshire, "Children's Perceptions of the Police: A Comparative Study of Attitudes and Attitude Change," *Journal of Criminal Law, Criminology, and Police Science*, 59 (June 1968): 183–190. This study is reprinted in *Race, Crime, and Justice*, Charles E. Reasons and Jack L. Kuykendall, eds. (Pacific Palisades, Calif.: Goodyear Publishing Co., 1972), pp. 144–155.

9. Robert Portune, *Changing Adolescent Attitudes Toward Police: A Practical Sourcebook for Schools and Police Departments* (Cincinnati: W. H. Anderson Co., 1971), p. 92.

10. Stanley Coopersmith, *Student Attitudes Toward Authority, Law, and Police: How They Are Affected by the Law Education Program of Davis, California* (Davis, California: Institute of Governmental Affairs, University of California, 1971), p. 44.

11. Ibid., pp. 45–48.

12. Victor I. Cizanckas and Carlton W. Purviance, "Changing Attitudes of Black Youths," *The Police Chief*, 40, no. 3 (March 1973): 42–45.

13. June Morrison, "The Controversial Police–School Liaison Programs," *Police*, 13, no. 2 (November–December 1968): 60–64.

14. David H. Bayley and Harold Mendelsohn, *Minorities and the Police: Confrontation in America* (New York: The Free Press, 1969), p. 206.

15. Robert M. Terry, "The Screening of Juvenile Offenders," *Journal of Criminal Law, Criminology, and Police Science*, 58 (1967): 173–181.

16. Clifford R. Shaw and Henry D. McKay, *Social Factors in Juvenile Delinquency*, National Commission on Law Enforcement and Enforcement, no. 13, vol. 2 (Washington, D.C.: U.S. Government Printing Office, 1931), p. 387.

17. Solomon Kobrin, "The Chicago Area Project—A Twenty-Five Year Assessment," *The Annals of the American Academy of Political and Social Science*, 322 (March 1959): 29.

18. Stanley L. Brodsky, "Models of Police Behavior," *Police,* 13 (May–June 1969): 27–28.

19. See Elaine Cumming, Ian M. Cumming, and Laura Edell, "Policeman as Philosopher, Guide and Friend," *Social Problems,* 12 (1965): 276–286.

20. See: John P. Clark and Eugene P. Wenninger, "The Attitude of Juveniles Toward the Legal Institution," *Journal of Criminal Law, Criminology, and Police Science,* 55 (1964): 482–489.

21. Kobrin, "Chicago Area Project," p. 29.

22. Steven V. Roberts, "Build Where Human Misery Is," *St. Petersburg Times,* September 9, 1967, News of Religion section, p. 3.

23. Richard W. Kobetz, *The Police Role and Juvenile Delinquency* (Gaithersburg, Maryland: International Association of Chiefs of Police, 1971), pp. 185–186.

24. David C. Couper, "The Delivery of Neighborhood Police Services: A Challenge for Today's Police Professional," *The Police Chief,* 39 (March 1972): 15.

25. A. C. Germann, "Community Policing: An Assessment," *Journal of Criminal Law, Criminology, and Police Science,* 60, no. 1 (March 1969): 95.

26. See Albert J. Reiss, Jr., *The Police and the Public* (New Haven: Yale University Press, 1971), pp. 173–221; and Richard N. Harris, *The Police Academy: An Inside View* (New York: John Wiley & Sons, 1973), pp. 171–182.

27. Nelson A. Watson, and James W. Sterling, *Police and Their Opinions* (Washington, D.C.: International Association of Chiefs of Police, 1969), p. 63.

28. John J. Hughes, "Training Police Recruits for Service in the Urban Ghetto—A Social Worker's Approach," *Crime and Delinquency,* 18 (April 1972): 176–183; Charles D. Reese, "Police Academy Training and Its Effects on Racial Prejudice," *Journal of Police Science and Administration,* 1 (September 1973): 257–268; and Harvey Treger, Doug Thomson, and Gordon Sloan Jaeck, "A Police–Social Work Team Model: Some Preliminary Findings and Implications for System Change," *Crime and Delinquency,* 20 (July 1974): 281–290.

29. Richard N. Harris, *The Police Academy: An Inside View* (New York: John Wiley & Sons, 1973), p. 177.

30. Gary B. Adams, "The Juvenile Officer and Prevention," *The Police Chief,* 40, no. 2 (February 1973): 54–57.

31. Joint Commission on Correctional Manpower and Training, *A Time to Act* (Washington, D.C.: The Commission, 1969), p. 56.

32. James H. Tenzel and Victor Cizanckas, "The Uniform Experiment," *Journal of Police Science and Administration,* 1 (December 1973): 421–424.

33. A. C. Germann, "Community Policing: An Assessment," *Journal of Criminal Law, Criminology, and Police Science,* 80 (March 1969): 94–95.

34. See Richard L. Block, "Fear of Crime and Fear of the Police, *Social Problems,* 19 (Summer 1971): 91–101; Nelson A. Watson, *Issues in Human Relations* (Gaithersburg, Md.: International Association of Chiefs of Police, 1973); and Hans Toch, "The Care and Feeding of Typologies and Labels," *Federal Probation,* 34, no. 3 (September 1970): 15–19.

35. See Ivan R. Gabor and Christopher Low, "The Police Role in the Community," *Criminology,* 10 (February 1973): 383–414.

36. Alfred J. Kahn, *Social Policy and Social Services* (New York: Random House, 1973), p. 13.

37. See George P. Tielsch, "Community Resource Field Training for Police Recruits," *The Police Chief,* 39, no. 11 (November 1972): 30–31. Also, an excellent listing of available social services for the youth of one community is: The Academy for Contemporary Problems and League of Women Voters of Ohio, *Open Doors: An Inventory of Social Services for Youth in Franklin County* (Columbus, Ohio: The Academy for Contemporary Problems, 1975).

38. Clorinda Margolis and Harry G. Fox, "Rap and Rapport: Police and Mental Health Pros," *The Police Chief,* 38, no. 12 (December 1971): 46–48.

39. See Edward W. Haurek and John P. Clark, ‘Variants of Integration on Social Control Agencies," *Social Problems,* 15 (Summer, 1967): 46–60; and, George H. Shepard, "Youth Services Systems: An Innovative Concept in Prevention," *The Police Chief,* vol. 40, no. 2 (Feb., 1973): 48–53.

40. For a provocative discussion see Edwin M. Schur, *Radical Non-Intervention: Rethinking the Delinquency Problem* (Englewood Cliffs, N.J.: Prentice-Hall, Inc., 1973).

41. Youth Services Division, Sacramento Police Department, Sacramento, California, "Crisis Intervention," mimeographed (Sacramento: Sacramento Police Department, 1972), p. 4.

DETENTION, JAILS, AND ALTERNATIVES

DETENTION
STANDARDS FOR DETENTION
JUVENILES IN JAILS
DETENTION GUIDELINES FOR POLICE
THE DETENTION HEARING
THE DETENTION CENTER
ALTERNATIVES TO DETENTION

Although the juvenile justice system sees rehabilitation as its goal, the first detention experience is traumatic for a youngster. Detention is defined as the secure custody of a youth, whether for overnight or longer, in an adult jail, a juvenile hall, or a juvenile detention facility. However, the evils of the detention suggest that treatment is not a primary goal at this point.

The case of William M., a sixteen-year-old with no prior delinquency record, illustrates a common—and improper—use of detention. William was arrested by a police officer on a warrant which charged him with selling marijuana to an undercover agent, seven weeks after the alleged offense was said to have occurred. A promise was made not to detain him because the minor's attorney indicated that William would appear for further proceedings. Yet he was held for eight hours until the detention hearing; neither the police nor the probation officer exercised his authority to release the minor from the detention facility to parental custody.

A court hearing was held the next day. The attorney for the minor offered proof that William M. would appear, that he was not a behavior problem in areas other than the alleged offense, that his parents were capable of controlling him and they wanted him at home, and that he posed no threat to the community. The court responded by indicating that continued detention was necessary because (1) the alleged offense was a serious one and (2) it was court policy to detain all minors charged with marijuana sales. Therefore, William M. remained in custody for one week until released by the California Supreme Court.[1] The higher court overruled the juvenile court, finding no necessity to detain William M. since seven weeks had elapsed between the time of the alleged offense and the day of arrest. The California higher court noted seven factors which should *not* be used as guidelines for detention:

1. Public outcry against the offense allegedly committed by the minor;
2. The need to crack down generally on juveniles in the area;
3. The nature of the offense per se;
4. The belief that detention would have a salutary effect on the minor . . . ;
5. Convenience of the police, the probation officer, or the district attorney for investigative purposes;
6. Concern that the minor will fabricate a defense to his case;
7. Inability of the minor to show good cause why he should be released.[2]

The function of detention is to provide secure or protective custody, not to give short-term treatment or to punish.

DETENTION

The mobile population in jail and juvenile facilities has hampered the study of who is detained, why, and what happens before the juvenile court hearing. Although the juvenile court movement began in 1899, not much was written about detention until 1930. Since then, field studies continue to document the inadequate conditions found in detention facilities.

Through its Jail Inspection Service, the United States Bureau of Prisons has compiled jail ratings for many years. When jails score very low on specific criteria—such as the number of personnel and programs—the Bureau of Prisons has the power to remove federal prisoners from these jails. The professional efforts of the bureau included the 1971 publication of *The Jail: Its Operation and Management*, by Nick Pappas (see Appendix D, General Bibliography). No federal agency is empowered to inspect and approve facilities for the detention of children and youth although 15 states indicate that their facilities are inspected. In only 14 states does the government take responsibility for detention, although such action has been sought by the National Council on Crime and Delinquency for many years. The 14 states are Alaska, Connecticut, Delaware, Georgia, Massachusetts, Maryland, Michigan, New Hampshire,

New York, Puerto Rico, Rhode Island, Utah, Vermont, and Virginia. Twenty-two states fail to maintain statistics on the detention of juveniles. California, Michigan, Ohio, and Pennsylvania have been identified as the states that provide the most complete statistics.[3]

Standards for detention are necessary, it is unfortunate that we have failed to provide our children with the same consideration given the federal adult prisoner. Children are housed in adult jails in many states. Connecticut is the only state which claims it has not used the adult jail for the detention of children. Howard James has said that the alternative to detention is attention. The recent White House Conference on Children formulated the following policy statement:

> We recommend that the use of detention prior to adjudication be minimized and that, where detention is absolutely necessary (for the safety of the child or the community), small community-based facilities should be provided. Such a facility should be totally separate from the county jail or other adult lock-ups. We urge the enactment of laws requiring that a hearing be held within 48 hours for all juveniles held in custody, and that a dispositional hearing be held within 15 judicial days if the youngster remains in custody, or within 30 days if the youngster is released to a parent or guardian. If these rights are violated, we recommend that the case be dismissed.[4]

The detention disgrace has been made public through the Research and Policy Committee of the Committee for Economic Development, the Advisory Commission on Intergovernmental Relations,[5] the Office of Youth Development, and the Law Enforcement Assistance Administration. These agencies and organizations, as well as many concerned citizens, are now supporting the struggle for juvenile detention standards.

STANDARDS FOR DETENTION

Overdetention, as in the case of William M., and the absence of legislation that prohibits putting juveniles in jails are serious issues in the administration of juvenile justice. Historically, the juvenile court movement has sought to separate juveniles from adults; this concern has led to a separate court for juveniles, and the construction of separate centers for the detention of youngsters in trouble. However, it is unfortunate that "the detention center developed more as a reaction against the jail than as something positive in its own right."[6]

Who should be detained? The National Council on Crime and Delinquency offers the following criteria for the admission of juveniles to a detention facility:

> Children apprehended for delinquency should be detained for the juvenile court when, after proper intake interviews, it appears that casework by a probation officer would not enable the parents to maintain custody and control, or would not enable the child to control his own behavior. Such children fall into the following groups:
>
> (a) Children who are almost certain to run away during the period the court is studying their case, or between disposition and transfer to an institution or another jurisdiction.
>
> (b) Children who are almost certain to commit an offense dangerous to themselves or to the community before court disposition or between disposition and transfer to an institution or another jurisdiction.
>
> (c) Children who must be held for another jurisdiction; e.g., parole violators, runaways from institutions to which they were committed by a court, or certain material witnesses.[7]

These criteria do not focus upon the wrongful use of detention practiced by certain juvenile justice personnel. There are those who assume that several days in the detention center will serve to discipline a youth. But the detention environment has been found to influence juvenile attitudes negatively. Others hope that "therapeutic detention" will act as a form of moral guidance strengthening juveniles so that they refrain from becoming intoxicated, from using drugs, and from sexual promiscuity. These simplistic positions do not engage the problem, which would be better served by allocating the costs of detention to community services that focus on the undesirable conduct.

JUVENILES IN JAILS

Many communities acquaint their children with the most infamous segment of the correctional system, the jail—they are put there from the time they are accused of delinquency until the court acts upon the allegation. About 93 percent of the juvenile court jurisdictions (totaling 2,800 counties and cities) in this country must use the local jail facilities when detaining children.[8] There are only about 300 juvenile detention facilities available. Jails are often the only available facility because communities have determined that they do not confine enough children to justify construction of a youth hall. Further, when a jail exists, the community has less need to find alternative forms of temporary detention. The 1970 National Jail Census states that youngsters may be held in designated adult jails in every state except Connecticut, Delaware, and Rhode Island where there are no locally administered jails and the state assumes responsibility for jail operations. The census provides the following information about juveniles in jails:

1. There are 4,037 locally administered jails in the United States which have the authority to retain adult persons for 48 hours or longer.
2. Of the 4,037 adult jails, nearly 70 percent or 2,785 receive juveniles.
3. On the day of the national census there were 7,800 juveniles confined in the 4,037 jails. It has been estimated that the number of juveniles in jail exceeds 100,000 each year.
4. 66 percent of the juveniles in adult jails can be classified under the "not convicted inmate" retention category; that is, two out of three juveniles were pretrial detainees or were being held for other authorities.
5. Only four states had *more* than 200 juveniles confined in local jails at the time of the census:
   a. New York—4,550 (although 3,943 of these are "youthful offenders" between the ages of 16 and 21 years, classified as juveniles in New York State).
   b. Pennsylvania—254
   c. Indiana—249
   d. Ohio—203

6. The following eight states detained as many as 100 juveniles, but no more than 200, on the day of the census:
    a. California—188
    b. Virginia—172
    c. Texas—169
    d. Florida—142
    e. Georgia—132
    f. New Jersey—126
    g. Maryland—106
    h. Illinois—106
7. *No* juveniles were being confined in the local jails of the following states on the day of the census: Hawaii, Massachusetts, New Hampshire, and Vermont.

The U.S. Law Enforcement Assistance Administration and the U.S. Bureau of the Census conducted the jail census in order to obtain basic facts about the nation's jails and their inmates (see Appendix D, General Bibliography). A supplementary report breaks down inmate data by county and by local jail within the county.[9] This report provides the following information about juveniles in county, city, and township jails: (1) whether they are housed separately in county and large city jails; (2) the number confined in each jail on the day of the census; and (3) the legal status (i.e., held for arraignment or transfer to other authorities, arraigned and awaiting trial, awaiting further legal action, serving sentence of one year or less, and serving sentence of more than one year).

The brutalizing nature of the jail environment has been documented. The abuses accompanying the detention of juveniles in jails have frequently resulted in short-term media publicity, but public apathy continues. During a recent jail riot in the District of Columbia the inmates angrily listed as one of their grievances the alleged sexual assaults on teen-age prisoners by other inmates. The prisoner demands led the jail administrators to separate 16- and 17-year-olds from the other prisoners. Since 1923, when the National Council on Crime and Delinquency first published the Standard Juvenile Court Act, it has recommended that juveniles be kept out of jails (see Appendix D, General Bibliography). In addition, it is strongly suggested that the jailing of juveniles under age 16 should never be tolerated. This recommendation was included in the platform of the Society for the Prevention of Cruelty to Children nearly a century ago. Children must be protected from the limitations of the jail with its misdemeanant population and its more serious adult offenders. New York is the first state to provide an answer to this problem. Recent legislation there makes it mandatory for every county to:

1. provide non-secure foster family or group home type facilities for delinquents,
2. place children in one of four regional detention centers, and
3. prohibit use of the jail without notification and approval of the New York State Division for Youth.[10]

A recent study of jailed children suggests that the need for detention must be reassessed when observing the following factors: (1) the offense that led to detention; (2) the duration of the detention period; and (3) the destination of the youth following release from detention. John Downey's study of juveniles detained in jails within 18 different states reveals the following: 41.6 percent of the children were apprehended for acts that would not be violations if committed by an adult; 70.4 percent of the children were confined in the jail for two days or less; and, 80.9 percent of the children were sent home or otherwise remained in the community following release.[11]

DETENTION GUIDELINES FOR POLICE

The decision to place a juvenile in detention is a serious action, especially since the local jail is likely to be the center for confinement. There are three decision points in the detention of the child:

1. The police officer making the arrest determines in the field whether or not it is safe to return the child to the parent, whether a referral to another community resource is appropriate, or whether he should be brought to the detention center.

2. The intake worker, once the child has been brought to detention, determines again whether the child should be detained. . . .
3. If detained by the intake worker, then the judge of the court should make the final decision regarding custody, and whether custody should be secure, i.e., detention, or minimal, i.e., shelter, in a detention hearing the next day.[12]

The intake worker for the juvenile court, then, makes the first decision about keeping the juvenile; detention decisions are the responsibility of the juvenile court personnel alone. The discretionary diversion authority of police officers should be increased. The police role is community oriented, but *not* oriented toward lockup and detention. The National Advisory Commission on Criminal Justice Standards and Goals recommends:

1. Police should have maximum discretionary authority, at the point of first contact, as well as at the police station, to divert juveniles to alternative community-based programs and human resources agencies outside the juvenile justice system, when the safety of the community is not jeopardized. Disposition may include:
    a. Release on the basis of unfounded charges.
    b. Referral to parents (warning and release).
    c. Referral to social agencies.
    d. Referral to juvenile court intake services.
2. When police have taken custody of a minor, and prior to disposition under Paragraph 3 below, the following guidelines should be observed.
    a. Under the provisions of *Gault* and *Miranda*, police should first warn juveniles of their right to counsel and the right to remain silent while under custodial questioning.
    b. The second act after apprehending a minor should be the notification of his parents.
    c. Unless a knowing and intelligent waiver is made by the juvenile, extrajudicial statements to police or court officers not made in the presence of parents or counsel should be inadmissible in juvenile court.

d. Juveniles should not be fingerprinted or photographed or otherwise routed through the usual adult booking process.

e. Juvenile records should be maintained physically separate from adult case records.

3. Police should not have discretionary authority to make detention decisions. This responsibility rests with the juvenile court, which should assume control over admissions on a 24-hour basis.[13]

The crucial police operation in detention is screening out those juveniles who do *not* require secure or protective custody. Detention is not to be used as an expeditious manner for disposing of all juvenile contacts with the police. It is often said that the police officer is very critical of juvenile court detention decisions because the juvenile may return to the community before the officer has completed his paperwork in the case. This criticism is more likely to be heard in jurisdictions where the police officer is allowed to do very little with juveniles or where community referral resources are limited. Actually the officer is really criticizing the matter of accountability for services, and this can be resolved with appropriate record-keeping procedures.

In a 1970 study of initial juvenile detention decisions in a number of counties, the National Council on Crime and Delinquency found that the majority of police agencies maintain very incomplete records of their contacts with juvenile offenders.[14] Because he knows so little about the case, an officer sometimes assumes that locking up a youngster probably affords the public the best protection. The record-keeping problem can be overcome if each police department tallies all juvenile apprehensions for a given time period (e.g., six months), then tallies all juvenile dispositions according to the available alternatives. Thereafter, the police department can follow up on the cases and determine whether the referral agencies did see the youngsters after they were apprehended. This system permits the department to identify the rate at which misbehaving youngsters return to the community (juvenile community absorption rate).[15] This rate shows the level of referral sources available and the level at which these resources are used. Coordination between the police and other agencies, whether criminal justice or social agencies, is more important than punitive use of detention. Services to youth, not lockup, will provide safety in the future; and public safety is the police goal.

The conflict regarding the use of detention may result from a failure to differentiate between police handling of adults and of juveniles. The adult offender, when apprehended and arrested, is transported to jail by the officer. The jailer accepts the prisoner without question. The courts determine at the time of the preliminary hearing, whether the actions of the arresting officer were appropriate. When the policeman apprehends a juvenile and transports him to custody there is no certainty that the youth will be deprived of his liberty while he awaits processing by the juvenile court. Therefore, temporary custody (i.e., apprehension) by the policeman does not necessarily imply that detention will continue.

Each police department should list its criteria for referral to juvenile court; these differ from one community to another. However, it is urgent that police administrators and juvenile court officials agree upon the written procedures for court referral and upon the information that the police will supply the court in the event a referral is made. Some or all of the following criteria might be used:

1. The particular offense committed by the child is of a serious nature.
2. The child is known or has in the past been known to the juvenile court.
3. The child has a record of delinquency extending over a period of time.
4. The child and his parents have shown themselves unable or unwilling to cooperate with agencies of a non-authoritative character.
5. Casework with the child by a non-authoritative agency has failed in the past.
6. Treatment services needed by the child can be obtained only through the services of the court and its probation department.
7. The child denies the offense and the officer believes judicial determination is called for, and there is sufficient evidence to warrant referral or the officer believes the child and his family are in need of aid.
8. Any case where a juvenile has been placed in detention.

9. Any case which would be non-criminal if the child were an adult, but total circumstances surrounding the case indicate the need for protective action for the welfare of the child.[16]

At the time of referral to juvenile court, the police department should be prepared to furnish, in writing, a full report of the allegation involving the alleged delinquent behavior. The information should include:

1. Nature and circumstances of the violation.
2. Date, time and place.
3. Jurisdiction date which shows that the offender comes within the scope of the State Juvenile Court Act.
4. Evidence obtained.
5. Name, address, parent's name and school attended by alleged delinquent.
6. Complainant's name and address.
7. Names and addresses of witnesses.
8. Statement of damages, stolen property and amount recovered.
9. Associates of alleged delinquent.
10. Previous police contact.
11. Police observations of home conditions.
12. Attitude of parents with police.
13. Previous referrals to social agencies.[17]

Decision for detention recommendations may be determined after careful consideration of the following points:

1. Protection of the child who is homeless or whose home is unfit by reason of neglect or cruelty.
2. Protection of the community because the juvenile is physically dangerous to the public.
3. Record of running away.
4. Lack of parental control and supervision.
5. Previous police contacts and juvenile court record.

6. Possible probation status of the juvenile with an accompanying history of violations.
7. Possible status of a youngster as a fugitive from another jurisdiction.

If a police department is making extensive use of diversionary programs, the criteria for juvenile court referral and recommendations for detention of juveniles transported to juvenile hall will be less extensive; emphasis will be placed upon agency accountability for services following the police contact.

The National Advisory Commission on Criminal Justice Standards and Goals recommends, as you will recall, that juveniles not be fingerprinted or photographed at the time of the police contact. This recommendation is very controversial.[18] Those departments which support the policy of fingerprinting and photographing juveniles do so under the following conditions:

1. The youngster is an habitual runaway and the information is needed to assist parents and guardians who are searching for their children.
2. The youngster uses a false name or fails to identify himself.
3. The offense is serious (i.e., an adult crime committed by a juvenile).
4. The youngster has a history of recidivism (i.e., repeated involvement in delinquent behavior).
5. Unidentified fingerprints are found when investigating a crime and a juvenile is a suspect in the case.

Another recommendation of the National Advisory Commission is that the parents of the youngster must be notified immediately of his apprehension. This requirement is usually found in the state statutes. However, intervention between parents and children should be accompanied by every safeguard to the rights of the family to remain together. The following guidelines are helpful:

1. Parents and guardians should be notified as soon as possible when a juvenile is taken into custody.

2. Notification is the responsibility of the officer-in-charge or the juvenile unit officer assigned. It is suggested that booking intake fact sheets provide a place for this information to be recorded.
3. A remark should be included on the booking form indicating parents were notified, the time of the notification, the notifying officer, and any reasons why parents were not notified.
4. Parents should be notified as to *why* the juvenile is in police custody and any reason for detention; and that for further information, they may contact the detention home.
5. If the juvenile in custody is from another jurisdiction, the appropriate police department should be contacted by telephone or teletype to notify parents or guardians.[19]

The right of the juvenile to communicate with his parent or guardian has been upheld in a 1971 decision of the California Supreme Court. The court ruled that police questioning of a juvenile arrested for a crime must cease when he asks to see one of his parents. The court decision reversed the conviction of Bozzie Bryant Burton III, then age 16, in the murder of two people. The youth had asked to talk to his father prior to questioning, but had been refused. Thereafter, he was properly admonished and he then made incriminating statements; the confession obtained by police was admitted in the jury trial. The 1971 California court opinion extended a 1966 U.S. Supreme Court decision requiring that police stop questioning when an adult in custody indicates the wish to remain silent or to talk with an attorney. This so-called *Miranda* rule is based on the Fifth Amendment privilege against self-incrimination. In Burton's case the California court held that his request to see his father effectively invoked his privilege not to answer police questions.[20]

Little controversy surrounds the police services to dependent and neglected youngsters. The number of such cases has increased in the 1970s. Because police are charged with the protection of the community, they do have an important function in handling cases of neglect and abuse of children. The neglected child suffers from parental mistreatment; the dependent child lacks proper food, shelter, or clothing. The following points are suggested for police evaluation and action in dependency and neglect cases:

1. Police are in the best position in any community to take immediate action, any time of the day or night, in acute cases.
2. Non-emergency complaints should be referred to a social agency or court during normal office hours.
3. Police juvenile unit officers and policewomen are specially trained and usually have more competence in handling these cases.
4. Police must decide if neglect or dependency exists as defined in the state Juvenile Court Act.
5. If police decide that there is a basis for juvenile court action involved in the complaint there are two distinguishable courses of action which may be taken: (a) action on behalf of the child, (b) action against the parents.
6. Police procedure in handling cases of neglect by parents should if at all possible be based on the philosophy of the continuing relationship between child and parents; it will need to be taken into consideration in deciding whether or not the adult is to be charged.
7. It is a police duty and responsibility to take children into custody for the prevention of injury, violence or abuse.
8. Police have a great deal of discretion in making decisions for appropriate action.
9. Before any criminal charges are proffered against parents, police are advised to confer with the District Attorney and appropriate casework agencies.
10. Where agencies exist, police may make referrals directly to community social agencies or to court.
11. In the absence of agencies, all cases should be referred to court after police investigation and evaluation.[21]

THE DETENTION HEARING

Very little has been written about the decision of court personnel to detain the juvenile once he is placed in temporary custody. This is unfortunate, especially in the 1970s when progressive police departments are skillfully referring youngsters for social services and the threat of detention is less likely. Some states have said that it should be established practice not to file delinquency charges against a youth who applies for help at a social agency. This procedure would work if the formal justice agencies can determine their juvenile community absorption rate. The time may arrive when only juveniles in need of detention will be referred to the juvenile court. Until then, however, the detention hearing remains an important decision for the child and his parents.

The juvenile court should provide printed admission policies and procedures which clearly state the criteria for detention. The judge is responsible for these procedures, which should be revised periodically. The policies of the police, the judge, and the probation department should be made explicit. Many states have specific statutes which limit or broaden the power of these three agencies.[22] The National Council on Crime and Delinquency found that police often made the decision about whether a juvenile would be detained even though such action was prohibited by statute in the state under study. In such cases, the judge and probation department have endorsed the decisions of the police officers.[23] In many other states the decision to retain a youth in detention is based on the whims of the person on duty when the youngster is brought to the hall for temporary custody. This practice, however, illustrates why detention centers are crowded rather than the fact that there is an excess of so-called dangerous juveniles.

The detention hearing takes place in juvenile hall within 24 hours after the youngster is taken there by the policeman and placed in temporary custody. The child should never be detained for longer than 48 hours before a hearing is held by the court. The purpose of the detention hearing is to determine whether the court shall release a child to his parents or continue the detention initiated by the police. The police agency operates 24 hours each day; the juvenile court does not. Therefore, many youngsters do not receive an immediate hearing. Most children are taken into custody at night or on weekends. For this reason, court personnel should be available on a 24-hour basis. The hearing is conducted by a member of the intake staff of the juvenile court.

The detention hearing is carried out in a formal, businesslike atmosphere, and can be a stressful period for the youngster unfamiliar with the experience. The hearing could continue for 30 minutes or it could end in only three. The youngster should be present with his parents, if possible; they are informed about their legal rights and the right to counsel. None of the participants are likely to engage in much conversation during the brief hearing. If the decision is to detain the child in custody, then he has a right to appear before the judge later and discuss his circumstances. This allows the judge to explain the purpose of the second detention hearing (see Chapter 7), determine whether he will continue holding the child in custody as recommended by the intake worker, and enumerate for the youngster the reasons for the decision.

The decision to detain a youngster is the responsibility of the probation officer (i.e., the intake worker) or the juvenile court judge. It is not the responsibility of the detention staff although they must handle the children. Unnecessary detention is the result of decisions made by the juvenile court staff. Consequent overcrowding should not be blamed on the police. Of course the superintendent of the juvenile hall and his staff are always concerned with this problem.

The National Council of Crime and Delinquency (NCCD) found that judges tend to decide on detention if the case exhibits three characteristics. There is an inclination to detain youngsters who have been held previously, those having a history of probation or who are currently on probation, and those alleged to be runaways at the time of referral.[24] When one or both parents accompany the child to the detention hearing, the probability of release is much greater. Since a number of guidelines for detention have been provided, one might assume that decisions are based upon the personal characteristics of the child. But this is not always true—some counties stress detention. NCCD found that the percent of children detained in 11 counties ranged from 19 to 66 percent for all those referred for temporary custody.

It may not be easy to find out which counties have a high detention rate. The court should be able to provide an actual statistical rundown of children detained or released. The reasons for detaining or releasing a child must be recorded in sufficient detail to reach a conclusion about the validity of the action taken by the intake worker or judge. This is important because the probability that a youngster will be detained is based upon whether the community is a high or low detention jurisdiction, not upon the social factors.

Displeasure with the detaining rate in a community is a step toward revising the written procedures for detention. These should be written, otherwise merely verbal methods may have taken their place. This should *not* be permitted! The writer compared the patterns of sentencing felons in a rural and in an urban county, and found that "The urban county sentenced less than one-third of the county jail felons to correctional institutions, but nearly three-fourths of the rural county offenders were imprisoned."[25] This rural county has continued its high prison commitment rate for nearly fifty years; as in the case of the high detention county, the judicial decision-makers, not the personal characteristics of the processed, determine the outcome. Those responsible for this high imprisonment rate point with pride to the postprison success of the offenders so treated. They avoid questioning what the wisdom of prison detention is in the first place.

In conclusion, the detention hearing must be based upon written guidelines. The county should be identified as a high or a low detention jurisdiction. Bear in mind that the decisions of those in charge of the detention hearing may be influenced by numerous personal opinions and attitudes. Some of these follow:

1. Attitude, appearance, and behavior of parents at time of contact with probation staff and at time of contact with law enforcement officers.
2. Opinion of arresting officer.
3. Child's behavior at time of apprehension.
4. Current juvenile court philosophy.
5. Availability of parents.
6. History of alcohol abuse.
7. Parents' behavior toward child.
8. Community pressures concerning particular offenses.
9. Physical appearance of child.
10. Probation status of child.
11. Parole status of child.
12. Repetitive nature of alleged offense.
13. History of narcotics involvement.
14. Whether alleged delinquency was an individual or "gang" act.[26]

THE DETENTION CENTER

The detention facility is not a treatment but a holding center for the youth who cannot remain free prior to the court hearing—which determines whether he receives probation, training school placement, or some alternate. The youngster is forced into association with many kinds of people: juveniles who have committed adult crimes; children who have committed status offenses (e.g., running away from home, truancy, or curfew violation); youngsters who are dependent or neglected; and of course the youth who recently committed the offense that everyone in the community is talking about.

The detention center is usually attached to the same building that houses the administrative offices and hearing rooms of the local juvenile court. Some communities build the detention facility a number of miles away from the juvenile court; however, this procedure is highly criticized by a majority of detention workers. There are several reasons for this objection: (1) it is difficult to transport the juvenile from the juvenile hall to the court room for hearings; (2) parents and relatives of the juvenile in detention expect juvenile hall to be located in or near the juvenile court facility; and, (3) geographical separation of the detention facility from the juvenile court administration building isolates the detention staff from the judge and the probation staff and creates severe morale problems.

The juvenile in detention can express many feelings. He may feel abandoned because he is separated from his family; maybe he realizes there is no caring adult person in his life; on the other hand, he may be angry and resentful. Whatever his range of feelings, the overwhelming emotion is failure. And he is concerned about his future, which will be determined by a judge's decision.

What are the functions of detention care? Ideally, the staff should try to provide a constructive experience for the child in an atmosphere which hampers growth. Practically it must do more than provide storage for the youngsters awaiting adjudication. Study and observation of the youngster is necessary if the probation officer is to provide a helpful report for the judge. Individual guidance helps the youngster in overcoming his hostility or fear. Gerald O'Connor has said that the child is open to influence and does change in feelings and attitudes during the initial detention experience.[27] However, this requires constructive individual and group activities. It is common for detention facilities to operate according to the latest management efficiency manuals. When efficiency is more important than the human experience, inevitably the functions of detention care are minimized. In such situations, the child may receive adequate physical care and the paperwork may be done with haste. Unfortunately, little else occurs to change failure into hope.

The youngster needs to know that someone is concerned about his future, otherwise he will hear nothing more than the exploits of the hardened juvenile offender. Therefore, it is important that a helping attitude characterize the relationship between staff and child. The environment of the detention center can usually be differentiated into one of the following: (1) a control environment with custody matters demanding most attention or (2) a personal care viewpoint which emphasizes positive activities or experiences for the youngster during this short-term experience.

The usual period of confinement in the detention center is three to 21 days. Most states insist that detention not continue over 48 hours without the filing of a petition which formalizes the requirements for the adjudicatory and dispositional hearing in the juvenile court. It is the period following the filing of the petition which extends detention to as much as 21 days. The statutes governing jurisdiction set varying limits on the length of detention.

The National Advisory Commission on Criminal Justice Standards and Goals recommends each juvenile court jurisdiction take the following principles into consideration in juvenile detention center planning:

1. The detention facility should be located in a residential area in the community and near juvenile court and community resources.
2. Population of detention centers should not exceed 30 residents.
3. Living area capacities within the center should not exceed 10 to 12 youngsters each. Only individual occupancy should be provided, with single rooms and programming regarded as essential. Individual rooms should be pleasant,

adequately furnished, and homelike rather than punitive and hostile in atmosphere.

4. Security should not be viewed as an indispensable quality of the physical environment but should be based on a combination of staffing patterns, technological devices, and physical design.
5. Existing residential facilities within the community should be used in preference to new construction.
6. Facility programming should be based on investigation of community resources, with the contemplation of full use of these resources, prior to determination of the facility's in-house program requirements.
7. New construction and renovation of existing facilities should be based on consideration of the functional interrelationships between program activities and program participants.
8. Detention facilities should be coeducational and should have access to a full range of supportive programs, including education, library, recreation, arts and crafts, music, drama, writing, and entertainment. Outdoor recreational areas are essential.
9. Citizen advisory boards should be established to pursue development of in-house and community-based programs and alternatives to detention.[28]

These recommendations seek to overcome many limitations associated with the detention center. The cost of constructing the physical plant has been estimated at $25,000 per bed. Good detention care costs $20 to $27 per day for each child.[29] A juvenile hall serving only a few cannot offer an adequate program. It has been estimated that counties with 250,000 population would have the minimum number of 300 cases, which justifies building a detention center. Regional detention centers on a state-wide basis are needed, therefore, statewide responsibility for detention, under the control of an existing state agency, is required if the regional detention plan is to operate successfully. This writer has spent many days trying to persuade contiguous counties to build regional detention centers—and these efforts have been unsuccessful. Each county hopes to maintain power and control, and so wants the center within its own boundaries. Even attempts to find neutral territory often fail. It is strange how the detention center, forgotten by the citizens it serves, becomes a symbol of power for city and county government. Worse, the problem is not limited to a specific region. There is no doubt that state responsibility for detention is necesary—less than 4 percent of the counties in the United States (122 out of 3,100 counties and other similar type political subdivisions) can plan minimum detention services for their own use.[30]

Much is said about the ongoing services which each detention center must supply its highly mobile population; the staff is concerned but insufficient. Every program should include a corresponding school plan for the short-term student who will decide that he does not fit into the detention environment. Medical and clinical services are necessary, but the small detention center is not equipped to handle anything beyond routine physical examinations and minor complaints. Recreation programs are needed to reduce the monotony, inactivity, and boredom of young people whose excessive energy needs an outlet. The detention center with trees, a patch of grass, recreational equipment, a gymnasium, or a tennis court is rare. Commonly, tattered books, a pool table and damaged furniture are found. Casework services are recommended; they are seldom provided. The introduction of volunteers, however much they care about children, is no substitute for caseworkers.

What about detention center staff? They are the forgotten participants in the whole program. Several years ago, Southern Illinois University at Edwardsville began a training program for detention staff members. Out of this has come a monthly newsletter published to exchange information by and for detention home personnel.[31] The National Juvenile Detention Association serves as the spokesman for these staff members. Detention personnel should not be isolated from their counterparts in juvenile courts and probation departments. Many people in the juvenile justice field began working in detention. For some it provides a rewarding experience and a chance to develop greater empathy for the child in trouble; others, reacting negatively, have found different vocational fields. A major goal of the juvenile court should be to select, train, and promote staff. It has been recommended that:

> Personnel should be selected on the basis of their humanness and maturity of character, their interest in the welfare of

> juveniles, their willingness to identify with the programs of various facilities, their potential for benefiting from increased training and their adaptability in different settings. Salaries should be commensurate with salaries received for a similar level of responsibilities in occupational roles in the public service outside juvenile corrections. Criteria for promotion should be consistent throughout the system.[32]

A program in Clark County (Nevada) reduces the barrier between the juvenile court and detention staff. A team relationship exists between the juvenile court judge, the director of county juvenile services, and the detention supervisor. This program, developed by Judge John P. Mendoza, is successful. When there is interaction between the juvenile court judge, the court administrator, and detention staff, then the future of the youngsters under confinement will be improved.

ALTERNATIVES TO DETENTION

The jail and the detention center are used when a youngster is in need of facilities that confine him physically for a temporary period. The jail is never an appropriate place for the juvenile. Detention is suitable under certain conditions discussed earlier, but it is not a solution. The runaway, the dependent, and the neglected child are in need of temporary placements, which are alternatives to detention. These children are often placed in detention centers because other facilities do not exist. Many counties have instituted new policies which remove from juvenile court jurisdiction the referral and processing of children in danger of parental neglect, abandonment, and physical abuse. These communities have transferred such cases to the local department of social welfare. Such changes should be instituted in all counties where possible. Until such action can be taken, the juvenile court ought to place continued emphasis upon shelter care in lieu of detention for the nondelinquent child referred to it.

Shelter care refers to the care of children in an open facility or substitute home where they can wait while being returned to their own or other homes (i.e., a group or foster home). Emergency shelter is required when children are abandoned, lost, or when one or both parents are arrested, physically injured, or killed. Shelter homes should always be open to receive children. They should be homelike, small, located in the community, and supervised by personnel sensitive to the situations which bring children to them.

Shelter care, under emergency conditions, is sometimes used unnecessarily. The following guidelines should be followed:

1. The child should be placed in a shelter facility only when an immediate danger is present which will harm the child either physically or emotionally.
2. The protective services unit of the county social welfare department should be used in lieu of emergency shelter care when possible. Homemaker services are sometimes useful as an alternative.
3. Relatives, friends, or neighbors may provide temporary care but such arrangements require careful planning with the assistance of staff members from the social welfare agency or the juvenile court.
4. Temporary detention without accompanying social services to the child and the parents (when possible) will not resolve the problem from which the emergency arose.
5. When the small child goes to a shelter facility it is important that he be allowed to take a toy or other personal possession so that he will have something familiar in his new environment. Sometimes there is a small pet in the home that the child must leave behind. It is appropriate to make arrangements for the care of the pet with friends, neighbors, or the local humane society. A child's anguish over the loss of a pet is enormous when compounded with an abrupt separation from his parents.

Group homes and foster care are appropriate alternatives to detention and may provide services once available only when a youngster was committed to a juvenile training school. The unavailability of foster home placements has forced many juvenile court judges to commit a juvenile to a correctional facility. The foster home is the residence of a private individual who has been licensed by the state for the care of one or more children in return for monetary payment. The foster home provides the child with an alternate family and the placement is usually long term rather than temporary. This type of service is appropriate for the preadolescent boy or girl. Placement is more difficult for the delinquent and the older youngster. Some foster homes accept the child with severe emotional problems and claim to be successful with these cases. Most communities are unable to find enough foster homes and waiting lists are customary.

The group home differs from the foster home. It is common for an agency to construct an open group home residence which houses from six to 20 adolescents, and uses the schools and services in the community. The child lives with a group that does not require the intense closeness which characterizes the foster home placement. The group home reflects the character of the adolescents assigned to it while the foster home mirrors the living habits of the foster parents. Staff of the group home are hired and supervised by the agency operating the facility. Most group homes are operated by the state although some are privately controlled operations approved by a state agency. Community involvement is the key to successful operation of the group home.

Some cities, such as Boulder (Colorado), operate attention homes, supported through the contribution of money and volunteer services from local citizens. The police, the juvenile court, and parents whose children have become discipline or behavior problems refer the majority of youngsters to the attention centers.[33] Local control of the group home by concerned citizens is helpful because lack of community acceptance is a major reason for the failure of the group home.

The juvenile runaway is best served by the short-term residence group home. This youngster experiences a crisis period following the runaway, and counseling with parents is necessary before the family can be reunited. Approximately half a million youngsters run away from home each year. Among the reasons are parental cruelty, unwanted pregnancy, and school failure. A number of the runaways occur after dinner when parent-child conflict seems to erupt more easily. Legislation is needed to provide assistance to local and state governments in establishing runaway houses to provide shelter, counseling, medical services, and a means of solving the problem. Such centers have been established in various cities: Runaway House in Washington, D.C., Huckleberry House in San Francisco, and the Bridge in Minneapolis. They provide shelter and a chance for the youngster to consider possible solutions to his problem. The runaway home should contact the parents of the youth within two days and honor the rights of parents according to the law in the jurisdiction where the child resides. The juvenile who goes to another city when running away requires services arranging his return to the home community; this can be accomplished with a two-day maximum stay in a low-security shelter while staff complete the appropriate arrangements.

Another method for assisting the transient runaway is the home away from home, which provides one to 10-day foster home placement in emergencies. A youngster may remain in the home away from home, with parental permission, until tensions with parents are reduced and counseling can be arranged. The YWCA, in El Paso (Texas) is operating a residential intervention center where teen-age girls can stay until age 20 if tensions are not reduced in their own homes. The center consists of four foster homes, each housing 8 to 12 teen-agers and their houseparents. Entrance to the center requires permission of the girl and her parent or legal guardian. Services for the runaway youth are important, otherwise he can easily become involved in delinquent or criminal activity while trying to survive. There is a movement underway to remove the runaway category from the laws of juvenile delinquency and request that children experiencing such a crisis be allowed child advocates who will act in their behalf when they are treated unjustly (see Appendix D, General Bibliography, Runaways).

These alternatives to detention represent a future trend in juvenile corrections. It has been suggested that all detention centers be replaced with neighborhood rehabilitation centers offering short-term temporary care or extended treatment programs. The advocates of such a policy contend that the vast majority of juvenile offenders, arrested for status offenses and minor crimes, should not be placed in the same institutions with hard-core offenders. Another recommendation argues that juvenile detention centers should be replaced with group homes in different neighborhoods and that boys and girls attend the public schools serving those areas. The staff in the group homes would be given regular consultation with the county mental health agency or local clinical psychologists to help them understand the problems of adolescents. Another proposal, patterned after a demonstration project in St. Louis (Missouri), urges that juveniles be detained in their own or foster homes during the period between arrest and the dispositional hearing by the juvenile court, and be given daily supervision by juvenile court workers to insure that they do not commit additional misbehaviors while awaiting court disposition. Careful assessment of the youngster and his family is necessary if the home detention program is to succeed.

Alternatives to jail and detention will not be used extensively until laws are enacted which prohibit the holding of children in jail or the detention of the less serious offender in juvenile hall. Each community must determine, according to its own standards, what is and what is not serious misbehavior. In many states and communities, dependent and neglected children are held in detention because shelter facilities are unavailable; in these situations the required programs should be provided and criteria established to determine who is in need of detention, shelter care, or other available alternatives. The growth of the youth service bureau concept will provide for the diversion of youth from the formal agencies of delinquency control.

Placing youths in jails and detention centers cannot be supported if lesser controls will adequately protect the community. Rosemary Sarri, codirector of the National Assessment Study of Juvenile and Youth Correctional Programs, offers a number of recommendations which should be enacted in order to eliminate the problems associated with jailing juveniles and using detention unreasonably.

1. Statutes should prohibit the commitment of juveniles to jail under any circumstances. Only those states which have strong prohibitions or have state control of jails have been successful thus far in eliminating the jailing of juveniles.
2. Statutes should provide for mandatory detention hearings with counsel provided and the detention decision the responsibility of the judge. Such hearings should be held within 24 hours of the juvenile's being taken into custody. It must first consider whether there is probable cause that he or she has in fact committed the act with which they are charged. The court then can decide whether detention is necessary because of the danger to others or because they are a serious risk in not being available to the court for subsequent processing. Although statutory provisions for mandatory hearing

are the exception rather than the rule, such provisions are essential if detention and jailing is to be controlled. . . . Furthermore, it is now possible to develop criteria as to what is a clear danger and who is a risk. This should be done so that statutes can contain the necessary provisions. We are in agreement . . . that jailing a child to protect him is inappropriate given the conditions for children in adult jails. It is difficult to see why self-destructive acts should ever be a basis for detention in jail. Hospitals and emergency clinics are far more appropriate referral agencies for the child who is a threat to himself.

3. Criteria for detention should be explicit and limited solely to acts which would be criminal felonies if committed by adults. . . . [It has been] proposed that special civil actions and quasi-judicial mechanisms be substituted for juvenile court action in cases of truancy, incorrigibility, and other status offenses. Obviously, for this proposal to be effective community resources would need to be greatly enhanced, but implementation of this proposal would reduce criminal handling of much juvenile misbehavior.

4. As indicated above, it is recommended that judges be given the responsibility for decisions to detain, and constitutional rights available to adults should also apply in the cases of juveniles in this decision-making.

5. Rapid development of alternatives to incarceration of juveniles charged with criminal violations must be given high priority. Foster and shelter homes can provide alternative 24-hour supervision but of equal or greater importance is home detention with supervision and consultation to parents. The use of release upon the promise to appear could be implemented immediately in most jurisdictions for the majority of cases. . . . Although bail is negatively viewed by most students of juvenile law, it is available in more than twenty states. Some mechanisms are needed to facilitate the immediate release of juveniles who are charged with acts for which adults can be released on bail.

6. In view of the fact that there are seven states in which jail is presently the only available detention facility, it is obvious that regional detention units are needed for

juveniles in these states. It is probable that some juveniles will have to be detained for limited periods of time, but because such centers are likely to be at a distance from the home of most offenders, the minimum age could be set at 15 years.

7. Jail inspections on a routine basis must be implemented in all states with the necessary resources and with inspectors responsible to the Department of Social Services or Supreme Court, rather than to the Department of Corrections, as is the case in many states today. These inspections must be frequent and mandatory so as to insure juveniles not being held in jail. Frequent inspections must be accompanied by a comprehensive system for state-wide information collection and processing, and feedback if accountability and quality control are to be achieved. Such a system should permit randomized checking of detention populations and practices. The lack of routinely collected information about organizational practice is probably the single greatest constraint on change in corrections today.
8. Obviously, the use of jails for sentencing juveniles also must be prohibited explicitly. If it is necessary to sentence a juvenile to an institution, then a public training school or a private residential facility is where he or she should be sent so that an appropriate rehabilitation program might possibly be provided for him. It is overwhelmingly apparent that neither jails nor juvenile detention facilities have the staff and other resources for even a minimally adequate rehabilitation program. Mandatory jail inspection should insure that this practice does not continue.
9. Given the development of various alternatives to the use of jails and detention, it appears likely that higher age limits (for example, 15 years) could be established for detention. Such an action would mean that children 8-14 years would not be placed with older adolescents who may have committed serious felonies and might only socialize the younger person to deviant values and behavior.
10. Court defined and state-wide detention standards need to be established and distributed widely to all relevant agencies. Such information would reduce variable inter-

pretations of statutes and highly disparate detention practices.

11. Legal counsel should be available to juveniles and parents immediately after detention takes place. Similarly, social investigations should not take place prior to a detention hearing and such information, when collected, should be made available to counsel.
12. The proposal of the National Task Force on Corrections for gradual state assumption of responsibility for all county and local detention is recommended. State consultation and supervision could begin immediately along with mechanisms for monitoring and supervising detention practices. . . . To encourage the development of alternatives for detention, the federal government could make special grants available for such purposes. In some states, activities of Youth Services Bureaus, for example, have resulted in the emergence of diversion and detention alternatives that are highly innovative and yet viable.[34]

Reform is imperative. It has been reported that:

. . . the use of detention is colored by rationalization, duplicity, and double talk. . . . Detention too often serves as storage, a means of delaying action. . . . In short, it serves as a substitute for the casework so urgently needed by both parent and child to begin unraveling the problem of which the delinquent act is but a symptom.[35]

STUDY QUESTIONS

1. What states were holding no juveniles in confinement on the day of the National Jail Census? More than 200 juveniles?
2. What percent of the juvenile court jurisdictions in the United States use the county jail or police lockup when detaining juveniles? What is the policy in your county?

3. Identify the states which have assumed responsibility for the operation of local jails.
4. What is the major police role in detention screening?
5. How might you determine the juvenile community absorption rate for your city?
6. Identify the procedures and policies for detaining juveniles in your local police department, juvenile court, and state legislation.
7. Which of the opinions and attitudes identified in the NCCD study of initial detention decisions appear to influence outcomes in your community?
8. Does your state conduct annual inspections of jails, juvenile halls, detention centers, and lockups which are used for the confinement of any minor under the age of 18?
9. Define the following: detention, shelter care, home detention, foster home, group home, and attention center.
10. Does your community support, through legislation and funding, programs which are identified as alternatives to detention?
11. Has your community implemented one or more of the recommendations of the National Assessment Study of Juvenile and Youth Correctional Programs?
12. Does your locality provide short-term residence group homes for the juvenile runaway? If not, what alternatives exist?
13. Identify guidelines which should be followed in determining whether emergency shelter care is required.

NOTES

1. *In re William M.*, 3 Cal. 3d 16 (August 24, 1970).

2. Ibid.

3. The President's Commission on Law Enforcement and Administration of Justice, *Task Force Report: Corrections* (Washington, D.C.: U.S. Government Printing Office, 1967), pp. 124 and 128.

4. *Report to the President, 1970 White House Conference on Children* (Washington, D.C.: U.S. Government Printing Office, 1971), p. 382.

5. *Reducing Crime and Assuring Justice*, A Statement of National Policy by the Research and Policy Committee of the Committee for Economic Development, June 1972 (New York: Committee for Economic Development, 1972); also Advisory Commission on Intergovernmental Relations, *State-Local Relations in the Criminal Justice System* (Washington, D.C.: U.S. Government Printing Office, 1971).

6. *Planning and Designing for Juvenile Justice*, U.S. Department of Justice, Law Enforcement Assistance Administration (Washington, D.C.: U.S. Government Printing Office, 1973), p. 48.

7. *Standards and Guides for the Detention of Children and Youth*, 2nd ed. (New York: National Council on Crime and Delinquency, 1961), p. 15. Reprinted with permission of the National Council on Crime and Delinquency, from *NCCD News* and *Standards and Guides for the Detention of Children and Youth.*

8. *Task Force Report: Corrections*, p. 121.

9. U.S. Law Enforcement Assistance Administration and U.S. Bureau of the Census, *Local Jails* (Washington, D.C.: U.S. Government Printing Office, 1973).

10. *NCCD News*, 51, no. 4 (September–October, 1972): 13.

11. John J. Downey, "Why Children Are in Jail and How to Keep Them Out," *Children*, 17, no. 1 (January–February, 1970): 21–26.

12. "Detention and Shelter Use and Practice," *Juvenile Court Judges Journal*, 23, no. 1 (Winter 1972): 21.

13. National Advisory Commission on Criminal Justice Standards and Goals, "Corrections: Role of Police Intake and Detention" (Working paper presented at the National Conference on Criminal Justice, Washington, D.C., January 23–26, 1973), p. C-152.

14. National Council on Crime and Delinquency, *Locking Them Up: A Study of Initial Juvenile Detention Decisions in Selected*

California Counties (San Francisco: National Council on Crime and Delinquency, Western Region, 1970), pp. 39–40.

15. Malcolm W. Klein, Solomon Kobrin, A.W. McEachern, and Herbert R. Sigurdson, "System Rates: An Approach to Comprehensive Criminal Justice Planning," *Crime and Delinquency*, 17, no. 4 (October 1971): 355–372.

16. Pennsylvania Department of Public Welfare, Office of Children and Youth, *Practice Guides, Child Welfare Series. No. 3: Police Work with Children* (Harrisburg, Pennsylvania: Bureau of Youth Development Services, 1963), p. 20.

17. Ibid., pp. 20–21.

18. For a discussion of the fingerprinting controversy and other issues, see Elyce Z. Ferster and Thomas F. Courtless, "The Beginning of Juvenile Justice, Police Practices, and the Juvenile Offender," *Vanderbilt Law Review*, 22, no. 3 (April 1969): 567–608.

19. *Pennsylvania, Practice Guides, No. 3:* pp. 22–23.

20. *People* v. *Burton*, 6 Cal. 3d 375 (December 28, 1971).

21. *Pennsylvania, Practice Guides, No. 3:* pp. 29–30.

22. See Elyce Z. Ferster, Edith N. Snethen, and Thomas F. Courtless, "Juvenile Detention: Protection, Prevention, or Punishment?" *Fordham Law Review*, 38, no. 2 (December 1969): 161–196.

23. *Locking Them Up*, p. 40.

24. Ibid., p. 162.

25. Thomas R. Phelps, "Pretrial Detention and Differential Sentencing of 1104 County Jail Inmates, Booked on a Felony Charge in an Urban and a Rural County of Washington State, 1954: A Comparative Analysis" (Master's thesis, University of Washington, 1959), p. 77.

26. *Locking Them Up*, p. 213.

27. Gerald G. O'Connor, "The Impact of Initial Detention upon Male Delinquents," *Social Problems*, 18 (Fall 1970): 194–199.

28. National Advisory Commission on Criminal Justice Standards and Goals, "Corrections: Juvenile Detention Center Planning" (Working paper presented at the National Conference on Criminal Justice, Washington, D.C., January 23–26, 1973), p. C-160.

29. John J. Downey, *State Responsibility for Juvenile Detention Care*, U.S. Department of Health, Education, and Welfare, Social and Rehabilitation Service, Youth Development and Delinquency Prevention Administration (Washington, D.C.: U.S. Government Printing Office, 1970), p. 6.

30. Ibid., p. 9.

31. Information regarding this newsletter may be obtained by writing Editor, Detention Newsletter, Box 24, Southern Illinois University, Edwardsville, Illinois 62025.

32. *Planning and Designing*, p. 40.

33. John E. Hargadine, Horace B. Holmes, and Ivan H. Scheier, "Attention Versus Detention," *Juvenile Court Judges Journal*, 19, no. 2 (Summer 1968): 74–78.

34. Rosemary C. Sarri, "The Detention of Youth in Jails and Juvenile Detention Facilities," *Juvenile Justice*, 24, no. 3 (November, 1973): 14–16.

35. *Task Force Report: Corrections*, p. 129.

THE JUVENILE COURT PROCESS AND PROBATION

JUVENILE COURT JURISDICTION

INCARCERATION ?

PROBATION FUNCTIONS AND SERVICES

The juvenile court movement emphasizes the protection of children's rights, especially in the areas of physical, moral, and mental development. This basic philosophy has always characterized the movement; its emphasis on procedural safeguards and due process does not minimize the protective functions of the court but, on the contrary, offers a more effective mechanism for their achievement. The *parens patriae* concept is basic; that is, the inherent power of the state passes to the juvenile court which acts in behalf of the child as would a parent. This requires that each child be seen as an individual, which is sometimes difficult in the court setting where everyone is overworked. In achieving these ideals, the primary function of the court—which is to protect the community while affording appropriate services to the child—must be kept foremost.

Although juveniles are frequently detained in jails temporarily, the juvenile court is useful in separating them from criminals in the court hearing. This separation has been effective, even though U.S. Supreme Court decisions have brought into the juvenile court many procedures which belong to the adult criminal court. When the *Standards for Juvenile and Family Courts* were revised in 1966 it was said that not a single state in the nation had achieved all the recommended objectives in services and organization, namely:

1. Every judge called on to serve in such a court should be both interested and fully qualified for his work and able to give time and thought to it.
2. The rights of parents and children should not be handled summarily or without proper provision for appeal to higher courts.

3. There should be an integrated court system rather than a multiplicity of specialized courts.
4. There should be uniformity in court practice and procedure throughout the State.
5. There should be adequate probation services throughout the State.
6. There should be uniform statistical reporting and record keeping—both legal and social.
7. There should be consolidated jurisdiction over justiciable issues involving interpersonal relationships within the family.
8. There should be effective working relationships between courts and agencies providing services through which the courts' decisions are rendered effective.[1]

Before these recommendations for a progressive court are discussed more fully, it is well to realize that several movements in the juvenile field have caused changes in the court's role. Child advocacy and the rights of children support the long-established idea that delinquency is made more severe when youth are denied social services. The diversionary movement permits a youngster to receive an alternative form of help—outside the juvenile justice system—when his problem might lead to labeling him a delinquent. The youth service bureau concept, the diversionary movement, and the helping police role all mean additional support for the juvenile court as a place of last resort. This concept is emphasized by Edwin Lemert:

> If there is a defensible philosophy for the juvenile court it is one of judicious nonintervention. It is properly an agency of last resort for children, holding to a doctrine analogous to that of appeals courts which require that all other remedies be exhausted before a case will be considered. This means that problems accepted for action by the juvenile court will be demonstrably serious by testable evidence ordinarily distinguished by a history of repeated failures at solutions by parents, relatives, schools, and community agencies.[2]

This viewpoint is supported further by Edwin Schur when he introduces the new term *radical nonintervention,* which

> . . . breaks radically with conventional thinking about delinquency and its causes. Basically, radical nonintervention implies policies that accommodate society to the widest possible diversity of behaviors and attitudes, rather than forcing as many individuals as possible to "adjust" to supposedly common societal standards. This does not mean that anything goes, that all behavior is socially acceptable. But traditional delinquency policy has proscribed youthful behavior well beyond what is required to maintain a smooth-running society or to protect others from youthful depredations. Thus, the basic injunction for public policy becomes: *leave kids alone whereever possible.*[3]

Adequate alternatives may be found to assist juveniles in trouble if the community explores possibilities and implements them. The late 1960s and the early 1970s brought an awareness that the court and the correctional institution could not of themselves reduce delinquency. These trends are noteworthy because it is now possible to use the juvenile court as one alternative and, in so doing, the effectiveness of the court is enhanced. The court exists for those children and youth who are not effectively helped by community programs. We need, therefore, to examine the juvenile court process.

JUVENILE COURT JURISDICTION

Eligibility for juvenile court processing is determined by state legislation (see Chapter 2). Juvenile court jurisdiction boundaries should be carefully formulated in state legislation, and should include only the non-adult crimes that the community wants retained. Neglect and dependency should not require court handling. The juvenile court should be asked to process *only* those children who cannot be served in diversionary programs. Chapter 6 discussed detention, the procedure for holding a juvenile before his hearing. Children processed by the court must pass through three hearings: (1) the intake or preliminary, (2) the adjudication or the fact-finding, and (3) the dispositional. The decision to detain the juvenile is reached by the intake staff at an earlier hearing. A time interval should occur between each of these stages. In some juvenile court jurisdictions there is no time between the adjudication and the dispositional hearing.

When the two hearings are scheduled and held on different days, one can say the juvenile court makes use of bifurcated hearings. The literature on juvenile court procedures authorizes or requires the three hearings but the question of using bifurcated hearings lies with the jurisdiction. The time interval between the adjudication and dispositional hearing, which identifies a bifurcated hearing, has important advantages. It allows the parents and counsel time to consider alternatives to institutionalization after the fact-finding hearing and before the juvenile court judge determines the disposition in the case. The family has a chance to mobilize its resources and offer appropriate care. The bifurcated hearing is also advantageous because it permits the youngster to spend a longer period of time with the judge. Some years ago, one juvenile court was alleged to have completed its case hearings in about three minutes. The bifurcated hearing protects the youngster against receiving such an accelerated hearing.

Intake

Legislation dealing with jurisdiction determines who is eligible for processing in the juvenile court. Intake is a procedure to help court personnel decide whether youngsters referred to the court can best be served by it. The most skilled people in the probation department, which is a part of the juvenile court, are the intake workers. In this preliminary hearing they seek answers to such questions as the following:

1. Does the complaint or the action appear to be a matter over which the court may have jurisdiction?
2. Can the interests of the child and the public be best served by court action (i.e., the filing of a petition) or by referral to another agency in the community?
3. If by referral to another agency, what agency?
4. If court action is indicated, what type of proceeding should be initiated?
5. If the child is in detention, is continued detention care needed or should the child be released.[4]

This screening of cases prevents unnecessary use of the judicial process and offers the youngster referral services in the community. Unfortunately, many social agencies are reluctant to help youngsters who have been referred to the juvenile court and released for alternate forms of help. They have come up against the resistant youngster who does not want services imposed upon him.

At the intake or preliminary hearing, the wishes of the community and the complainant collide with the reality of the services the juvenile court can provide the child. The privilege against self-incrimination (i.e., *Miranda* rights) plays an important role in the preliminary hearing. However, it will be remembered from the earlier discussion of the decisions of the U.S. Supreme Court that the rights of the juvenile place emphasis on the next stage of the process, the adjudication hearing. Intake is a form of preliminary screening that determines whether a formal charge will be placed against the juvenile. The charge must be filed in a document known as a petition. The offense charged must be clearly understood by the parents and the child. There must be adequate time for the interested parties to prepare a defense and this means giving notice of the right to counsel. To cite the delinquency statute, which refers to alleged misbehavior of a youngster, is not enough. Specific facts are needed such as the following:

1. Proceedings in which a child is alleged to be delinquent or neglected or a person in need of supervision.
2. A statement . . . that the child is in need of supervision, care, or rehabilitation.
3. The name, birth date, and residence address of the child.
4. The names and residence addresses of his parents, guardian, or custodian, and spouse, if any.
5. Whether the child is in custody, and, if so, the place of detention and the time he was taken into custody.
6. When any of the facts herein required are not known, the petition shall so state.[5]

Approximately 50 percent of the cases referred to the juvenile court do not move beyond the intake hearing. Sometimes the worker evaluating the case will decide that a formal petition is not required although there is some need for a period of informal adjustment in order to assure the court that the child has received the required attention. The period of informal adjustment should be limited to no more than three months; this decision should be made less often when adequate diversionary programs are available. When the juvenile court fails to file a petition in a case, the case is said to be handled nonjudicially. A majority of such cases are dismissed by the court, but sometimes a period of informal adjustment is sought in order to determine whether the juvenile stays out of trouble. During this time he will be free of court controls, although he may be advised to participate in programs recommended by the court.

The use of informal adjustment must be accompanied by appropriate legal safeguards: the juvenile and his parents should be advised of their right to counsel; voluntary participation in the court program is to be stressed; the major facts of the case should be undisputed. The right to formal adjudication, when requested by the parents and the child, is to be honored. If, at a later time, a formal proceeding is sought on the original complaint it is important that any statements made during the period of informal adjustment be excluded. Informal adjustment, sometimes called informal probation, is helpful to the probation officer who questions the need for a formal petition. The availability of skilled services such as counseling, tutoring, and other pertinent programs is crucial during this period. The absence of programs reduces informal supervision to nothing; some say that the youngster cannot respond when in reality no services were there.

The filing of the petition by the court worker, not merely the signing of the document, is the important step which determines whether the juvenile moves to the adjudicatory hearing. The decision to file a petition lies with the probation staff and these same people may later be asked to serve as treatment workers for the child. Most parents and youngsters are unable to differentiate between the role of the probation staff in filing a petition and the later role of the probation worker which may then be defined as a "helping relationship." The passage of a few days between the preliminary and the adjudicatory hearing does not minimize this difficulty. For this reason the right to counsel can be useful to parent and child.

An adjudication hearing is in order when: (1) requested by the complainant or the juvenile; (2) there are substantial discrepancies about the allegations of a serious offense or its denial; (3) protection of the community is a concern; and (4) court attention is appropriate because of the gravity of the offense or the special needs of the juvenile.

Adjudication

The filing of the petition is followed by the issuance of a summons which states that a fact-finding or adjudicatory hearing has been scheduled. Each summons to appear should be accompanied by a copy of the petition and a notice of the right to counsel. The summons should reach the juvenile at least one day before the hearing.

In earlier years, the adjudication hearing was considered an uneventful interim period between the preliminary hearing and the disposition of the case, a period when the court could switch from the role of sifting cases into the role of how best to serve the child. The introduction of the right to counsel and the other changes brought about by the U.S. Supreme Court have revolutionized the adjudication hearing in a manner undreamed of by its founders. At the fact-finding hearing, the court decides from legally admissible evidence whether the child is guilty of the alleged delinquency, whether he is a neglected child, or whether he is in need of supervision.

This hearing is conducted in the informal and sensitive manner characteristic of the juvenile court. The court presumes the innocence of the child at the hearing. It hears evidence attempting to determine beyond a reasonable doubt whether the juvenile has committed the alleged delinquency. The probation staff refrains from submitting a social evaluation of the child at the time of the fact-finding hearing. This is necessary so that hearsay and subjective evaluations of the child's environment do not influence the evidence, which focuses on the alleged delinquency alone. The presence of a lawyer at the adjudicatory hearing is helpful because he can assure the parents that appropriate procedures for the determination of guilt or innocence are followed in the assessment of the evidence at hand.

Some difficulties were encountered when lawyers were first introduced into the juvenile court hearing. Traditional training in the adversary procedures of the criminal court did not prepare the lawyer for the different atmosphere of the juvenile court. This problem has been resolved with the passage of time and the concurrent interest in juvenile justice held by those now completing law school.[6] The informality and privacy of the court hearing often overwhelms the parents. They are likely to equate due process of law with the machinelike, noisy, and impersonal proceedings characteristic of the open, adult criminal-court atmosphere.

When the facts alleged in the petition presented in the fact-finding hearing have been substantiated the juvenile court proceeds to the third stage, the dispositional hearing.

Disposition

The period between the end of the adjudicatory and the beginning of the dispositional hearing is used for gathering and preparing the relevant information necessary for determining the action to be taken by the court in the individual case. Concern for the child, the basis for the juvenile court movement, is expressed in this third stage of the proceedings. The nature of the decision and the value of this court depend upon the sensitivity and knowledgeable skills of the juvenile court judge. Few people have such power in the administration of justice. Communities should pay careful attention to the selection of their juvenile court judges. The juvenile court movement is fortunate in the quality and probity of a vast majority of its presiding judges.

The most important information prepared by the court for the disposition hearing is the social study investigation. This study focuses upon the child and not the evidence surrounding the offense. The report familiarizes the judge with the social conditions of the child's environment. Assumptions made by the probation officer who prepares the report will influence the decision. A carefully prepared social history focuses on the youngster's background —relationships with the parents and siblings, the peer group, the school; health and medical history; an identification of significant people in the life of the child; identification of areas of conflict created by the behavior of the youngster in his relations with other people in the community; earlier contacts with social agencies, the police, and other formal social institutions; previous delinquent history whether known or unknown to official processing agencies; and a search for positive relationships, helpful in reducing the recurrent misbehavior that would mean future court appearances. The probation officer accompanies the report with recommendations regarding the appropriate treatment program for the youngster. The parents, the child, and counsel should be familiar with the facts upon which these recommendations are made. The court then determines the disposition of the case with the best interests of the youngster in mind. Therefore, secrecy is incompatible with the philosophy of the juvenile court. The court indicates that a juvenile should remain in his own home so long as the community is not endangered.

The options open to the judge are: (1) dismissal; (2) probation; (3) placement of the child in a foster or group home; (4) commitment to a county correctional institution if the youngster is considered too sophisticated for a foster home but not in need of the severe sanction represented by placement in the state-wide correctional facilities; and (5) sentencing to the state juvenile correctional system. The judge must be sure that the services recommended for the youngster will be made available.

The three stages of the juvenile court process are critical experiences for the juvenile and should be handled with care by the judge and the probation staff. They can damage the youngster or provide him with constructive relationships in which authority figures are influential. Some years ago, a judge in a certain community decided that delinquency might be curtailed if extensive newspaper publicity were accorded the juvenile being processed in his court. Violating the concept of privacy in juvenile hearings, he assumed that the publishing of the names of juveniles and their families would teach everyone a lesson. Visibility of court hearings replaced the availability of services to children. He claimed a great reduction in the amount of delinquency in his town—but he overlooked several important issues. Juveniles in trouble are sometimes seeking recognition; they have been known to keep scrapbooks, including newspaper accounts of their exploits, as methods for gaining status. When a youngster knows that his parents are embarrassed by the publication of their names, his pleasure shows his hostility toward them.

In addition, a juvenile court that does not provide appropriate services may find very few children referred to it. An unthinking community may conclude that delinquency is decreasing. Unfortunately, it works the other way; the installation of a new juvenile court judge or additional proven programs may increase referrals. People should be alert to extreme fluctuations in the number of court referrals. Reasons will vary, but the following frequently occur: more attention given to existing community resources by the court, the capacity of the court to utilize these resources, and the concern of the court in understanding the treatment needs of the child.

The attitudes of children to the court hearing are varied. The child appearing in court for the first time is more likely to express a positive attitude toward the probation officer once his fears are reduced. Cynicism is a common response among juveniles who have been brought before the court repeatedly. The judge receives a positive rating from the youngster when he takes the time to talk with him and shows concern for his problems. Of course the attitude of the youngster is more favorable when the judge grants him probation. Children are often concerned about the response of parents to the juvenile court hearing, especially when the parents express negative feelings toward their children in the presence of the judge. It is common for the youngster to comment that the hearing allowed him to reassess the behavior that led to the offense. There is little evidence that the hearings, in themselves, turn children from delinquent activity if such an orientation is well established and it is doubtful that greater respect for law and order occurs. A 1972 study of boys who had committed adult crimes and were known to the police and juvenile court supports this viewpoint. According to the boys interpersonal relationships with family members and friends were not strained; however, increased police surveillance and probable employment difficulty concerned them. They counted on their youth at the time of the offense, the secrecy of juvenile records, and their own subsequent good conduct to protect them from further liabilities.[7]

INCARCERATION?

A majority of juveniles processed through the juvenile court find their cases dismissed or handled by informal adjustment. The remainder experience more restrictive decisions; the most severe sanction is referral to the statewide correctional system for a period of confinement. The decision to confine a youngster in a state institution requires thoughtful consideration. Each state should set a minimum age below which a youngster may not be confined in a state training school. The minimum age should be specified in the juvenile delinquency statutes. In California no ward of the juvenile court who is under the age of eight years may be committed to the state correctional system (i.e., California Youth Authority). The statute further states that no youngster who is suffering from an infectious or contagious disease which will endanger other inmates may be confined in such an institution.

Guidelines are needed to determine which youth should be considered for incarceration in a state correctional institution. The following three categories represent appropriate types of cases for this severe sanction:

1. Sophisticated delinquent youth whose behavior cannot be adequately modified in the community.
2. Wards involved in very serious offenses and who require relief from community pressures.
3. Aggressive or assaultive wards who pose a threat to the lives or property of others and are not in need of treatment under the mental health system.[8]

It is possible that other states will follow the recent trend in Massachusetts where all the correctional institutions were closed. In such situations it will be necessary for the counties to establish medium security institutions for the confinement of wards meeting the above criteria. No community should accept incarceration as a measure which will protect it from the youths confined in state institutions; protection exists only so long as the juvenile is locked up. Confinement without social services assures a community that the dangerous behavior will continue upon release; it might cease if the juvenile lived in the community without being incarcerated. Social services and a competent staff devoted to the treatment of difficult youth increase the probability of positive change. Existing knowledge about the treatment of youth who require incarceration is not effective.

We do know, however, that the following types of youngsters should *not* be committed to state correctional institutions and that if they are, the youngsters suffer:

1. Youths who are dependent or primarily placement problems. For these youths in need of a home and peer acceptance, as well as accepting adults, life in an institution might be totally fulfilling, resulting in an orientation to an institutional experience.
2. Unsophisticated, mildly delinquent youths for whom commingling with the serious delinquents who make up the bulk of the Youth Authority population might result in a negative learning experience and serious loss of self-esteem.
3. Pregnant girls, since the Youth Authority is not equipped to provide imminent pre- and postnatal care or placement planning for the child.
4. Mentally retarded or mentally disturbed youths for whom the probable benefits of treatment within the mental health system exceed those of programs within the Youth Authority. The Youth Authority has no programs for the mentally retarded nor psychiatric treatment for the mentally ill.
5. Homosexuals who pose no threat to the life or morals of others. Confinement of homosexuals usually deepens the problem, endangers the individual, and achieves little resolution to the deviant behavior.[9]

A number of anxious citizens assume that confinement is the answer to the delinquency problem; these individuals usually believe that the training school should be tough, that few luxuries should be allowed, and that harshness will change behavior. These supporters of indiscriminate incarceration are likely to reject budgets which might provide services directed toward changing the behavior of the delinquents. These people, who have never visited a prison and are unaware of the complexities of the juvenile justice system, do not realize that their thinking makes the danger worse. For this reason the guidelines for the selection of youngsters for confinement are important. Those who should not be confined are in the majority when the preceding criteria are followed. Advantages inherent in the formal processing of youth are found through the services of the probation department or through the alternate referrals made by the probation staff.

PROBATION FUNCTIONS AND SERVICES

The functions of the probation department include the following:

1. The officer prepares the background investigation, the social study and diagnosis, which assists the court in determining the amount of control and surveillance required if the youth is to remain in the jurisdiction of the court and if services are to be recommended.
2. The officer provides supervision and treatment when the youngster is returned to the community. Treatment services offered while on probation are accompanied by varying levels of surveillance. The same social services offered in a diversionary program would be characterized by no surveillance, no coercion, and the right to terminate at any time.

There is much controversy as to whether treatment services are the same when accompanied by coercion and surveillance. The question is, does the juvenile need the careful observation of the probation department? Probation permits the youngster to remain at home, withholding the more severe sanction of removal. Treatment is helpful during the first probation period, especially if the youngster is permitted to tour a correctional facility—unknown consequences produce little fear or trepidation. Services, when offered outside of the juvenile justice system, have been found more effective than when youngsters are provided identical services on probation.

Ideally the probation officer might effectively use surveillance to identify the positive factors in the youth's neighborhood; coercion when the youngster requires support because ambivalence might lead him back to crime and delinquency. Actually, the probation officer, with his two different tasks, is bogged down and unable to be effective at either. The writing of the social summary places so much emphasis on paperwork and background information that the probation officer seldom includes information showing the youngster in his arena of action. Instead, unfortunately, many social histories are merely impersonal accounts of youngsters from low-income or middle-class neighborhoods. The content of these summaries does not reveal patterns of vitality, apathy, giving, coping, and striving which provide the youngster with inner skills and controls to survive there as he continues his probation.

The second function of the probation officer is supervision and treatment. Supervision is defined as determining the whereabouts of a youngster and accounting for him on probation. Caseloads are assigned each officer and he may be asked to supervise 100 or more youngsters. A smaller caseload is recommended, usually 50 cases, but it is seldom possible for a court to reduce the caseload. Unfortunately, the myth of caseload size hampers much that could be done for the child; it is easy to say one cannot provide much time to 100 youngsters. However, each caseload is made up of many kinds of children: some require little attention because they submit periodical reports to the probation officer and request his assistance when needed; others need specific services available at the court and have demonstrated their ability to use such help. Only a small number should be seen by the probation officer weekly. Supervision, however, requires a great deal of paperwork and can get in the way of treatment and counseling. Probation officers concentrate either on the counseling or on the recording aspect of their work, but unfortunately they are asked to perform all the functions. So they always have practical reasons for not serving the needs of the youngster: the judge wants an immediate social study for the court, the caseload is too large, and there are those difficult cases which require an unreasonable amount of time. In these situations it is easy for the worker to blame his failure on resistance to treatment.

Diversionary programs offer the same treatment services as the probation department but the workers are not required to spend a major part of their time on duties which have nothing to do with helping the youngster. The great criticism of probation is the dilution of the staff time to duties which can be performed by clerical staff and volunteers. This limitation is being overcome through court-administered services. The probation officer is the key worker; casework, the one-to-one relationship, is the treatment of choice. Progress is likely when the probation counselor is allowed to treat and does not spend excessive time on other duties. Some probation officers should write social study evaluations, while others should counsel and treat those on probation. In addition, the basic individual counseling or casework approach should be supplemented with group work and the use of the probation team who make joint decisions about the services needed by the youngster and who assist in providing these services. A leader directs the many professionals who make up the team: a caseworker, clinical psychologist, psychiatrist, group worker, occupational therapist, music therapist, recreation therapist, and psychiatric technicians.

The probation departments offer the same quality of services as do local diversionary programs. It is clear that a probation officer cannot perform effectively the diverse roles assigned to him. A further dilemma is, do court-administered or community-administered social services best help youngsters in trouble? Those who favor court-administered programs argue that nonjudicial agencies resist referrals from juvenile courts and the courts offer duplicate services. Those who support community-administered programs believe the juvenile court should limit itself to the legal processing of youth who need such action. Advocates of community-administered programs believe in using diversion and the youth service bureau when the youngster is not in need of county or state institutionalization. They get additional support from those communities where the juvenile court and the probation department are unable to assign staff to either the social evaluation writing chores or to the supervision and treatment activity. The argument against the court-services approach is even greater if the time spent on paperwork and nontreatment actions reflect a high failure on probation rate for the youngsters in the community. Robert D. Vinter has said ". . . the behavior of significant numbers of boys who become involved in illegal activity is not redirected toward conventional activity by the institutions created for that purpose," and he provides a number of arguments critical of court-administered programs.[10]

Manpower Issues in Upgrading Court-Administered Services

The juvenile court must be strengthened to attract and retain the best-qualified individuals, including judges, chief probation officers, and probation counselors. One cannot introduce the concept of probation subsidy and at the same time overlook the recruitment and training of court judges and staff.

Probation subsidy is a plan that gives county probation departments monetary incentives to reduce their commitments to state training schools. The idea is good. Money used to strengthen local probation programs results in better services to children in their own homes. Unfortunately, more money cannot by itself remove the problems enumerated earlier; youngsters may remain out of correctional facilities but innovative services are not provided for them. In fact, a review of counties making use of probation subsidies often reveals *no* attempt to do the following:

1. Increase the number of probation counselors available to provide services to youth through smaller caseloads.
2. Use in-service training and community involvement to increase staff skills in coordinating available services.
3. Train volunteers to work effectively with children while gaining additional skills from the probation staff. Too often volunteers are viewed as budget-saving "do-gooders."
4. Permit probationers to assess programs, in order to vitalize the processing of children and adjust it to the changing life styles of today.

Too many probation subsidy programs operate like public school systems where children are viewed as impersonal bodies that do not bring money to the school district unless the bodies are present. The agency should give up the usual pattern of projecting blame upon those it is delegated to process.

Judges. The selection of judges for the juvenile court must be re-examined. They should be trained in a law school, have passed the state bar examination in the state where they are to serve, and have some experience in the practice of law. Undergraduate education should include a major in criminal justice, criminology, or corrections, with a concentration of courses in sociology and psychology. In addition to academic training, the judge should be:

1. Deeply concerned about the rights of people.
2. Keenly interested in the problems of children and families.
3. Sufficiently aware of the contribution of modern psychology, psychiatry and social work that he can give due weight to the findings of these sciences and professions.
4. Able to evaluate evidence and stituations objectively, and make dispositions uninfluenced by his own personal concepts of child care.
5. Eager to learn.
6. A good administrator, able to delegate administrative responsibility. (Applicable when administrative judge.)
7. Able to conduct hearings in a kindly manner and to talk to children and adults sympathetically and on their level of understanding without loss of the essential dignity of the court.[11]

Many are opposed to the requirement that a juvenile court judge be trained in the behavioral and social sciences. There is some justification for this viewpoint especially because law-school training focuses upon renewed sensitivity for the child and his rights, child advocacy, and the changing role of law in human relations; revisions in the traditional law school curriculum afford the kind of training formerly found only in the behavioral and social sciences. In addition, the judge has available a number of excellent training programs sponsored by the National Council of Juvenile Court Judges. Attendance at these sessions should be required of newly appointed or elected juvenile court judges. The training of the juvenile court judge has been an area of serious concern for a number of years (see Appendix D, General Bibliography, Court Judges), because he is the chief agent for change in his area. The judge influences the relationships existing between the police and the juvenile court, provides in-house training for his staff and determines the level of juvenile justice and community protection in his jurisdiction. Every community deserves a juvenile court judge with the sensitivity of Judge Ben Lindsey, a reformer in the early 1900s. Lindsey, a poor newsboy in his youth, became a judge in 1901 and by 1914 his campaign for children's legislation put him on a national list of the ten greatest living Americans. He claimed to have set up the first juvenile court in Colorado, before the passage of the juvenile court law in Illinois; Colorado set up a separate court for juveniles through an educational law in 1899.[12]

Probation officers. The chief probation officer is the manager of the court and probation services. He is responsible to the judge, the court personnel, and the community. His probation department may be a small rural office or a large metropolitan department with thousands of personnel. A probation department is only as good as the chief probation officer because he must implement the program of the court. He may be committed to the provision of court-sponsored services to youth or he may believe that the juvenile court is a junior criminal court. His education can range from two years of college to the master's degree in social work. Some work has been done in training court managers at the Institute for Court Management at the University of Denver under the direction of Ted Rubin, formerly judge of the Denver (Colorado) Juvenile Court. The chief probation officer is responsible for management of the intake unit; control over the detention facility even though it is operated by the detention supervisor; and hiring, firing, and upgrading the probation staff.

The probation officer is most important in implementing the philosophy and policies of the judge and the chief probation officer. As the primary contact between the juvenile and the court after the dispositional hearing, he may act out this role as a sensitive, concerned counselor or as a punitive figurehead who must control. About his training, there is disagreement. For many years the baccalaureate degree was required; then progressive probation departments recommended the master of social work degree. Most schools of social work did not emphasize corrections and few graduates selected the juvenile court for employment; nonetheless, juvenile courts, which required the M.S.W. degree for employment and succeeded in attracting such a staff, have been successful.

With the increase in criminal justice programs and the number of graduates, it is increasingly common for the court to require one or two years experience in the field, in addition to the undergraduate or graduate degree. Usually, the applicant gets experience as a counselor at a juvenile or detention hall.

It is unfortunate that the civil service requirements often state that, for the probation officer position, only the minimum of six or 12 hours in the social and behavioral sciences and the baccalaureate degree are necessary. There are many dedicated, articulate, and concerned undergraduate majors in the new criminal justice programs and in the programs of the behavioral and social sciences which emphasize delinquency prevention and control. Failure to recruit these people as probation officers is a hypocrisy as tragic as granting probation to a youngster and then denying him services.

Juvenile justice and community protection will exist only when there is care in selecting the juvenile court judge, chief probation officer, probation staff, and other court personnel. The hopes of the juvenile court movement cannot be realized, and have often been unfulfilled, because such selection is a routine and unchallenging pursuit. Careful staffing can assist the court in overcoming the harsh reality documented by Edwin Lemert:

> Neither the modern state nor an harassed juvenile court judge is a father; a halfway house is not a home; a reformatory cell is not a teenager's bedroom; a juvenile hall counselor is not a dutch uncle; and a cottage matron is not a mother. This does not mean that the people referred to should not be or are not kindly and dedicated, but rather that they are first and foremost members of organizations, bound by institution controls and subject to its exigencies; they are enforcers of superimposed rules. Where conflicts arise between the interests of a youth and those of the organization to which these functionaries are bureaucratically responsible there is no pattern of action which can predict that they will observe an order of value satisfaction favorable to the youth's interest.[13]

The juvenile court movement should engage in immediate self-evaluation. If not, the recommendation of the National Advisory

Commission on Criminal Justice Standards and Goals will be implemented in a number of states within the next decade. The commission recommends the abolishment of the juvenile court and calls for the establishment of a family court as a replacement for the juvenile court. The recommendation reads:

> Jurisdiction over juveniles of the sort presently vested in juvenile courts should be placed in a family court. The family court should be a division of the trial court of general jurisdiction, and should have jurisdiction over all legal matters related to family life. This jurisdiction should include delinquency, neglect, support, adoption, child custody, paternity actions, divorce and annulment, and assault offenses in which both the victim and the alleged offender are members of the same family. The family court should have adequate resources to enable it to deal effectively with family problems that may underlie the legal matters coming before it.[14]

STUDY QUESTIONS

---

1. Has your state achieved the objectives in services and organization recommended for the progressive juvenile court? If not, why?
2. Define radical nonintervention.
3. What is a petition? When is it filed in the juvenile court?
4. What is the bifurcated hearing?
5. Discuss the traits and the training recommended for the juvenile court judge.
6. What is the purpose of the preliminary hearing? Dispositional hearing? Adjudication hearing?
7. What is a social history? Who prepares it? When is it introduced into the juvenile court hearing?
8. Should the names of juvenile offenders be published in the newspaper? Substantiate your answer.
9. Identify the attitudes of youngsters toward juvenile court hearings.

10. When is probation the preferred juvenile court disposition? Incarceration? Diversion?
11. What is the role of the chief probation officer?
12. List and explain the functions of the probation officer.
13. Define court-administered social services.
14. What is the purpose of probation subsidy? Is it used in your locality?

NOTES

1. William H. Sheridan, *Standards for Juvenile and Family Courts,* U.S. Department of Health, Education, and Welfare, Welfare Administration, Children's Bureau (Washington, D.C.: U.S. Government Printing Office, 1966), pp. 27–28.

2. Edwin M. Lemert, "The Juvenile Court—Quest and Realities," in the President's Commission on Law Enforcement and Administration of Justice, *Task Force Report: Juvenile Delinquency and Youth Crime* (Washington, D.C.: U.S. Government Printing Office, 1967), pp. 96–97.

3. Edwin M. Schur, *Radical Nonintervention: Rethinking the Delinquency Problem* (Englewood Cliffs, N.J.: Prentice-Hall, 1973), pp. 154–155.

4. William H. Sheridan, *Standards,* p. 54.

5. William H. Sheridan, *Legislative Guide for Drafting Family and Juvenile Court Acts,* U.S. Department of Health, Education, and Welfare, Social and Rehabilitation Service, Children's Bureau (Washington, D.C.: U.S. Government Printing Office, 1969), pp. 10 and 16.

6. See W. Vaughn Stapleton and Lee E. Teitelbaum, *In Defense of Youth: A Study of the Role of Counsel in American Juvenile Courts* (New York: Russell Sage Foundation, 1972).

7. Jack D. Foster, Simon Dinitz, and Walter C. Reckless, "Perceptions of Stigma Following Public Intervention for Delinquent Behavior," *Social Problems,* 20 (Fall 1972): 202–209.

8. *Criteria and Procedure for Referral of Juvenile Court Cases to the Youth Authority* (Sacramento: Department of the Youth Authority, June 1971), pp. 2–3.

9. Ibid., p. 2.

10. *Task Force Report: Juvenile Delinquency and Youth Crime*, p. 113; see also Appendix D. General Bibliography, Courts.

11. *Standards*, pp. 103–104.

12. See Charles Larsen, *The Good Fight: The Life and Times of Ben B. Lindsey* (Chicago: Quadrangle Books, Inc., 1972); and Anthony M. Platt, *The Child Savers: The Intervention of Delinquency* (Chicago: The University of Chicago Press, 1969), pp. 137–175.

13. *Task Force Report: Juvenile Delinquency*, p. 92.

14. National Advisory Commission on Criminal Justice Standards and Goals, *Report on Courts* (Washington, D.C.: U.S. Government Printing Office, 1973), p. 293.

JUVENILE INSTITUTIONS AND AFTERCARE

HISTORY: JUVENILES AND INSTITUTIONS
ORGANIZATION OF INSTITUTIONS
THE RECEPTION CENTER
OPERATION OF INSTITUTIONS
THE COTTAGE SYSTEM
WAYS TO CHANGE STAFF
PROGRAMS
AFTERCARE OR PAROLE

The correctional institution should be used only when the juvenile is not amenable to diversionary programs or probation. Confinement protects the community from the youngster temporarily. Equating confinement and protection, otherwise known as warehousing, without accompanying services directed toward treatment is shortsighted. It is also expensive—to keep a youth in a training school ranges from $2,000 to $11,000 per year; costs are highest in the reception center, less in the training school, and least in the forestry camp.

A recent survey identifies 343 public institutions for delinquent children. The majority are traditional training schools (235), but there are also forestry camps or ranch facilities (94), and diagnostic-reception centers (14). The total daily population may reach 50,000. Twice this number are admitted and released each year.[1] The ideal training school should not exceed 150 juvenile offenders. Forestry camps most often meet this standard; only 50 percent of the training schools do. Diagnostic and reception centers are sure to be overcrowded but the temporary nature of confinement in these facilities makes the problem less serious.

Approximately one-third of the juvenile institutions are overcrowded. The delinquent may stay three months at the reception center, ten months in the training school, and eight months in the forestry camp. Only 71 out of 343 public facilities for delinquent youth are operated by the counties. Usually under state control, the number in a single state may range from 1 to as high as 61 in California, 29 in New York, or 20 in Illinois.[2] The recent trend away from state juvenile institutions will reduce these figures in the future. Massachusetts closed theirs in January 1972. Several months later the National Council on Crime and Delinquency issued a policy statement asking that construction of all juvenile training schools be halted until full use of community-based programs is achieved.[3] In the 1980s the community correctional center will replace the multi-purpose training school in states following these guidelines.

Nonetheless, communities will continue to demand that dangerous juveniles be confined. Moving the youngster closer to his home is beneficial, but it cannot be considered revolutionary. The services in the community must be as good or better than those in the state institution but the methods for handling groups of offenders, juvenile or adult, may be no better than those in operation at the time the training schools were closed. Change is miserably slow in corrections, especially the congregate handling of youngsters. Buildings constructed as early as 1826 are still being used. Conditions in training schools, revealed by Albert Deutsch in 1950, were not corrected two decades later when Howard James revisited a number of them.[4]

HISTORY: JUVENILES AND INSTITUTIONS

The earliest institutions for children in this country were known as houses of refuge. John Griscom (1774–1852), a Quaker and concerned educator, introduced separate housing for children; the first was established in New York City in 1825. During the next twenty years others opened in Boston, New Orleans, and Philadelphia. Their goal was to retrain the youngster, relying heavily on academic and work programs. Because of the stigma attached to these facilities the names were changed—to Boys Village, Girls Town, Greenhill, Lookout Mountain, and Maple Lane. But the environment remained the same. From these originals have come the modern industrial and reform schools.

Today's correctional institutions are better—youngsters do live long enough to be released, and all of them return to the community. When juveniles were first separated from adult offenders, the life expectancy of children in adult institutions was one year. Many of the early reformers were content simply to remove children from adult institutions; treatment meant confinement in separate facilities. Rehabilitation did not yet include care, compassion, and individualized programs.

The history of child care reveals the following pattern: a large population in institutions and orphanages in the early 1900s; the foster home replacing orphanages in the late 1920s; the closing of institutions for the mentally ill in the 1960s; and the introduction of community-based correctional programs with the concurrent reduction in training schools in the 1970s. The closing of institutions is not a new idea. In Massachusetts a study recommended that training schools be closed in 1896 but not until 1972 was the policy carried out. An important question for correctional administrators is whether staff energies should be used to improve and humanize institutions or be diverted to creative alternatives. Group homes and foster homes are two such innovations, not new except when used in place of training school.

Most juveniles sentenced to institutions come from families on public welfare, from broken homes; they function two years behind their peers in school. Institutions have little success with juvenile delinquents (or orphans or the mentally ill). This is not a criticism of staff and administrators who have expressed concern for these youngsters. Rather, the problem is that the facilities are located in the country away from where the delinquents reside. We hide our children in trouble, and so we find resistance to establishing confinement alternatives. And yet we know that most such children do well in shelter homes, group homes, or by using other community services. Let us separate these children from those who require close confinement because they are dangerous. This cannot be done until communities provide the kind of services previously offered in the correctional institution. Impetus for adopting alternatives lies in the realization that youngsters respond more favorably to programs outside the coercive setting.

ORGANIZATION OF INSTITUTIONS

A state agency is responsible for operating juvenile institutions in all states. A majority also administer the aftercare services required for approximately 60 to 70 percent of released juveniles. Ideally, the institutions and aftercare programs should be operated by the same state agency in order to assure continuity of service. The following 12 states do not: Alabama, Louisiana, Mississippi, New Hampshire, New Mexico, North Carolina, North Dakota, Pennsylvania, South Dakota, Utah, Virginia, and Wyoming.[5] Ordinarily, the agency responsible for training schools oversees other state services such as mental health, welfare, and adult corrections. The consolidation of services into super-agencies appears to be increasing.

The youth authority movement of the 1940s, which emphasized the central state agency for delinquency prevention and control, is decreasing. The movement began when a number of states (i.e., California, Minnesota, Wisconsin, and Texas) adopted portions of the Model Youth Correction Authority Act prepared by the American Law Institute.[6] Not all states established youth authorities. The movement has been successful in states that have professional staffs, innovative programs, adequate budgeting, and a climate of cooperation between local juvenile courts and law enforcement. Diversion and a renewed emphasis on the local community has probably ended the youth authority and the closing of institutions will reduce their personnel. Youth authority's new role is to be consultative, to provide state guidelines for the prevention and control programs in the counties.

The youth authority movement offered responsible programming and supervision of the youth in trouble from his arrival at the reception center until his release from aftercare supervision. It was a self-contained system. The state agency administering juvenile facilities can hardly offer a variety of services unless there are special-purpose confinement centers. A very large number of states have less than five institutions and it is not uncommon to find only one facility for juveniles. It would be good to establish some continuity among all the agencies involved in the administration of juvenile justice to offset the isolation which has always characterized juvenile corrections. The Joint Commission on Correctional Manpower and Training identifies three pervasive themes which run through correctional management:

> First, the goals of restraint and reformation have helped to reenforce correctional administrators' perceptions of offenders as morally, psychologically, physically, and educationally inferior human beings. They must be upgraded, and in the meantime they must be controlled. As a result of this perception, correctional administrators focus the resources at their command primarily upon the individual offender.
>
> A second persistent attribute of correctional management has been a particularistic approach to program development and

> change. This approach has been characterized by faddism, a somewhat frivolous subscription to "new" ideas and generally nonrigorous, nonscientific rules of thumb, for determining what to delete from the old system and what to add to it. The predominant conservatism of system managers has militated against deviations from familiar ways and has led to tokenism in the launching of new measures.
>
> A final theme which has its roots in the "prison culture" of the past and still runs through correctional management today is the syndrome of isolationism and withdrawal. This condition has helped to conceal the realities of life in institutions . . . from the public, and has thus acted to perpetuate stereotypes and myths.[7]

This is why the reception center experience is so important to a youngster being committed. Now for a review of the indoctrination process accompanying confinement.

THE RECEPTION CENTER

The juvenile offender is not sentenced to a specific state institution. The juvenile court transfers the minor to the director of the statewide juvenile corrections agency or to whichever agency is responsible for the operation of the training schools. Sometimes all the facilities are filled and the youth remains in the local detention center until space is available. The first stop in the transition from court to institution is the reception diagnostic center.

The reception center is a separate entity in states that have diverse juvenile facilities. The center holds the youngster for a period of four to six weeks, while he is studied and evaluated. Where there is no separate diagnostic center the evaluations are completed at the receiving facility; thereafter, he commences his confinement in another unit at the same institution.

The reception center staff should be able to begin their evaluation of the youngster with background material from the courts. The county of sentencing always transports the youth to the reception center, but the case material prepared by the judge at the dispositional hearing seldom precedes the youth. When it is necessary to write for the materials, there is another week of delay. The reports prepared by the probation officer for the judge usually reflect the decision to commit to an institution. They may observe that the youth did not deserve a milder disposition from the court; thus, the probation officer's report is not likely to include a favorable prognosis for treatment. From the point of view of the child or the court staff, confinement would be unnecessary if an agreeable rehabilitation program could be worked out. For this reason the guidance center staff are likely to commence their interviews with little background material. The reception center should, therefore, obtain all information from original sources.

It is common for the youngster to get more attention and consideration at the reception center than during the remainder of his confinement. The staff members interview and test the youth and determine the correctional strategy or treatment plan which best suits him. The staff includes a large number of social workers, clinical psychologists, and a full-time or consulting psychiatrist. Since the reception center is a place for temporary confinement the staff spends its time in short-term diagnosis rather than long-term treatment.

Its skilled professionals, on a machinelike work schedule, usually prepare two social evaluations per day. Their report attempts a careful analysis of the youngster. The evaluations increase the skills of the worker, but the treatment needs of the youth are not met.

When there is an appropriate program for a youth and a facility to provide it, then the objective of classification has been met. The traditional classification criteria determine placement. In fact, custom is so important that its more easily identified factors—age, custody risk potential, and earlier delinquent history—actually govern assignment. However, the treatment plan should be worked out even if security considerations delay its implementation, and alternate programs available at the chosen facility should be integrated into this plan.

The important contributions of the reception center staff are their diagnostic skills and their prescription for treatment. Their social evaluations are limited because reception center staff cannot visit the various facilities in the system and familiarity with institutional programs can be obtained only by on-site visits and by continuing feedback about program effectiveness. Also the disparity between intention and result in such programs is common knowledge to anyone in the field. For example, individual or group counseling is more effective in a treatment setting than in an institution where it might conflict with custodial goals. One juvenile facility put trusted agency personnel in the counseling groups. Afterward, these informers would give the superintendent the names of all those who had criticized the administration. As a result the superintendent decided that each session should be devoted to a specific topic such as citizenship, strengthening family life, or moral guidance. The emphasis of juvenile corrections on the noncontroversial spoils the effectiveness of its far flung programs!

Although the minor may receive an excellent work-up, the reception center is an isolated operation; it does not represent the probation department, juvenile court, or the institution where the youngster will actually stay. This separation creates problems. The institution that receives the youngster conducts its own classification hearing which determines housing assignment, degree of custody required for public safety, attendance at school, participation in work programs, and whether a vocational program is appropriate. The training school staff should find the reception center report a helpful resource, but each institution is a separate empire within a statewide juvenile corrections system. So the wisdom of the diagnostic staff is overlooked because of a distrust of outsiders determining programs. The reports prepared by reception staff are seldom read.

Therefore, it is advantageous to have the reception center at the same place where the delinquent will be confined. Then the staff, as members of the institution, are familiar with the available programs. Had the institutions used the reception center when it was first introduced, it might be possible to justify the use of training schools for treatment services. Here was their opportunity to show that individualized programs were possible and that mass processing was not the primary activity of juvenile prisons. Juvenile offenders understand that their transfer elsewhere for individualized treatment does not necessarily follow the recommendations made in the interviewing session. Instead, the reception process is a time for noisy rhetoric. The transfer decision is based more on the staff's evaluation of the youth as a risk than on his treatment needs.

The reception center concept never did belong in the post-adjudication phase, to be implemented once the youngster was committed to a training school. Furthermore, the guidance center, with its diagnostic skills, should be located on the county level; its report determines whether the needs of the youngster can be met within or outside the community. If secure custody is required, then it should be available at the county level or, should there be none, at a regional center. It is shortsighted to involve a minor in the state correctional machinery if ancillary county services are not provided. The nearer home he can be kept, the better.

The "non-prison" plan permits a community to use reception center staff in both a diagnostic and treatment situation, and avoids the extended period of incarceration accompanied by an abrupt return to community living. Under this program the young offender meets with a committee and together they develop an individualized progress plan. The programs should reflect the activities in which the minor takes an interest, possibly including an academic program, vocational training, or counseling. The young person's responsibility in selecting programs helps to develop attainable behavioral objectives. When these objectives are achieved early, then the youth can be given more responsibility and he needs less staff supervision.[8] Specific behavioral objectives for an academic program in a community correctional center include the following:

1. The juvenile offender expresses an interest in the academic program of the center. Initially, he participates in a testing program, which emphasizes both interest and aptitude in educational and vocational areas.
2. He may begin with a regular full-day academic program.
3. At a later time the full-time school program at the correctional center may be supplemented with one class at an adult education center near the facility.
4. If the earlier programs are successful and the person continues accepting more responsibility, then he may choose to attend the local high school or community college full time.

The reception center remains apart from the training school. The institution experience is entirely different and is closely examined next. First some general observations about how juvenile corrections institutions operate.

OPERATION OF INSTITUTIONS

The statewide agency is responsible for the operations of juvenile correctional facilities; it establishes specific procedures dealing with the acceptance and processing of youth received from the courts. Its procedural manual emphasizes treatment and rehabilitation although it is likely that the agency is more successful in confining the individual than in changing him. Unfortunately, confinement in itself does not protect us from the juvenile offender after his release. In the institution, effective services rather than excessive leisure time are needed. The demise of the reformatory movement, except for those 15 percent requiring continuous incarceration for reasons of public safety, is the result of excessive concern with processing and reduced commitment to effective service delivery.

The success or failure of a juvenile institution is determined by its administrator. Hopefully, the superintendent will emulate the philosophy of the state-wide agency director. Not that he always does. Ineffective superintendents may be criticized, but they are seldom removed. Lack of concern for the youngster in trouble is no reason for his discharge. No matter how many institutions are found in a state system, each operates as a separate kingdom under the direction of its superintendent.

There are other handicaps: the institution is often located in a rural area; trained staff will not accept positions there because of the isolation from professional colleagues; line staff are recruited locally and their commitment to juvenile matters is slender while their suspicion of the professional staff is strong; and the juveniles confined are usually from urban areas.

It is undeniable that, in the history of juvenile institutions, the emphasis is upon revenge. That is why the discipline-oriented facility is the most common; staff members are promoted for their effective use of control measures. Lateral transfers to different agencies in the juvenile justice system don't happen; reassignment to other units within the same agency are possible. These limitations curtail innovation among career employees. An emphasis on custody need not be accompanied by supportive concern for treatment programs. However, the staff member committed to treatment has to understand the custody function of the training school in order to gain credibility for his work.

Although most training schools do little to resocialize the delinquents so that they may return to the community, in the 1970s efforts are being made to provide an atmosphere and an education that may help rehabilitate these youngsters. We review these efforts next—the cottage system, ways to change staff, and the programs.

When study and evaluation are completed, reception center processing concludes with a recommendation for placement, and the youngster is transported from the center to the receiving institution by departmental bus or automobile, but not necessarily to the place recommended by the staff. Placement need not have been discussed with the youngster. Arrival at the new permanent facility is followed by a period of restrictive observation. The classification process is repeated again.

THE COTTAGE SYSTEM

Through financial support from the community, training schools can seek a more humane, homelike environment. The introduction of the cottage system permitted the renaming of housing units; what is called a cell block or dormitory in an adult institution becomes a cottage. Further facelifting is applied by setting aside rooms for the cottage parents, who supervise wards in eight-hour intervals. These adult caretakers are often in short supply, so a college student supplementing his income has to fill in for them. This staffing pattern is acceptable. The students should be selected from criminal justice majors but experience shows that they often are not; at the same time, students who volunteer to assist institutional staff, or who complete working internships, generally major in disciplines allied to delinquency control.

The smaller institutions, especially for youngsters between the ages of 8 and 13, have been most successful in implementing cottage housing systems. The cottage parents are more likely to be a mature couple whose concern for the youngsters is evident. Each cottage has a manageable population, four to ten children, not the 45 to 75 of the larger facility. Institutions for older juveniles begin to resemble adult facilities. The cottages become structures that consist of several floors and there is a greater emphasis on custody. We are talking about the kind of multipurpose institution which houses two-thirds of all youngsters committed to state juvenile facilities.

Renewed interest in prison architecture has accompanied the emphasis on community correctional centers. More humane design is found in the new plans for secure custody. The National Clearinghouse for Correctional Programming and Architecture at the University of Illinois is pioneering in this area.[9] Some feel that buildings are secondary in the corrections program, and see staff and programs as the key to rehabilitation. They are correct. It would be good to have more programs headed by charismatic administrators whose hand-picked staff could then assume new directions. Allan Breed did this at the Fricot Ranch School for Boys near San Andreas, California, in the late 1940's. Fricot traditionally housed the youngest boys committed to the California Youth Authority, those 8 to 14 years of age.

WAYS TO CHANGE STAFF

The Joint Commission on Correctional Manpower and Training found over 111,000 persons employed in corrections. Only 16 percent of them were recruited from recent graduates in colleges and universities that train personnel for the field. Although juveniles comprise about one-third of the total correctional workload, nearly 50 percent of the corrections workers were 30 years old when they were hired. In addition, 74 percent of the employees are 35 or older; 88 percent are male; 87 percent are white; and 20 percent have been employed in corrections for three years or less (while 47 percent have been working in the field for 11 or more years).[10] The alienation between adults and juveniles cannot be reduced unless these patterns change. A recent Wisconsin study concludes that the juveniles who are indifferent toward adults during confinement are the ones who return often.[11] Some states have upper age limit requirements for employment as a youth counselor, usually 35 or 36; traditionally, the twenty-first birthday is the lower age limit. States might experiment with a lower age to use for recruitment, perhaps the eighteenth birthday.

Milton Luger has pioneered in the use of ex-offenders as staff members in the New York State Division for Youth. He suggests four general qualities as characteristic of the ex-offender who is successful in corrections:

1. Ability to relate to others.
2. Verbal communication skills in understanding instructions and conveying information to others.
3. An interest in helping others.
4. Evidence of a reasonably satisfactory community adjustment upon discharge . . .[12]

These characteristics should be present in all staff members, and Vernon Fox speaks of basic competencies which should be developed:

1. Ability to understand and withstand provocative behavior without becoming punitive.
2. Development of objectivity in accepting relationships with all clients in a nonjudgmental manner, without either punitive or sentimental emotional involvement.
3. Competence to accept an inmate or person on the caseload without personal involvement, with neither punitive nor sentimental views, much the same as a physician views a patient—This does not mean complete detachment.
4. On-the-job counseling techniques.
5. Ability to say "no"—with reasons when necessary, and to say "yes" with equal reason.
6. Sensitivity to pathological behavior as compared with normal random behavior, sufficient to permit intelligent referral to professional staff.
7. Ability to assess strengths of an individual, to determine what the treatment team has to build on in the treatment of an offender.
8. Making referrals to all staff, community resources, and other specialties with some sophistication.
9. Ability to use tact to avoid creating or aggravating problem situations.

10. Ability to use tact to ameliorate developing problem situations.
11. Willingness to augment and support the therapeutic process in the institution and the community programs.
12. Ability to observe and accurately record:
    a. Individual behavior
       —Pathological behavior needing referral to professional staff.
       —Escape, manipulation, or other suspicious behavior in which the safety and security of the institution or community may be concerned.
    b. Group behavior
       —Beginning of disturbance.
    c. Miscellaneous behavior.
       —Incidents that might be recorded that may crescendo into major difficulty or be part of an organized illicit activity.
13. Ability to assess the community-reintegration model, including attitudes toward the returning offender.
14. Constructively interpret administrative decisions, actions, and procedures to inmates, probationers, and parolees.
15. Serving as upward communicator from the inmate body to the administration and from the probation and parole caseload to the judge and field services supervisor with the view toward improving correctional services.
16. Maintaining discrete silence on some critical issues and "classified" information to maintain *(a)* staff morale, *(b)* inmate and caseload morale, and *(c)* good public relations.
17. Capability of exerting external controls on individuals who need containment with physical force or firearms when necessary without using more force than the situation requires.
18. Knowing specific procedures that might be modified or elaborated in the in-service training program of the correctional agency or institution—such as classification procedure, preparole planning, probation and parole revocation hearings, and procedures at a similar level.

19. Knowledge of the civil and constitutional rights of prisoners, whatever their status, and the incorporation of that knowledge into the supervisory process.
20. Knowledge to interpret the system of justice, including laws of arrest, judicial procedure—and the total correctional process of probation, prison, and parole, together with knowledge of revocation hearing procedure and pardon procedure.[13]

Staffing and recruitment in juvenile institutions deserve renewed attention. Diversion has kept many youngsters from incarceration. This means, of course, that training school wards are more serious offenders than in the past. There is greater need for staff to understand the hostility of the young prisoner. Then his rejection of adults can change and he will be able to establish a meaningful relationship with a staff member, whether it be the social worker or the cottage parent. The staff worker must understand his own prejudices and feelings about delinquents so it may be possible for a youngster to relate to him. A few guidelines:

1. The worker should not claim perfection. The youngster knows better because the adult world gives him inconsistent responses. He looks for honesty, guidance, and the limits which prove real interest in his welfare.
2. He should not tell the ward that conformity in the institution will assure acceptance when he is released; there is little relationship between a clear record and post-institutional success. This does not suggest that violence should be approved or condoned. It is just that the success of institutional programming is judged by return to the home community. What happens then depends upon the ability of a youngster to avoid a delinquent peer group, engage in worthwhile activities, and find a place in the labor force so as to support himself without returning to crime.
3. He should not violate the helping relationship through acts of hypocrisy. Some staff members make promises such as reducing custody, immediate placement in programs, and transfers. When such promises cannot be carried out the staff member will sometimes absolve himself of all blame and claim the fault lies with custody or treatment. Again, staff people may say one thing to the juvenile and something quite different when he

is not present. Violations of trust are usually discovered. At training schools the walls have ears!

PROGRAMS

The program is the heart of the training school operation. Grouping large numbers of children into various activities is called mass treatment, and it impairs the effectiveness of individualized programs. The reformatories and schools of industry accented academic and vocational training. Later, individual and group counseling were introduced.

Education

A number of teachers choose to work in corrections because the small classroom allows personalized instruction. Unlike the public school system, the academic program has to be tailored to students who have experienced difficulties in earlier learning situations. Instructors work with other staff members in preparing youngsters for various future goals. Many enter high school or the university upon release from confinement; some get jobs and receive no further schooling; a smaller number participate in special classes offering basic educational skills or remedial work.

The school program is a good example of cooperation with other staff members. Full-time school should be available for those who desire it; however, half-day academic programs are more common. It is important that other work assignments and cottage activities not interfere with time set aside for classroom instruction. The teacher should be involved in the evaluation of the youngster's progress in the total instructional program; such participation will further protect the student from work details and other activities incompatible with the school experience. This is imperative because so few are enrolled in full-time academic programs. It is unusual for more than 40 percent of the youngsters to be involved in the educational portion of the program. The curriculum should emphasize resocialization and provide the student with skills which aid him in reentering the community after he is released: (1) self-discipline, (2) respect for authority, (3) development of useful work habits, and (4) social adjustment.

Training-school wards do not differ markedly from the general population in intellectual ability. They are likely, however, to be functioning several grades behind their peers in the public schools. Although conflict usually accompanied a ward's life style and school experience on the outside, the institution may provide the neutral environment in which he can operate. He then has an educational goal. Diplomas are issued by the local school districts and do not carry the name of the correctional agency. National standards recommend that the academic program be administered within the state agency responsible for juvenile institutions. When this procedure is not followed, the local or county school district provides a program. The school year is more flexible and classes may operate 12 months.

The Newgate Project, which operates in a number of communities, assists youthful offenders who wish to enroll in college or university programs following release; it has been introduced by the National Council on Crime and Delinquency. Enrollment commences two years before release from the institution. At that time a battery of tests—which determine intelligence, grade achievement level, and personality characteristics—are administered. Test findings and counseling sessions help to identify the capacity of the youth to achieve a satisfactory adjustment in a college setting. It is common for Newgate students to reside in a halfway house near the campus while they complete their education and parole or aftercare obligations. A similar program for the younger student has been initiated at the Fred C. Nelles School for Boys in California; its purpose is to reduce the school failure when individuals return home. A team at the institution prepares the program to be followed there; it consists of the cottage staff, one teacher, cottage caseworker, parole or aftercare agent, parents, and the appropriate public school personnel. The team, a liaison among institution, school, and community, emphasizes goals to be met at the institution, a joint evaluation of the youngster's functioning while confined, and an introduction of the boy to his parole program before his release. This endeavor has improved communications among parents, the public school, institutions, and parole.

Vocation

Vocational training programs are emphasized in some training schools for older youth. Staff members are limited by numerous restrictions when they offer training, not the least of which is the nine or 10-month average sentence.[14] Adequate training cannot take place in such a short period. Furthermore, many vocational programs require a certain academic grade level for enrollment. Tests can determine the range of an individual's vocational interests. The major contribution of the staff may lie in the strengthening of work habits rather than in providing specific employment skills.

The youth service bureaus find that employment counseling is frequently requested, and it is more appropriately offered outside the correctional setting. Because training schools do not have the time to provide specific work skills, it is common for institutions to substitute on-the-job training (work on the school grounds) for vocational programs. This is one way they hope to overcome the limitations mentioned earlier; the solution is comfortable for the staff who assume that good work habits are being developed. Each facility requires a number of gardeners, janitors, and kitchen workers—building maintenance, the culinary arts, and nursery or gardening are always important vocational training programs. These programs do assist in the beautification and day-to-day operation of institutions; work habits are observed and rewarded. But there is little reason to believe that these skills are needed in the local community. Such educational and vocational programs must be up-dated and minors given an array of ideas which will help them readjust in the community. Because this goal is best accomplished in full-time programs, one institution could emphasize the academic while another could stress vocational training and work-related experiences. The single-program institution can then assess its real accomplishment. A state with only one or two juvenile facilities can emphasize certain programs in separate housing units.

Counseling

In earlier years, individual casework services, a method for counseling on a one-to-one basis, were employed. Many factors made this system unsatisfactory—the few social workers and psychologists could not devote much time to each youngster; the rapport established between counselor and youth in brief sessions was often undone by later pressures and alliances in the delinquent population and frequently the youngster experienced additional difficulties; institutional staff demeaned the clinical program or retaliated with changes in work assignments or restrictions; individual members of the clinical staff departed and other counselors were assigned the case.

In the early 1950s, it was decided that individual counseling was very limited in confinement settings. Group meetings, involving all youngsters in a certain housing area, were introduced. Those staff members possessing undergraduate and graduate degrees were designated group therapists; those without degrees became group counselors. They all did the same thing: that is, they led groups of offenders in open discussions at specified times.

Since 1955, outside of the juvenile institution, the group approach has been much used, and supported strongly by its followers. The goal of treatment may be personality change or greater competency in dealing with daily problems. Each new approach seems to provide a more easily acquired body of knowledge. A few staff members will train incoming employees and soon an entire institution reflects one viewpoint.

The psychoanalytic approach of Sigmund Freud, because it was the philosophical basis for the social casework approach, fell into disuse as the group treatment method came into prominence. Freudian psychoanalysis emphasized that which brought discomfort to the person, stressed the lonely war between the individual and his inner self, and endeavored to assist the youth in uncovering the information which created the conflict; this could take place only when a close, trusting relationship with a therapist occurred. A current approach, guided group interaction, tries to give participants more options in coping with basic needs. The attitudes of the individual are explored, the impact of his behavior on others is verbalized, and he is asked to use the group to rechannel unacceptable behavior.

At the training schools, the group focuses upon the discomfort the minor causes his associates; peer influence is the key to change in this approach to counseling. Groups are composed of those youngsters residing day-to-day in the same unit. Pioneered by the Highfields Project in New Jersey and the Provo Experiment in Utah,[15] these programs invested considerable decision-making power in the group and the group culture was built around each delinquent helping the other with his problems. The assumptions of this movement have led to its popularity:

1. The psychoanalytic approach focuses upon personality development as the major cause of delinquency. Acceptance of the sick role by an individual is not likely to deter delinquency, which is usually a group activity. The psychoanalytic role permits excuses for delinquency while the guided group interaction approach demands responsible accountability for harmful activity by the individual.
2. Effective counseling requires recognition of group membership by the individual delinquent. The group committed to delinquency must be changed and when this occurs the group is the primary change agent for the individual.
3. Delinquents are comfortable with their way of life. Anxiety must be present if new values are to be introduced. Amenability to change is hastened by participation in groups composed of others who have made such a commitment.

The guided group interaction approach has been implemented by a number of principles found in William Glasser's reality therapy, Eric Berne's transactional analysis, and behavior modification.[16] Reality therapy emphasizes present behavior and minimizes the past. The worker stresses responsibility and community reward for approved behavior while providing emotional support for action toward more positive relationships. Transactional analysis deals with the games people play; maturity is measured by the manner in which we satisfy the search for gratification. The strategy is to identify the reaction that group members are using in relation to the three categories: adult, parent, or child—most approval is offered by the adult label and least by the child. The approach does rank solutions to problems and provides the youngster with a range of actions with which to work in the future.

The behavior modification approach goes further; it gives rewards for good behavior, when the staff has defined what that conduct should be. It looks at what a minor is actually doing, and judges it for its social acceptability. Thereafter, the staff can help the individual increase his capacity for making the right decision. Contract goals are set up which explain in very understandable language the manner in which treatment objectives can be met. Immediate rewards are forthcoming when the individual moves along and achieves the goals of the program. This is helpful because training schools are slow to praise those who have made progress in their programs. A review of case files in an institution always reveals infractions but seldom recognizes special merit.

Individual and group treatment in correctional facilities has been beneficial. It has reduced the isolation between youngsters and staff, and has made real the programs which formerly existed only on paper. Congregate care is more humane because of group treatment. The effectiveness of these programs in the institutional setting is unknown; but a review of the literature on group treatment reveals severe limitations which those adopting current group treatment models have not understood, such as the following:[17] (1) Without anonymity the juvenile has no place to hide once he has told all about himself. (2) It is impossible to evaluate the person involved in various methods of treatment concurrently. (3) There are no statistics which separate individuals who have maintained continuous attendance at group meetings from those who malinger. (4) There is almost no information about what occurs in the sessions and how this is affected by different group leaders or individual juveniles. (5) The most important limitation is the absence of follow-up studies; we need to know more about group participants after their release from confinement. A mode of treatment which is perhaps effective outside the institutional setting may falter inside. This is important because fewer minors are being confined and these wards require more intense, knowledgeable assistance since behavioral change is required if community protection is to be assured.

The individualized program has been called the catalyst for reform. Study, vocational training, and individual or group treatment compete for the youngster's time. Sometimes he gets none of these. In such cases, leisure time and boredom are the program. The custody vs. treatment philosophy can dilute effective programs. A response to these problems is to introduce only one of these treatment programs to an institution. This reduces conflict and allows staff to mobilize existing resources around the program it is equipped to carry out. Transfers between institutions can occur when a youngster is prepared for another treatment resource. Such policies will reduce the historical tendency to house juveniles according to age, previous delinquency history, and the risk of his escaping.

AFTERCARE OR PAROLE

Release from confinement depends on the corrections agency determination that the youngster is ready to reenter his community. An independent parole board makes this decision in adult corrections, but in the juvenile field it is uncommon except where the youth authority concept is used. Parole is defined as release to the community under supervision; parole and aftercare are the same, and each state determines which designation to use. Personnel are assigned to help the youth during his transition from confinement to freedom. Release with supervision has a long history in juvenile corrections. It was used as early as 1876 at Elmira Reformatory in New York.

Most youngsters are released on parole, and find the first few months the most difficult period. The juvenile was docile while in the institution, and supervision implies a continuation of this same relationship under the control of the parole officer. It is important that the youngster receive assistance with reentry when he requests it. A recent Minnesota study found the intensity of the parole supervision experience did not influence parole adjustment for juveniles. These youngsters ranked their difficulties on parole in the following order: family related problems, school difficulties, problems in the area of work, and pressures associated with the use of alcohol and drugs. They preferred to discuss their problems with close relatives and friends rather than the parole officer or staff in local social agencies.[18]

The problem areas mentioned by parolees in the Minnesota study are similar to those noted in referrals to the youth service bureaus. Referral to the youth service bureau is a diversionary type of program; the youngster using such services maintains community contacts and supports. The parolee must reestablish these contacts and the transition is easier if temporary housing in a halfway house can be arranged as part of the aftercare program. This living arrangement, where 10 to 25 individuals may reside, sometimes is used as part of probation and sometimes as a pre- or post-release interim form of housing. It is not a new experiment. In 1896 the Volunteers of America opened a residence in New York for men released from the New York State Prison at Ossining. A few years later, in 1916, a halfway house was opened in the same city for adolescent girls discharged from the Hebrew Orphan Asylum who were unable to adjust in other residential settings. Rachin describes the halfway house as ". . . a kind of decompression chamber through which institutional releases are helped to avoid the social-psychological bends of a too rapid reinvolvement in the 'real world.'"[19] The halfway house movement is promising. More research is needed to determine which juvenile parolees:

1. Will succeed either with or without exposure to halfway house living.
2. Will succeed only with exposure to halfway house living.
3. Will not succeed with or without halfway house living.[20]

The International Halfway House Association provides a resource center for communities interested in developing the versatile programs possible in this type of facility.[21] Community support is necessary for the success of the halfway house.

Aftercare is more than supervision, it is a source of help in the search for community acceptance.

STUDY QUESTIONS

1. When should a training school commitment be recommended?
2. Identify the juvenile institutions in your state. Describe the treatment programs available in each.
3. Do some counties commit greater numbers of youngsters to state institutions? Why?
4. Trace the history of institutional child care in your state.
5. Find out whether the county or the state is responsible for the administration of the following in your area: probation, juvenile correctional facilities, and parole or aftercare.
6. What is the youth authority movement?
7. List and explain the goals of correctional management.
8. What is a reception diagnostic center? Why is it used? Where is it located?
9. What are the objectives of the academic program in an institution? Vocational program? Individual or group treatment?
10. Have new forms of correctional architecture been employed in the construction of recent juvenile facilities in your state? Has new construction been halted in the past few years? Explain reasons for the policy.
11. What recruitment policies are used in staffing the institutions and parole agency in your state? Are student volunteers used in these agencies?
12. Are ex-offenders employed in your state juvenile correctional system?
13. List the major tasks of personnel employed in corrections. Identify the basic competencies required to carry out these tasks.
14. What are some of the pitfalls to be avoided in trying to help a youngster in trouble?

15. Identify the objectives of the Newgate Project.
16. Why have group methods replaced social casework as the choice of treatment in juvenile facilities?
17. What is aftercare or juvenile parole?
18. What is a halfway house?

NOTES

1. *Statistics on Public Institutions for Delinquent Children: 1970,* U.S. Department of Health, Education, and Welfare, Social and Rehabilitation Service, Office of Program Statistics and Data Systems, National Center for Social Statistics (Washington, D.C.: U.S. Government Printing Office, 1971).

2. See American Correctional Association, *Directory of Correctional Institutions and Agencies.* Issued annually. Available from American Correctional Association, Woodridge Station, P.O. Box 10176, Washington, D.C. 20018.

3. "Institutional Construction: A Policy Statement," *Crime and Delinquency,* 18 (October 1972): 331–332.

4. Albert Deutsch, *Our Rejected Children* (Boston: Little, Brown and Co., 1950) and Howard James, *Children in Trouble* (New York: David McKay, 1970).

5. Advisory Commission on Intergovernmental Relations, *State-Local Relations in the Criminal Justice System* (Washington, D.C.: U.S. Government Printing Office, 1971), pp. 282–286.

6. A most articulate and moving discussion of the youth authority movement is the following: John R. Ellingston, *Protecting Our Children from Criminal Careers* (New York: Prentice-Hall, 1948).

7. Elmer K. Nelson, Jr., and Catherine H. Lovell, *Developing Correctional Administrators,* Research Report of Joint Commission on Correctional Manpower and Training (Washington, D.C.: The Joint Commission, 1969), pp. 5–6.

8. Harold B. Bradley, et al., *The Non-Prison: A New Approach to Treating Youthful Offenders* (Sacramento: Institute for the Study of Crime and Delinquency, 1970).

9. Current trends in correctional architecture are discussed in the informational resources available from the National Clearinghouse for Correctional Programming and Architecture, Department of Architecture, University of Illinois, Urbana, Illinois 61801.

10. Rudy Sanfillipo and Jo Wallach, "We Need People to Change People," *Federal Probation,* 34, no. 3 (September 1970): 5–14.

11. *Social Worker Prognosis Study,* Bureau of Research, State Department of Public Welfare, Division of Corrections, Research Bulletin C-11, Madison, Wisconsin, April 1966.

12. Milton Luger, "Selection Issues in Implementing the Use of the Offender as a Correctional Manpower Resource" (Paper delivered at a Workshop on The Offender as a Correctional Manpower Resource: Its Implementation, Asilomar, California, Sept. 8–10, 1966), pp. 6–7.

13. Vernon B. Fox, *Guidelines for Corrections Programs in Community and Junior Colleges* (Washington, D.C.: American Association of Junior Colleges, 1969), pp. 18–19.

14. *Statistics on Public Institutions,* p. 6.

15. See H. Ashley Weeks, *Youthful Offenders at Highfields* (Ann Arbor: University of Michigan Press, 1958); and LaMar T. Empey and Jerome Rabow, "The Provo Experiment in Delinquency Rehabilitation," *American Sociological Review,* 26 (October 1961): 679–696.

16. See William Glasser, "Reality Therapy," *Crime and Delinquency,* 10 (April 1964): 135–144; Eric Berne, *Games People Play* (New York: Grove Press, 1964); and Rosemary C. Sarri and Robert D. Vinter, "Group Treatment Strategies in Juvenile Correctional Programs," *Crime and Delinquency,* 11 (October 1965): 326–340.

17. Karl A. Slaikeu, "Evaluation Studies on Group Treatment of Juvenile and Adult Offenders in Correctional Institutions: A Review of the Literature," *Journal of Research in Crime and Delinquency,* 10 (January 1973): 87–100.

18. C. H. Hudson, *An Experimental Study of the Differential Effects of Parole Supervision for a Group of Adolescent Boys and Girls,* U.S. Department of Justice, Law Enforcement Assistance Administration, National Institute of Law Enforcement and Criminal Justice (Washington, D.C.: U.S. Government Printing Office, 1973), p. 21.

19. Richard L. Rachin, "So You Want To Open a Halfway House," *Federal Probation,* 36, no. 1 (March 1972): 30.

20. *Graduated Release,* U.S. Department of Health, Education, and Welfare, National Institute of Mental Health, Center for Studies

of Crime and Delinquency (Washington, D.C.: U.S. Government Printing Office, 1971), p. 19.

21. International Halfway House Association, 2316 Auburncrest, Cincinnati, Ohio 45219. Also see John M. McCartt and Thomas J. Mangogna, *Guidelines and Standards for Halfway Houses and Community Treatment Centers,* U.S. Department of Justice, Law Enforcement Assistance Administration, Technical Assistance Division (Washington, D.C.: U.S. Government Printing Office, 1973).

PLANNING FOR DELINQUENCY PREVENTION AND CONTROL

THE COMPREHENSIVE STATE PLAN
STATE AND REGIONAL PLANNING AGENCIES
THE CRIMINAL JUSTICE PLANNER
THE PLANNING PROCESS
THE CITIZEN'S ROLE IN PLANNING

Crime was declared "essentially a local problem" by Congress in 1968. State and local governments were encouraged to prepare comprehensive plans calling for the control of crime and delinquency based upon an evaluation of their current problems. A comprehensive state plan permitted a state to receive funds for programs through a designated state planning agency. The local community would assess the problem, the federal government would offer guidelines for action, and crime as well as delinquency might be reduced.

THE COMPREHENSIVE STATE PLAN

Legislation created two new federal agencies in 1968, the Law Enforcement Assistance Administration (LEAA) and the Office of Juvenile Delinquency and Youth Development. The Omnibus Crime Control and Safe Streets Act declares:

> It is the purpose of this title to . . . encourage States and units of general local government to prepare and adopt comprehensive plans based upon their evaluation of State and local problems of law enforcement.[1]

The Juvenile Delinquency Prevention and Control Act adds:

> In order to encourage States and localities to prepare and adopt comprehensive plans covering their respective jurisdictions, based on a thorough evaluation of problems of juvenile delinquency and youths in danger of becoming delinquent in the

State, the Secretary is authorized to make grants to any State or local public agency to assist in preparing or revising such a plan.[2]

The Safe Streets Act created the first comprehensive anti-crime program in the nation's history. Administered by the Law Enforcement Assistance Administration, an agency of the Department of Justice, this act gives the primary responsibility for the control and improvement of the criminal justice system to state and local governments. They receive the bulk of the financial aid given by LEAA.

The heart of the LEAA program is the block grant concept, so named because grants are awarded as a lump sum. States receive block grants to plan and carry out law enforcement and criminal justice improvement programs. With the aid of planning grants, based upon population, each state cooperates with its cities and counties in drafting a plan for statewide, comprehensive criminal justice improvements. The plan must deal with all segments of the system as well as the following priority areas:

1. Public protection, including the development, demonstration, evaluation, implementation, and purchase of methods, devices, facilities, and equipment designed to improve and strengthen law enforcement and reduce crimes in public and private places.
2. The recruiting of law enforcement personnel and the training of personnel in law enforcement.
3. Public education relating to crime prevention and encouraging respect for law and order, including education programs in schools and programs to improve public understanding of and cooperation with law enforcement agencies.
4. Constructing buildings or other physical facilities which would fulfill or implement the purpose of this section, including local correctional facilities, centers for the treatment of narcotic addicts, and temporary courtroom facilities in areas of high crime incidence.
5. The organization, education, and training of special law enforcement units to combat organized crime, including

the establishment and development of State organized crime prevention councils, the recruiting and training of special investigative and prosecuting personnel, and the development of systems for collecting, storing, and disseminating information relating to the control of organized crime.

6. The organization, education, and training of regular law enforcement officers, special law enforcement units, and law enforcement reserve units for the prevention, detection, and control of riots and other violent civil disorders, including the acquisition of riot control equipment.
7. The recruiting, organization, training and education of community service officers to serve with and assist local and State law enforcement agencies in the discharge of their duties through such activities as recruiting, improvement of police-community relations and grievance resolution mechanisms; community patrol activities, encouragement of neighborhood participation in crime prevention and public safety efforts; and other activities designed to improve police capabilities, public safety and the objectives of this section: *Provided,* That in no case shall a grant be made under this subcategory without the approval of the local government or local law enforcement agency.
8. The establishment of a Criminal Justice Coordinating Council for any unit of general local government or any combination of such units within the State, having a population of two hundred and fifty thousand or more, to assure improved planning and coordination of all law enforcement activities.
9. The development and operation of community based delinquent prevention and correctional programs, emphasizing halfway houses and other community based rehabilitation centers for initial preconviction or postconviction referral of offenders; expanded probationary programs, including paraprofessional and volunteer participation; and community service centers for the guidance and supervision of potential repeat youthful offenders.[3]

Once the planning is completed, each state then receives a block action grant, again based on relative population, to put the city and county programs into effect. In each state, the program is carried out by a state planning agency (SPA) which works closely with units of local government in both planning and initiating improvement programs. There are 55 planning agencies serving the 50 states, American Samoa, the District of Columbia, Guam, Puerto Rico, and the Virgin Islands (addresses in Appendix C). Most states have a number of regional planning councils, which assist local units of government in effective use of local resources and are operated independently of the state planning agency. For example, California has 21 separate criminal justice planning regions. Comprehensive state plans must be updated each year by the SPA's. The California plan, probably the nation's largest, contained 5,896 pages; the later 1972 comprehensive plan, when bound and printed, was only 434 pages.[4]

LEAA defines the comprehensive state plan as one which:

> . . . will focus on the problems of crime: how much there is, what causes it, how to prevent it, how to control it, how to treat people who commit crimes, and how to improve and expedite justice. It will examine the physical and human factors that produce crime. It will analyze the needs of police, prosecutors, defense attorneys, courts, the correctional processes and the offenders. Each State plan should offer realistic, specific goals; it should be action-oriented; and it should weigh costs and benefits.[5]

In turn, the regional plans prepared within each of the states represent the united efforts of a number of agencies and organizations. Such a plan includes the proposals of this group which appear most suitable in aiding the region in meeting its planning goals.

The second federal agency created by Congress in 1968 was the Office of Juvenile Delinquency and Youth Development; in 1970, it was renamed the Youth Development and Delinquency Prevention Administration (YD/DPA), and in 1973 it received another designation, Office of Human Development, Office of Youth Development (OYD). It is housed within the U.S. Department of Health, Education, and Welfare. The Juvenile Delinquency Prevention and Control Act of 1968 (Public Law 90-445) created the agency. In addition, this legislation (in Title I, parts B, C, and D) calls for the development of separate comprehensive state plans dealing only with the improvement of delinquency prevention and control programs.

The states did not respond immediately to requests for the delinquency plans. Both LEAA and YD/DPA required submission and approval of a comprehensive state plan as a prerequisite for funds. Unfortunately, the money available from YD/DPA was substantially less than that available from the more powerful LEAA. The YD/DPA appropriation from Congress during fiscal year 1970 totaled $10 million and was increased to $15 million in 1971. At the same time, the LEAA appropriation was $268 million in 1970 and $529 million in 1971.[6] This trend has continued.

In spite of handicaps, the dedicated staff of YD/DPA was able to assess the comprehensive state plans submitted to it during the first two years of operation. The YD/DPA viewed comprehensive juvenile delinquency planning as the development of a state's capability to deal with delinquency and youth problems. Planning was divided into two phases:

1. Phase I—Data Collection and Analysis
    a. Data collection on juvenile delinquency and youth problems
    b. Assessment of existing state and local programs
2. Phase II—Planning of Priorities and Projects
    a. Assigning priorities to service needs
    b. Development of programs.

A written comprehensive plan is essential to success in the field of delinquency prevention and control for the following reasons:

1. The written plan is a result or record of decisions and assignments made;
2. Decisions on goals and objectives are stated;
3. Written plans are more likely to be clear and definite than plans not reduced to writing;

4. Written plans provide an orderly history which is readily available. Future plans are better made when it is possible to go back over what has and has not worked in the past. Referring to past plans insures that more care and thought will be put into current plans and wiser decisions can be made concerning the priorities of service to be rendered;
5. Written plans promote increased probability of success since there is more certainty that plans will in fact be made if they exist in writing;
6. Written plans promote an increase in leadership ability. The skills of those involved in planning will be sharpened and leadership growth in administration and in elementary human relations will be accelerated;
7. Written plans provide a vehicle for communicating what is done, and why, to all parties concerned in the implementation of the plan.[7]

The staff of YD/DPA found that the comprehensive plans for delinquency services submitted by the states fell short of these expectations. Their assessment of these plans revealed:

1. There is little coherent national planning or established priority structure among the major programs dealing with the problems of youth development and delinquency prevention.
2. There is a strong indication that although bits and pieces of the Federal response to the problems of youth and delinquency may be achieving their discrete objectives, the whole, in terms of the overall effectiveness of Federal efforts, may be less than the sum of its parts.
3. There is a lack of effective national leadership dealing with all youth including delinquents. The present array of programs demonstrate the lack of priorities, emphasis and direction in the Federal Government's efforts to combat delinquency.
4. Although there is a lack of resources devoted to delinquency prevention, in many cases grantees have not made maximum use of existing resources.
5. Grantees have not sufficiently coordinated either the development or implementation of programs with State

Planning Agencies. One factor is that there may have been many State Planning Agencies which were not ready for such coordination. Because data were frequently unavailable on the extent and nature of delinquency and on gaps in existing services, action projects were not linked with the development of the State comprehensive plan and/or were not directed to the most pressing state-wide delinquency problems.

6. State planning has been spasmodic and ineffective. This is due in large part to the fact that a sufficient theoretical knowledge base was lacking and only an extremely limited amount of technical assistance was forthcoming. For the same reasons, many of the projects submitted were of poor or limited quality.
7. There has been a noticeable lack of joint funding or use of other outside resources by grantees.
8. No model systems for the prevention of delinquency or the rehabilitation of delinquent youth have been developed or implemented. Nor has there been feedback of knowledge, gained from funded research, for use in the development of such systems.
9. Severe budget constraints negate the effective implementation of Title I (grants for planning, preventive and rehabilitative services) of the Juvenile Delinquency and Control Act of 1968.[8]

These findings led the YD/DPA to make a major change in program emphasis. The new focus is upon prevention rather than control: community services to those in danger of becoming delinquent, personnel training for staff engaged in providing such programs, and technical assistance when necessary. These changes are reflected in the amendments to the original act, now known as the Juvenile Delinquency Prevention Act of 1972 (Public Law 92-381).

It is not surprising that comprehensive state planning experienced a slow beginning. Few states possessed criminal justice planning agencies prior to 1968. Only a small number of personnel in the system had been trained. Such courses were usually found in departments of political science, public administration, or social work on university campuses. The initial comprehensive plans submitted to YD/DPA ranged from a few sheets to over

400 pages. Some of the plans were little more than a series of agency annual reports which had been bound, while others served as useful supplementary reading in this field.

With the creation of LEAA and YD/DPA a new specialization has emerged in this field. This career cateogry requires knowledge of comprehensive state planning and familiarity with such agencies on the state and regional level.

STATE AND REGIONAL PLANNING AGENCIES

Now, at last, the problem of crime and delinquency was before the public. Unfortunately, the practical skills required to solve the problems of the criminal justice system did not appear along with the plans.

Personnel throughout the criminal justice system were long accustomed to viewing their jobs as stationary niches—in which they stayed pretty much all their working lives. But suddenly, in 1968, everything changed. People in the field were asked to view the administration of justice as a system involving police, courts and corrections. Personnel were expected to assume a more comprehensive and less parochial position. Only one group had understood the total operation of the criminal justice system. The offenders. But they had never been consulted.

Who was recruited for the state planning agencies? A staff drawn from law enforcement, the courts, and corrections. It was a good mix; representatives of different parts of the system were working together for the first time. Or, more accurately, they shared offices until there was the common cause of reducing crime and delinquency. Of course, some state planning agencies diluted this challenge by recruiting from only one segment of the justice system (i.e., law enforcement or corrections). Fortunately, colleges and universities now train personnel for the criminal justice field, and give people a much broader conception of the area they may decide to specialize in. This background is prerequisite to later work in criminal justice planning; total isolation in any one segment of criminal justice is limiting and hardly produces the vision needed for state and regional planning positions.

The newness of planning creates its own difficulties. Those who were employed in 1968 acquired much of their knowledge on the job. Now it is usual to require either academic degrees, experience, or both. Because few applicants are so well prepared, students who wish such jobs should plan to get both. It would also be useful to become familiar with the comprehensive state plans. Annual reports are published by the Law Enforcement Assistance Administration and Office of Youth Development. The student can review the press releases and research of his state planning agency as well as his county or regional criminal justice planning board. These resources serve as an informational support system for planning and program development.

State planning agencies, not always easy to locate, can be found in Appendix C, which includes names and addresses. Both the comprehensive state plan submitted to LEAA and the delinquency services state plan required for OYD funds are handled through the listed state planning agency. However, six jurisdictions have separate delinquency planning agencies: Alabama, Colorado, Florida, New Jersey, Oklahoma, and the District of Columbia.

Each community has a county or regional criminal justice planning board or coordinating council. The name of the local board may be obtained from the state planning agency. It is necessary to become familiar with the comprehensive county plan in order to compare it with its counterpart at the state level.

The activities and responsibilities of the state planning agency include:

1. Preparing and updating long-range comprehensive plans for improving their criminal justice system.
2. Coordinating planning efforts among the various units of state and local government.
3. Administering and monitoring subgrants for program planning and implementation.
4. Evaluating the planning and effectiveness of funded projects and programs.

5. Providing technical assistance to state and local government agencies in planning and carrying out programs to improve the criminal justice system.[9]

Approximately 15 percent of the block action grant funds are set aside for discretionary use. They provide "the means to advance national priorities, draw attention to programs not emphasized in state plans, and provide special impetus for reform and experimentation."[10] Examples of discretionary use: a program designed to establish an effective range of police services in multistory or high-rise apartment complexes; the development of community-based correctional programs to serve as alternatives to the institutionalization of offenders; and well-planned management studies of major criminal courts designed to improve operating efficiency.

Juvenile justice can get much help from the state planning agency; as an important resource, the agency helps us to understand and take into consideration regional and state priorities. Access to the standards of these two federal agencies, which exist to fight crime, can only clarify the problems. The federal guidelines are supposed to insure reasonably uniform requirements in the state planning operation. Wittman has said, "This approach permits comparisons of the relative standards of services within a state as between states themselves."[11]

THE CRIMINAL JUSTICE PLANNER

The expertise of the planner determines whether a state solves or merely controls its crime and delinquency problems. Crime and delinquency need not be handled on a crisis-first basis; where it is, the question may not be one of priority so much as a lack of criminal justice planning capability.

The planner must provide the rationale to develop and implement the comprehensive state plan. This very difficult task includes the art of devising strategies which effectively utilize the full range of agencies and involve the community. The planner should also locate mechanisms for change and assess their long-term contribution to community safety. He must have the sensitivity to hear citizen complaints or agency criticism and explore ways to reduce them. His most important weapons are expertise, rational thought, and the ability to make money achieve results.

A narrow, dogmatic approach to planning can be avoided by considering the following factors mentioned by Hazel Kerper, Charles Friel, and Donald Weisenhorn:

1. Much study and research has already been done.
2. Nonprofessional personnel generally staff the planning agencies.
3. Planning participants should do their homework.
4. Control of crime and delinquency involves behavior change.
5. Programs come before buildings.
6. Basic knowledge and correctional skills already exist.
7. Communications systems should communicate.
8. No program should be recommended or given high priority without careful consideration of the availability of trained manpower to carry it out.
9. The worker "on the firing line" can contribute to knowledgeable planning.
10. Scapegoating should be avoided.[12]

This advice is helpful to the planner in carrying out his functions. The U.S. Department of Health, Education, and Welfare together with the U.S. Department of Justice have said the function of the planner is to:

1. Gather background material on the subject of delinquency prevention, control, and treatment from a variety of sources including other local, State, national and international governmental and private agencies and organizations;
2. Analyze such material in relation to the community for which he has planning responsibility;
3. Evaluate existing programs in the community;
4. Identify needs of the community which are not being met by existing programs;
5. Develop programs to meet the needs of the community;

6. Serve as a channel of communication to those interested in or affected by the communities' programs;
7. Involve the affected organizations or individuals in the development of a comprehensive plan;
8. Provide leadership in the development of a comprehensive plan for delinquency prevention and rehabilitation.[13]

The job descriptions for criminal justice planner positions vary from state to state. The title may not include the word planning; for example, in one state the euphemism is criminal justice specialist. The position is described in the following manner:

> A Criminal Justice Specialist advises and assists State and regional task forces, local governments and other organizations involved in planning and implementing programs for crime prevention and control; motivates and assists local governments and agencies in the development of innovative plans, studies and programs applicable to the area; collects information and data for the improvement of, and use by, organizations involved in the criminal justice system; coordinates local studies and programs with those under consideration or already implemented elsewhere; makes analyses of, and recommendations on, proposals for grants of financial assistance according to established requirements, State and local needs, and the potential impact of the proposed program; monitors approved projects to assure conformity with contract and other requirements; gives advice and assistance to contracting entities during the course of projects; acts as the staff representative of the agency at meetings of local government agencies and other organizations; may serve as the staff expert on other State and Federal programs which are concerned with crime and crime related problems, and act as liaison between the agency and the agencies which administer related programs; actively participates in educational and informational programs related to criminal justice; and does other work as required.[14]

In order to become a criminal justice specialist the following requirements must be met: (1) the baccalaureate degree, although experience may be substituted for a maximum of two years of the required education on a year-to-year basis; and (2) experience of one year or more in a first line supervisory position performing staff work in a police or correctional occupation; this work should involve responsibility in manpower utilization, planning, program development, or research. These prerequisites apply in states where such work classifications are under civil service. Many states do not use civil service; appointments are made by the governor. When this happens, even minimum standards may not be observed.

Hopefully, such formidable job descriptions will, in the future, include more specific experience and educational qualifications. If not, planning will attract the person who is tired of practicing his profession and wants a respite from its pressures. This motivation is not appropriate because the planner must seek innovative, challenging change in a system which has failed in the past.

THE PLANNING PROCESS

The planning process is the most promising strategy against delinquency; its primary purpose is to provide direction for goal-oriented action. "Planning is the design of a desired future and the selection of ways of bringing it about."[15] Planning is action. We need information that focuses upon the existing situation, the predictable future, and the desirable situation. A comprehensive attack on delinquency requires maximum use of community resources and agency participation. Until this attack is viewed systematically in a state plan, it will not be possible to determine where comprehensive modification should occur.

A most useful guide to the planning process is found in a recent publication of the U.S. Department of Justice, Law Enforcement Assistançe Administration entitled *Planning and Designing for Juvenile Justice*. This lengthy volume is summarized below:

THE COMPONENTS OF PLANNING

1. *ENDS.* These are classifiable as objectives or goals.
   a. *Objectives.* Ends which we do not expect to attain during the planning period but progress toward

which we nevertheless believe to be possible within it.

b. *Goals.* Ends which we intend to attain during the period planned for. . . . The goal over any particular planning period would be to reduce juvenile offenses (especially in terms of recidivism) to a specified level by allocating a specified amount [of resources] in specific ways.

c. *Principles.* A planner has to take account not only of the objectives of the juvenile justice system but also of the larger society of which it is a part. Every society pursues certain ideals and objectives which put limits on the means which can be employed in their pursuit. These means are normally expressed as *principles:* rules of conduct intended to assure compliance with general values. "Humanness and justice for all" are such principles. The ways in which such principles are applied in juvenile justice depends upon the values of the local community. More immediately, they depend upon the values of those in charge of its various phases. The ways of application should be *specified* to assure consistency.

d. *Ideals.* An end which is unattainable in any time period but progress toward it is never cut off. . . . The ideal of juvenile justice may be broadly stated as follows: to minimize offenses and the resources expended to maintain this condition. Juvenile justice may approach this ideal directly by continuously improving its own methods and indirectly by continuously educating public opinion to become more aware of those aspects of society which promote delinquency.

e. *Measures of performance.* Goals and objectives should be defined in such a way as to provide appropriate measures of progress toward them.

2. *MEANS.* Planning involves selecting means from among perceived alternatives and, more importantly, discovering or developing alternatives not previously perceived or conceived.

   a. *Courses of action.* The selection of means by which to obtain the goals sought. Means are generally divisible into two major classes, those concerned with changing: 1. the resources available, 2. the way existing resources are used.

b. *Practices.* [These are] repeated courses of action.

c. *Programs.* [These are] sequences of courses of action.

d. *Policies.* [These are the] rules for selecting courses of action.

3. *RESOURCES.* A planner has to determine . . . how much of each [resource] he will require for the programs and policies he may wish to select. What he finds is already, or can later be, made available to him, in each of these resource categories, and will determine what he must in the end accept as feasible.

   a. *Personnel.* [The] number and kinds of skills required.

   b. *Facilities and equipment.*

   c. *Materials and services.*

   d. *Money.*

4. *IMPLEMENTATION.* Organizational planning should be directed toward identifying the task required to accomplish organizational objectives, grouping them into jobs and assigning them to individuals and groups. Responsible personnel should be provided with relevant information, appropriate measures of performance and motivation to act in the organization's interests. A five-phase procedure can be used to accomplish these objectives.

   a. *Decision flow analysis.* This identifies each type of decision and action required to run an organization. A flow diagram of decisions and actions shows their precedence relations.

   b. *Model construction.* The conceptions of the system that are used in making each type of decision, or at least the important ones, are explicitly formulated in models. (In some cases, these models can be formulated so that they can be manipulated to yield best decisions, using the techniques of Operations Research.)

   c. *Informational requirements.* The variables in his models which the decision maker cannot control are those about which he needs information.

Where models are not available, judgment of what information is relevant must be used.

d. *Decisions and jobs.* Decisions should be grouped into jobs that minimize informational requirements. Each decision should be assigned to an individual or group. If a group, the decision making procedure should be specified. In addition, responsibility for implementation, evaluation and recommendation for change of each decision should be assigned.

e. *Measures and motivation.* Measures of performance should be developed for each decision maker or group compatible with overall organizational units. Existing incentives should be evaluated for consistency with overall objectives. New ones should be developed where possible to encourage behavior efficient for these objectives.

5. *CONTROL.* [This] is the evaluation of decisions that have been carried out. It includes examining the consequences of deciding to do nothing. Control makes possible the correction of error and the modification of plans. . . . All decisions . . . should be subjected to control.

   a. *Prediction.* Predicting the outcome of decisions in the form of performance measures.
   b. *Collection.* Collecting information on actual performance.
   c. *Comparison.* Comparing actual with predicted performance.
   d. *Diagnosis.* Diagnosing discrepancies.
   e. *Correction.* Removing the causes of discrepancies and correcting for their consequences.[16]

Further familiarity with the components of planning can be acquired by reviewing juvenile and criminal justice planning materials prepared by the states. For up-to-date information regarding availability of these materials, consult any issue of the *Document Retrieval Index*, especially listings under the subject heading Planning and Evaluation.[17] Figure 9-1 illustrates the planning task, incorporating many of the planning components.

FIGURE 9-1

The Planner's Task

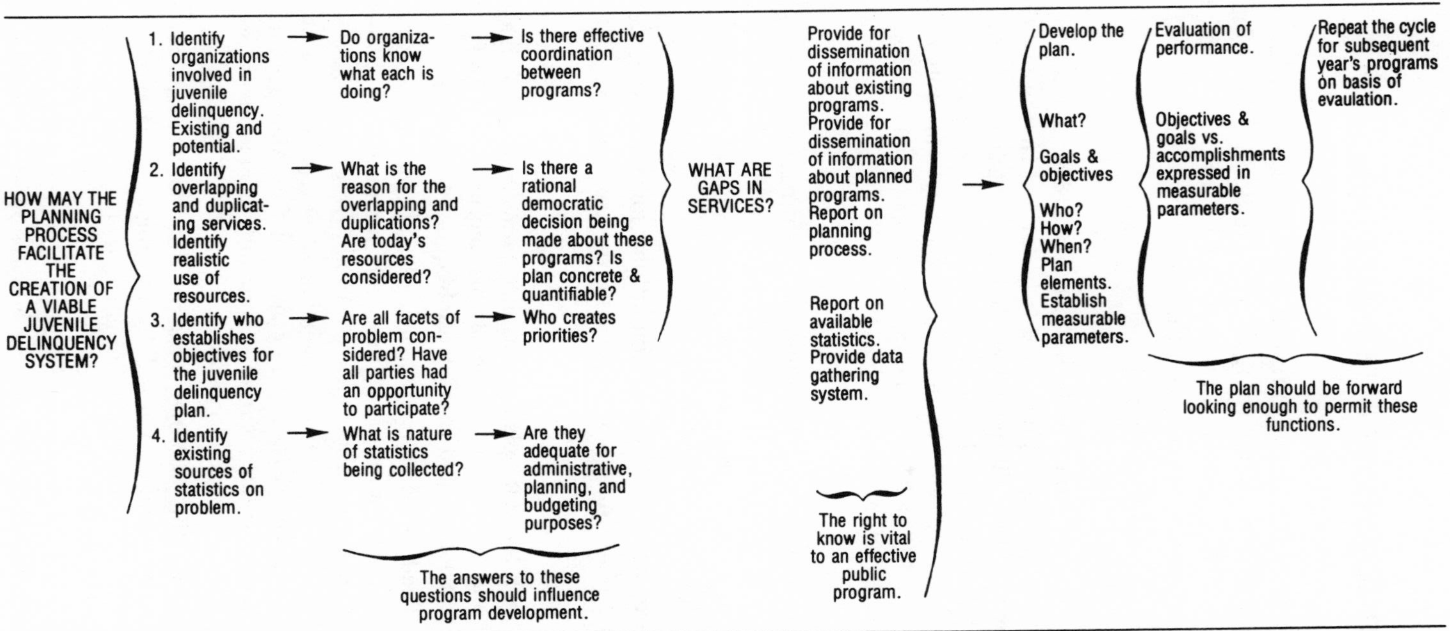

HOW MAY THE PLANNING PROCESS FACILITATE THE CREATION OF A VIABLE JUVENILE DELINQUENCY SYSTEM?

1. Identify organizations involved in juvenile delinquency. Existing and potential. → Do organizations know what each is doing? → Is there effective coordination between programs?
2. Identify overlapping and duplicating services. Identify realistic use of resources. → What is the reason for the overlapping and duplications? Are today's resources considered? → Is there a rational democratic decision being made about these programs? Is plan concrete & quantifiable?
3. Identify who establishes objectives for the juvenile delinquency plan. → Are all facets of problem considered? Have all parties had an opportunity to participate? → Who creates priorities?
4. Identify existing sources of statistics on problem. → What is nature of statistics being collected? → Are they adequate for administrative, planning, and budgeting purposes?

The answers to these questions should influence program development.

WHAT ARE GAPS IN SERVICES?

Provide for dissemination of information about existing programs. Provide for dissemination of information about planned programs. Report on planning process.

Report on available statistics. Provide data gathering system.

The right to know is vital to an effective public program.

→

Develop the plan.

What?

Goals & objectives

Who? How? When? Plan elements. Establish measurable parameters.

Evaluation of performance.

Objectives & goals vs. accomplishments expressed in measurable parameters.

Repeat the cycle for subsequent year's programs on basis of evaulation.

The plan should be forward looking enough to permit these functions.

SOURCE: *Juvenile Delinquency Planning*, a joint publication of the U.S. Department of Health, Education, and Welfare, Social and Rehabilitation Service, Youth Development and Delinquency Prevention Administration and the U.S. Department of Justice, Law Enforcement Assistance Administration (Washington, D.C.: U.S. Government Printing Office, 1971), p. 14.

THE CITIZEN'S ROLE IN PLANNING

Citizens demonstrate an interest in planning if they want to live in a community doing things for its children. Planning is the catalyst which transforms concern for children into services for them. Howard James has said that his search for the ideal county is based upon four premises:

> (1) The local community has a responsibility to children in trouble; (2) crime prevention is better and far cheaper than crime fighting; (3) the answer lies in strengthening both the child and the family, not in hurting children or tearing the family apart; and (4) the efforts of a single institution (the school, the police, or the court, for example) are not sufficent to resolve the problem.[18]

Armed with an awareness of planning one is prepared to support programs which move the community closer to the ideal. Where there is apathy among representatives in local government it should be called to account.

Here are some recommendations for increasing familiarity with state planning while improving the community:

1. Ask the state planning agency to make available the research submitted to it. Much of this information is useful although catalogued and circulated infrequently.
2. Read newsletters from federal and state agencies. The Law Enforcement Assistance Administration publishes *LEAA Newsletter*. The Office of Youth Development issues *Youth Reporter*. Each state planning agency publishes a bulletin on a regular basis. The International City Management Association circulates *Target*, a bimonthly bulletin of "successful" projects funded by LEAA.
3. Determine whether local priorities for delinquency services have been recognized by the regional planning agency. If not, transmit this information to the state planning agency through local legislators or the office of the governor. Priorities of the regional planning agency should reflect those of LEAA. If not, determine how the federal priorities might be

reexamined to meet the needs of each locality. If this fails, contact congressional representatives.

4. Develop an interest in one or more promising programs in delinquency prevention or control. Review grant requests submitted to state and federal agencies in these specific areas. Examine successful programs and become familiar with those recognized as good projects because the results are carefully evaluated.
5. Do not prejudge the state planning agency. There are good reasons for rejecting the many individuals who apply for grants. Some are rejected when the proposals fail to meet existing needs; usually, these people have not reviewed ongoing programs. There is little reason to fund action projects which have failed elsewhere. Systematic planning should precede a request for grant funds. There must be a funding source for every idea. Too many individuals respond to available money sources without having anything original to offer.

Specific planning efforts in delinquency prevention, control, and treatment have failed in the past because

> First, they have generally ignored the fact that community conditions and organizational arrangements significantly contribute to and differentiate who is to be or not to be a delinquent. Second, they have been built on the assumption that the label "delinquency" denotes a population to be dealt with as though "all their members were relatively similar." Third, and most important, communities have been too willing to accept the individual agency and institution as the planning unit. Fourth, communities have reacted spasmodically and irrationally to delinquency, mainly in punitive terms, instead of in rehabilitative and preventive terms.[19]

The comprehensive state plan has introduced a new way to determine appropriate community responses to juvenile delinquency. The involvement of new people in the search for solutions has exciting potential. The preceding chapters have dealt with the activities of the police, juvenile court, and corrections (i.e., probation, institutions, and parole). Some of our programs are being tried out in the local community; others have been rejected; some localities may ignore their crime. Even so, all communities express concern about youth crime. Whoever would be effective in this field ought to take pains with the planning aspect.

STUDY QUESTIONS

1. Identify the federal legislation which was instrumental in introducing comprehensive state planning to this field.
2. What is the name of your state criminal justice planning agency? Your regional planning board?
3. What is a block action grant? A discretionary fund grant?
4. List the limitations of the comprehensive state delinquency plans submitted to YD/DPA.
5. Does your state have a separate delinquency services planning agency? If so, why?
6. Review the activities and responsibilities of a state planning agency.
7. What are the functions of a criminal justice planner?
8. Identify and explain the five major components of planning.
9. What is the citizen's role in planning for delinquency prevention, control, and treatment services?
10. Review a current copy of the newsletter published by your state planning agency.

NOTES

1. *Omnibus Crime Control and Safe Streets Act of 1968* (Public Law 90-351), Title I, p. 1.

2. *Juvenile Delinquency Prevention and Control Act of 1968* (Public Law 90-445), Title I, p. 1.

3. *Omnibus Crime Control and Safe Streets Act of 1968* (Public Law 90-351), Title I, Part C, pp. 2–3; and *Omnibus Crime Control Act of 1970* (Public Law 91-644), Title I, Part C, p. 2. References to "law enforcement" in the nine priorities are expanded to include "law enforcement and criminal justice" in a later amendement to this legislation, the Crime Control Act of 1973 (Public Law 92-83).

4. *1972 California Comprehensive Plan for Criminal Justice* (Sacramento: California Council on Criminal Justice, 1972).

5. *A United Strategy for Crime Control,* U.S. Department of Justice, Law Enforcment Assistance Administration (Washington, D.C.: U.S. Government Printing Office, 1968), p. 9.

6. *Attorney General's First Annual Report: Federal Law Enforcement and Criminal Justice Assistance Activities* (Washington, D.C.: U.S. Government Printing Office, 1972), pp. 42 and 97.

7. *Juvenile Delinquency Planning,* a joint publication of the U.S. Department of Health, Education, and Welfare, Social and Rehabilitation Service, Youth Development and Delinquency Prevention Administration and the U.S. Department of Justice, Law Enforcement Assistance Administration (Washington, D.C.: U.S. Government Printing Office, 1971), pp. 5–6.

8. *Annual Report of Federal Activities in Juvenile Delinquency, Youth Development, and Related Fields,* U.S. Department of Health, Education, and Welfare, Social and Rehabilitation Service, Youth Development and Delinquency Prevention Administration (Washington, D.C.: U.S. Government Printing Office, 1971), p. 9.

9. *Third Annual Report of the Law Enforcement Assistance Administration, Fiscal Year 1971,* U.S. Department of Justice, Law Enforcement Assistance Administration (Washington, D.C.: U.S. Government Printing Office, 1972), p. 42.

10. Ibid., p. 44.

11. Gerald P. Wittman, "Comprehensive State Planning for Delinquency Services" (Paper delivered at the Midsummer Planning and Evaluation Conference on Statewide Juvenile Delinquency Prevention and Control Programs, Gulf Shores, Alabama, July 30, 1970), pp. 12–13.

12. Hazel B. Kerper, Charles M. Friel, and Donald J. Weisenhorn, "Planning Under the Omnibus Crime Control and Safe Streets Act," *Federal Probation*, 33 (September 1969): 30–31.

13. *Juvenile Delinquency Planning*, p. 3.

14. *California State Personnel Board Examination Announcement*, Number 5933-5934, December 9, 1972.

15. *Planning and Designing for Juvenile Justice*, U.S. Department of Justice, Law Enforcement Assistance Administration (Washington, D.C.: U.S. Government Printing Office, 1973), p. 6. See also Appendix D, General Bibliography, Planning.

16. Ibid., pp. 25–45.

17. See *Document Retrieval Index*, U.S. Department of Justice, Law Enforcement Assistance Administration, National Criminal Justice Reference Service.

18. Howard James, *Children in Trouble* (New York: David McKay Co., 1970), p. 298. Copyright © 1970 by the Christian Science Publishing Society. Reprinted by permission of the publishers.

19. Irving A. Spergel, *Community Problem Solving: The Delinquency Example* (Chicago: University of Chicago Press, 1969), p. 234.

SCHOOL AND EMPLOYMENT

10

THE SCHOOL AND ITS EXPECTATIONS
VIOLENCE AND THE SCHOOL
THE DELINQUENT PUPIL
YOUTH AND THE LABOR FORCE
CAREER EDUCATION
UNEMPLOYMENT

The community concerned with delinquency will explore the role of the school and its contribution to reducing youth unemployment. As Lloyd Ohlin has said, "A person comes to reflect the qualities of help, opportunity, and hope which are built into the institutions surrounding him."[1]

In the compulsory American educational system, motivation is not uniformly strong; children are both negative and positive about their school experience. Polk and Schafer found that school plays an important role in defining success:

> First, we live in a society that places a heavy emphasis on success. . . . Second, our theory assumes that schools, fundamentally, are about success. . . . The school has become the gatekeeper of success. . . . Third, we assume that schools will, as a consequence, develop mechanisms for processing students, differentially with regard to their access to the avenues leading to success. . . . Fourth, the impact of technological changes may be functioning to change the nature of the connective links between class origins, school status, and class destination. . . . Fifth, it is assumed that placement into educational categories is an important determinant of the stake an individual student has in conformity. . . . Sixth, it is assumed that the implication of deviance for success is of such importance that the school will develop organizational procedures for misbehavior comparable to those developed around ability, except that these operate in reverse. . . . Seventh, we assume that as the school makes clear through its mechanisms that the youngster is not wanted, a group response of pessimism and hostility results.[2]

The fact that students are labeled *bright* or *dull* indicates how embedded our success ideology is. And even if they are more correctly called *the committed* and *the uncommitted,* the same negative psychology is put to work. When the discomfort and ego denigration of academic failure reaches a certain point, the most attractive option appears to be "dropping out" of a difficult situation.

Compulsory attendance, far from dealing with this problem, only makes matters worse. The juvenile who does not meet the school's standards of success will never be happy there. He is kept against his will and becomes sullen. Or if he causes too much trouble, he is removed along with his delinquent counterparts. He is not likely to find a job as he wanders the streets. These same dropouts often come to the youth service bureaus on their own for vocational counseling, remedial education, or tutoring.

Schools rank high among the agencies that refer students to the bureaus for help. Many activities can be incorporated into an existing youth service bureau; those dealing with the school and work area include the following:

1. *"Self-study" groups* in the schools, whereby students and faculty come together to analyze and then deal with problems that are of concern to students, such as drug use, racial conflict, police-youth relations.
2. *Special work projects* which would give young persons an opportunity to demonstrate their potential to contribute valued services to the community. Examples would be:
   a. *youth-tutor-youth programs,* where young persons of all ability levels would have a chance to help younger children learn,
   b. *drug education programs,* where adolescents take responsibility for educating both students and adults (parents, teachers) about the youthful drug use scene, or
   c. *crisis centers,* where young persons are made available to deal with a range of crises faced by youth, including rumor control, drug problems, and other emergencies faced by youth.
3. *Youth oriented "new careers" programs,* devoted to expanding the potential of the new careers concepts so that they are applied to youth, thus gaining access for youth to both jobs and alternative forms of educational experiences.

4. *Youth involvement programs,* whereby the Youth Services Bureau negotiates with a range of institutions and agencies (schools, school boards, county commissions, city councils, private agencies) to provide for participation of young people in decisions of these agencies, especially in areas of public policy.
5. *Community involvement programs,* where the Bureau negotiates mechanisms at the neighborhood level for participation of adults in correctional and other agency functioning.[3]

The National Commission for the Reform of Secondary Education has concluded that compulsory attendance is an unworkable idea. Most states require school attendance until the age of 16, 17, or 18. Many of them, including California, now require youngsters to attend school until they are 18 years old although students may leave regular high schools after they are 16; however, these pupils must attend continuation schools on a part-time basis. It is obviously difficult to enforce attendance laws on a 16-year-old. The national commission recommends lowering the compulsory attendance age to 14. It further proposes that those youngsters who do not wish to continue in traditional high schools be given alternatives like occupational education, on-the-job training, or entry into the labor force. Many school administrators oppose this recommendation. Those who disagree accept age 16 as the cutoff point for compulsory attendance because of the enforcement problem. The commission urges school administrators to face the reality that daily attendance at inner city schools may lack 50 percent of enrollment. Other recommendations include: (1) improving curriculum materials; (2) emphasizing student rights; (3) banning the use of corporal punishment; (4) eliminating racism and sexism in schools; (5) reducing the size of most high schools; and (6) legalizing smoking.[4]

THE SCHOOL AND ITS EXPECTATIONS

For many students school is a jail. A place where they are sentenced to spend a large part of their lives. The classroom in the urban ghetto is tragic—an inspection shows broken windows, writing on the walls, and trash in the hallways. There is no pride. Total teacher, parent, and student involvement are needed to restructure the learning environment.

The frustration of poverty is not easily penetrated by teachers, including those who claim to work effectively with the disadvantaged. It should be understood that poor families feel trapped and helpless in the endless cycle of daily stresses and deprivations; that they are loathe to call on the police, housing authority, school, public welfare, or the juvenile court for help. Conversely, they don't always know when to reject interference. They may feel self-conscious about their speech or clothing, and uncertain; they may have nothing to say or be full of irrelevant facts about the school problems of their children. The youngster in trouble with the school should be studied in several ways. It is important to determine how the pupil is perceived by the teacher, the student's self perception, and the parental overview of the child. If the student is seen as aggressive he is much more inclined to react aggressively. It is helpful to know and understand the dominant values of people who live in the school area. Do they regard education as a vital necessity or do they resent and distrust educators?

Academic success, measured by grades received in school, has been found to be an important variable in determining whether a student remains in school. Delos Kelly and William Pink explored the problem of school dropout, academic failure, and participation in school social activities. High grades were found to be related to school attendance regardless of social class (i.e., working class or middle-class) or level of participation in extracurricular activities. Failing grades were correlated with school dropouts.[5]

There is a tendency to publicize the advantages of staying in school which ignores the success pattern of the system. In a recent study of tenth grade boys who left school, Jerald G. Bachman noted that failing students find less hostile environments beyond the school. When the dropouts returned to school (1) they were four times as likely to have academic failure while in school; (2) their delinquency rate was higher than their more academically successful peers; and (3) their self-esteem scores were lower on tests measuring their personal, family, and social situations. Tested once more after leaving school, these academically unsuccessful dropouts then enjoyed an increase in self-esteem.[6]

The pupil is also likely to do badly in school when the teacher anticipates poor work. It is a case of the self-fulfilling prophecy; students do what they are expected to do. This view is reinforced by an experiment carried out recently. The teachers in an urban school were told that children in their classes would show remarkable intellectual gains during the forthcoming year. The encouragement was based upon psychological tests given to the youngsters. What the teachers did not know was that they were selected at random. Nevertheless, during the academic year these students showed significant achievement over their classmates. The teachers expected them to learn, so the children did. Of course, the instructors should not receive all the criticism. Many families downgrade formal schooling. Conditions in the home do not provide an environment for learning—i.e., there is no study area set aside for the youngster, rooms are too noisy, the diet is improper and interferes with the well-being necessary to study, and the emotional crises of others in the child's environment keep him in a state of confusion.

The aspirations of low-income minority youth are found to be similar to those held by middle-class students. Michael Lalli and Leonard Savitz explored the educational aspirations of a number of black youngsters (N=693) aged 13 enrolled in the Philadelphia school system as of October 1970. Interviews with 400 of them and their families revealed the following: (1) the desire to at least complete high school was expressed by 97 percent; (2) those with delinquent histories were less likely to express an interest in a college education and for these students there were signs of disengagement from formal education at an early age; and (3) a delinquent career tends to increase the possibility that a student will eventually drop out of school. Almost all the boys in the sample supported a number of middle-class values, regardless of delinquency records. The values are those which underlie the success goals of the school system: (1) getting a steady job; (2) having a pleasant and comfortable home; (3) possessing good clothes; and (4) residing in a good neighborhood.[7]

The goal of public education is to equip youngsters for adult responsibilities, but the critical skills, such as reading and writing, are not being transmitted to students in many urban areas. School districts within the same state have very unequal success. Schools do not develop the cognitive skills of youngsters (i.e., the ability to manipulate words and numbers, assimilate information, and make logical inferences). Ability grouping, also known as tracking, does not reduce the number of dropouts nor improve the performance of students. Successful students in this system have the necessary qualities to score high on intelligence tests and thus find themselves in the high ability group; the other pupils are firmly assigned to non-academic programs. This is creating serious problems in schools located in the central areas of many large cities.

VIOLENCE AND THE SCHOOL

The effectiveness of the traditional school for character building is challenged by increasing disorder, vandalism, and assaults upon teachers and students. Presently, the school resembles a maximum security prison. In a recent three month period the Los Angeles Unified School District alone reported assaults on 60 teachers, 123 pupils, and 31 police officers; also, there were 83 cases of weapon possession.[8] In the first three months of 1974 the Los Angeles city schools recorded 437 criminal assaults.[9] This pattern is repeated throughout the country.

In response to the problem of school violence and vandalism, the U.S. Senate Subcommittee on Juvenile Delinquency issued a preliminary report in 1975. The report studied only 747 of the 16,600 school districts in the country, but it concludes that in the districts studied there are approximately 70,000 serious physical assaults on teachers, and more than 100 student murders each year. Property losses, through vandalism, amount to $500 million annually. This figure compares to the entire investment on textbooks for the nation's schools in 1972. Senator Birch Bayh, Chairman of the Senate Subcommittee, has continued nationwide hearings to explore the problem and seek solutions.[10]

The reason for this high school criminality is not well understood. Students blame school violence on: (1) the uneven application of discipline by staff; (2) unfair and authoritarian administration practices; (3) poor counseling services; (4) the absence of a student role in decision making (i.e., youth involvement); and (5) oppressive school policies such as outmoded dress codes. Administrators, counselors, and teachers list different causes: (1) excessive administrative paperwork; (2) poor facilities; (3) teacher disinterest; (4) extensive use of drugs by students; and (5) apathy about educational values in the home. Parents have their own ideas including: (1) crowded schools; (2) lax discipline; (3) irrelevant curriculum; (4) poor communication between schools and police; and (5) outside agitators.[11]

Whatever causes crime in the schools, it is evident that improvements are needed. At the same time it is important for principals and school districts to report the extent of crime in their localities. The school administrator sometimes denies the magnitude of offenses committed on school grounds; records of school crime patterns would help identify areas of greatest need. It accomplishes nothing to blame factors such as poverty, racism, poor housing, and inadequate health care—that they contribute is understood.

The frequency of crime seems to be related to the size of the school and the income of parents. Obviously the larger schools have overcrowded hallways, classrooms, and locker areas, and more crime occurs in schools in low-income areas. The control of such crime requires immediate action. Measures being tried include: (1) the use of security guards or parents in the halls and on school playgrounds; (2) implementation of an emergency plan for violent situations similar to that used for fires and civil defense; and (3) limited access to campuses through the use of photographic identification cards. Assigning police to junior and senior high schools is preferable to calling for police assistance in emergencies. Only a police officer trained in counseling should be given a school assignment; he is alert to the unique problems of the specific school and he also enlarges an inadequate counseling staff. Traditional counselors have failed to exert much influence on crime because of: (1) high caseloads; (2) excessive paperwork; (3) underrepresentation of minority counselors; and (4) limited time available for crisis intervention counseling. Very few teachers and counselors prepare themselves with juvenile delinquency courses, and this limitation is overlooked in most recommendations for teacher training improvement. Courses in criminal justice would equip prospective educators with: (1) improved classroom management; (2) group dynamic skills; and (3) sensitivity to ethnic and cultural differences.

Between 1960 and 1969 the number of black teen-agers rose by nearly 75 percent in the central districts of the largest cities; the number of white teen-agers rose by only 14 percent in these same areas.[12] This unprecedented increase in minority pupils underlies the need to intensify minority teacher recruitment, a more reasonable approach to the problem than mere emphasis upon teacher training. Recipients of teaching credentials have always preferred teaching in middle-class schools. More volunteers are needed to teach in low-income areas and in juvenile correctional institutions. Therefore, greater emphasis upon the qualified minority teacher should be a critical concern. In addition to reforms in teacher recruitment and training it is necessary to review the importance of an open campus. To reduce violence it might be helpful to limit the access of nonstudents to school grounds. This will become increasingly important if the compulsory age of school attendance is lowered. Dr. Marcus Foster, the late Superintendent of Schools in Oakland, California, was murdered by members of a radical terrorist group because he had approved a policy requiring enrolled students to carry identification cards. The Symbionese Liberation Army took credit for Foster's murder at the time it occurred, saying he was executed with cyanide bullets for allegedly attempting to control students with police state tactics.

Mount Clemens, Michigan (a suburb of Detroit), has found that the appointment of an ombudsman alleviates school tensions. The individual occupying this position meets the following requirements: (1) a college degree in the social sciences; (2) prior experience supervising student activities with an emphasis upon proven skills in interpersonal relations; and (3) an empathy and ability to work with minority students. He is employed by the school district. The ombudsman has helped to renew students' faith in the school's ability to respond to their needs. Accomplishments during the first year of operation included the establishment of parental biracial committees, meetings with probation officers about students involved with the police, and establishment of a high-school tutorial center. Channels of communication are thus developed with all elements of the community and school system. During the first year of operation school suspensions dropped from 400 to 226, and expulsions from 22 to four.

School crimes are not limited to armed robberies, extortion, and assault. Vandalism, the destruction of buildings and equipment, costs the largest school districts more than $1 million per year. National surveys of school damage have been conducted by the research division of the Baltimore school district since 1964.

Destruction of school property becomes more serious as tighter budgets reduce maintenance and a building looks vacant; it does not seem to belong to anyone, no one has the pride to protect it, and it becomes a playground for vandals. A number of precautions have been taken to reduce destruction of school property by juveniles, including: (1) making parents pay for vandalism by their children; (2) the installation of tamper proof locks and motion and sound detectors; (3) use of closed circuit television for surveillance both inside and outside of buildings; and (4) installation of break-proof windows or walls.

THE DELINQUENT PUPIL

In one school district an administrator announced over the public address system that a pupil had just returned from juvenile hall. He asked that anyone observing improper behavior from the culprit report it. This delinquent's offense was not school related, and his future was dim. The importance of a good school experience has been emphasized by the Youth Development and Delinquency Prevention Administration (recently renamed the Office of Youth Development):

> The tie of the young person to the school as his "institutional home" is maintained and reinforced by (a) the direct rewards of approval for valued academic and social performance; and (b) by the indirect rewards of a credible promise of a desirable occupational future.[13]

The youngster who has been in trouble will find that a return to school, when accompanied by some success in that setting, is an excellent way to show others that he wishes to amend his behavior and avoid further involvement in crime and delinquency. One state has vitiated this goal by establishing a truancy school in its largest city. A youngster must attend the truancy school before being readmitted to the traditional junior and senior high schools. Any juvenile justice contact, whether status offense or an adult crime, is basis for placement in the truancy school. Unfortunately, teachers in the truancy school are not selected for their understanding of problem children; untrained in special education or delinquency prevention and control, they prepared to discipline the delinquent. In another city a contrasting situation can be observed. There, a high school teacher was selected to handle a group of students defined as troublemakers. The instructor was trained in the field of delinquency control, and accepted his pupils as students, not as troublemakers. In an effort to bridge the gap between the assigned material and their street language, he had surprising results with the most unlikely book, *Canterbury Tales* by Chaucer. The course even became popular with other students. So the delinquents came to view theirs as a program with status and honor. The stigma of delinquency and the problem of school discipline were removed. Many of those assigned to the program developed a new interest in classroom activities and were returned to more traditional programs with improved study habits.

The teacher-probation-officer program has been successful for juveniles who attend school while on probation. The program was developed in Ohio and spread to Indiana, Michigan, and Virginia; in it, a full-time teacher serves the juvenile court on a part-time basis. The school principal chooses a member of his junior-high-school faculty to take this dual role; the teacher may work with the delinquent during or after school hours. The juvenile court pays the teacher a nominal part-time salary in exchange for his supervising the probationers of his own school. The program has been successful, promoting cooperation between the schools and the juvenile court.

Another recognized program is operated by the Passaic (New Jersey) Public Schools. From its beginning in 1937, their Division of Pupil Personnel Services (formerly known as the Passaic Children's Bureau and Special Services) has emphasized delinquency prevention and readjustment. Four police officers, assigned to Pupil Personnel Services, form the Investigative Unit; they are selected by the Board of Education; their salaries are paid by the Department of Public Safety; they are referred to as investigators and one of them is a woman. When a police officer apprehends a juvenile, he immediately turns the suspect over to the Investigative Unit, which assigns an officer to the case. The Investigative Unit is responsible for presenting to the county courts those cases which need to be heard by a judge of the juvenile or adult court.

The division uses the child study team approach to develop methods for alleviating the problems of the school youngster. The child study team is comprised of a psychologist, a social worker, a learning disability specialist, and the principal of the school. The team can be expanded, when necessary, to include a psychiatrist, physician, nurse, a remedial specialist, guidance counselor, or a concerned teacher. The team initiates the action required to help the youngster resolve his problems. The methods employed include: (1) school program adjustment; (2) changes in the home situation; (3) guidance in school activities; (4) assessment of the impact of factors in the school milieu or the community; or (5) various school programs such as special classes, group counseling, therapy, or other therapeutic programs. The team can give more concerted attention to the pupil than is possible for classroom teachers who have to think in group terms.

An alternative method for handling minors within the juvenile justice system is the school attendance review board. The SARB concept was developed by the Schools–Juvenile Court Liaison Committee of Los Angeles County in 1974. The committee was organized in 1971 and includes representatives from the Probation Department, Sheriff's Department, Department of Public Services, nine school districts, the Juvenile Court, and the office of the Los Angeles County Superintendent of Schools. A single school attendance review board is set up in each school district. The 6-to-8 member board is made up of representatives from the public schools, probation, mental health, community services, and public social services. A representative from law enforcement should be included on the board.

The purpose of the board is to: (1) remove school behavior problems from the jurisdiction of the juvenile court; (2) consider school attendance problems as indicators of many potential situations which might affect a child's participation in school—not merely the matter of truancy or tardiness; (3) review all earlier efforts made on behalf of a child and determine the availability of services which might be used in lieu of the juvenile court; (4) coordinate the services of those agencies having major responsibility for the welfare of children and youth; and (5) promote the development of resources where none exist. Implementation of this proposal will require action by the state legislature and passage will support the current view that compulsory school attendance is necessary. Its value lies in its intent that mandatory schooling should not help manufacture official delinquency when violence or property damage have not occurred.

The diversion of pupils with attendance problems away from the juvenile court to agencies offering services affecting the underlying cause of such behavior is commendable, as are also the attempts by the school to help those who return to class after an encounter with the formal justice system. These are piecemeal solutions. Alternative educational experiences should be explored. The National Advisory Commission on Criminal Justice Standards and Goals recommends that schools provide programs of education based on:

1. An acknowledgement that a considerable number of students do not learn in ways or through experiences that are suitable for the majority of individuals.
2. A recognition that services previously provided through the criminal justice system for students considered errant or uneducable should be returned to the schools as an educational responsibility.

   A variety of methods and procedures could be established to meet this goal. Among these are the following:

   a. Early identification of those students for whom all or parts of the regular school program are inappropriate; and
   b. Design of alternative experiences that are compatible with the individual learning objectives of each student identified as a potential client for these services, including:
      (1) Shortening the program through high school to 11 years;
      (2) Recasting the administrative format, organization, rules of operation, and governance of the 10th and 11th grades to approximate the operation of junior colleges;
      (3) Crisis intervention centers to head off potential involvement of students with the law;
      (4) Juvenile delinquency prevention and dropout prevention programs;

(5) Private performance contracts to educational firms; and

(6) Use of State-owned facilities and resources to substitute for regular school settings.[14]

Examples of an alternative education program is San Francisco's BEAM Project (Behavioral Evolvement through Achievement Management) and Girls' Adventure Trails in Dallas. Project BEAM is administered by the YMCA and receives seventh and eighth graders residing in a high delinquency area of the city. They are referred for underachieving, truancy, dropping out of school, or because of severe family problems. The BEAM curriculum is devised to modify the negative behavior patterns that resulted from their inability to cope in school and in social settings. Those referred to the program were doing poorly in reading and many were under the supervision of the juvenile court. The teachers in the program undertook to improve the youngster's ability to learn by combining instruction in graded reading material with a programmed schedule of rewards for improvement. Right answers resulted in the award of one chip which could be converted into a penny at the end of the week. One hour and forty-five minute tutoring sessions twice a week were supplemented with one group counseling session weekly, and cultural enrichment activities. Program results were positive: (1) after one year the number of pupils still under juvenile court supervision dropped from 40 percent to 4 percent; (2) unsatisfactory classroom behavior dropped from 52 percent to 25 percent; and (3) student reading accuracy increased dramatically.

The Girls' Adventure Trails is a community service for emotionally disturbed girls between the ages of 10 and 15. It consists of a 26-day wilderness camping trip that combines recreation with individual and group counseling. The Dallas Independent School District, the largest referral source for this program, claims that this alternate learning situation has resulted in improved classroom conduct, academic motivation, and personal behavior.

Functioning at school is but one of the problems of childhood. Achieving competency for adult living and gaining an employable skill remains a challenge sometimes overlooked by the school and the pupil.

YOUTH AND THE LABOR FORCE

A majority of adults consider work the most important of their obligations; therefore, the transition from school to work is a critical experience for youth. It is more difficult for the dropouts and those with official delinquency histories. The young person has not been considered useful in the labor force. Public policy emphasizes keeping youngsters in school as long as possible, and this pattern delays the entry of young workers into the labor force.

Before the advent of child labor laws, there was severe exploitation of youngsters in employment. Later, the age for entering the work force was raised and the school inherited these youngsters. At the same time it became more difficult to get jobs. A number of laws prohibit hiring 14- and 17-year-olds in occupations considered hazardous. Other laws prohibit employment during regular school hours or late at night. There is even legislation which refuses a youngster employment in hotels or restaurants where alcoholic beverages are sold.

Flexible arrangements are needed to provide for continued education and work training. Vocational education in high school should be something better than an expedient for students not going to college. Preparation for a career should begin in grade school. The Committee for Economic Development, a nonpartisan group of 200 businessmen and educators, strongly recommends:

> Effective functional education requires the introduction of children to the world of work in the primary grades and a continuous infusion of job information and counseling throughout the school years. The schools and prospective employers should jointly plan educational programs that will ensure not only adequate instruction but also satisfactory employment.[15]

A career is the usual goal of young people, whether or not the preparation requires college training. Education should include employment certainty. Adult continuing education should point the way to steady work. The young person looking for a job is discouraged at the crucial point where he might become a productive part of society.

Cloward and Ohlin, in their theory of the delinquent's attempt to achieve success through adherence to the basic norms of society, observe:

> Whether the "failure" blames the social order or himself is of central importance to the understanding of deviant conduct. When a person ascribes his failure to injustice in the social system, he may criticize that system, bend his efforts toward reforming it, or disassociate himself from it—in other words, he may become alienated from the established set of social norms. He may even be convinced that he is justified in evading those norms in his pursuit of success-goals. The individual who locates the source of his failure in his own inadequacy, on the other hand, feels pressure to change himself rather than the system. . . . By implication, then, attributing failure to one's own faults reveals an attitude supporting the legitimacy of the existing norms.[16]

It is important for the individual who experiences failure to direct himself toward greater competency. This means narrowing the gap between vocational and academic schooling.

Failures in work and school are always related. Stinchcombe tells us that "high school rebellion . . . occurs when future status is not clearly related to present performance."[17] He adds, "A high school student wants to grow up into an adult who is successful by adult standards."[18] Stinchcombe calls for closer alliances between school vocational programs and potential employers. The high school diploma suggests to a potential employer that the graduate is trainable. Training for a specific job is best left to the employer. Secretarial training is recommended for high school boys in order for them to compete in the white collar job market when the blue collar area is closed.

Closer ties are needed among industry, business, and schools so students can have an idea of where their education will lead them in terms of a livelihood. One organization, ORT or Organization for Rehabilitation Through Training, maintains a network of 650 vocational schools in 22 countries. ORT volunteers and lecturers visit high schools and junior colleges encouraging students to study technical courses. Advisory career education committees have been established in various communities to acquaint parents and students with available careers. These programs are valuable for youngsters. Bridging the gap between school and work reduces the conflict for school failures who naturally expect like conditions in the labor force. Cohen, in his sociological theory of delinquency, emphasizes that many boys internalize enough middle-class values to desire success. But this heightens their awareness of the barriers to success. If conformity doesn't work, delinquency may. Recognition through delinquency is more satisfying than conformity and failure.[19] Christopher Jencks, a severe critic of the existing educational establishment, admits that schooling is very important; he makes this assumption even though he found that luck is sometimes as important as school-related skills.[20] Perhaps career education will increase the luck of youths entering the world of work.

CAREER EDUCATION

Everyone wants to enter the job market with a salable skill. Students are better able to pay for their college studies when they have some kind of training. High school pupils are more certain to select a satisfactory career if preparation and careful selection accompanies their choice. Too many leave school without being able to do anything. The search for employment by such individuals becomes a haphazard activity. There are serious, long-term results, among them the problems of (1) job discontentment; (2) the dead-end nature of the work; and (3) the sense that life has fallen short of earlier established goals. A worker's response to boredom on the job can lead to alcoholism, drug abuse, and episodes of violence. Many firms have introduced rehabilitation programs to deal with the personal difficulties of employees. The United Auto Workers and Ford Motor Company have started a joint program aimed at helping workers overcome drug- and alcoholic-related conflicts. Profit-sharing programs and greater employee participation in company decision making is being introduced by many corporations to reduce the meaningless nature of work.

Career education can reduce the personal crises associated with work. Preparation for employment is the goal of career education. It involves:

1. The provision of instructional environments and learning goals that relate education to the world of work—its scope, its opportunities, and its significance—from pre-school through high school.
2. The provision of opportunities to explore and be trained in special subjects leading toward a particular career or career pattern.
3. The provision of opportunity for students to leave and reenter the educational system or the labor force or to obtain instruction in both in order to advance toward specific career objectives.[21]

Children should become familiar with occupations and work categories beginning in the first grade and continuing through high school and college. The importance of work may be emphasized in grades 1-6. The information ought to focus on the wide variety of available jobs and the requirements for obtaining them. The *Dictionary of Occupational Titles,* published by the Manpower Administration of the U.S. Department of Labor, identifies and briefly describes 22,000 jobs found in the American economy. It is used primarily by the U.S. Employment Service and its affiliated state agencies to facilitate counseling and job placement. In addition, government agencies and officials in industry, education, and labor use it as a source of information. Be sure that you consult the most recent edition.

Education for employment should continue in grades 7-9 where specific emphasis can be given occupational preference clusters. A talent or skill need not be related to any one occupation. Vocational education identifies 15 occupational clusters encompassing 45,000 jobs. The junior high school can familiarize the pupil with these clusters through pertinent study materials. Field trips and lectures by business representatives are also valuable supplements. Where possible, some actual experience in the chosen job would help indicate whether the choice is realistic; this is best accomplished in the classroom since it is too early for work-study internships. The clusters should be emphasized at the junior high school level and include:

1. Business and Office Occupations
2. Marketing and Distribution Occupations

3. Communications and Media Occupations
4. Construction Occupations
5. Manufacturing Occupations
6. Transportation Occupations
7. Marine Science Occupations
8. Health Occupations
9. Hospitality and Recreation Occupations
10. Personal Service Occupations
11. Fine Arts and Humanities Occupations
12. Environmental Control Occupations
13. Homemaking-Related Occupations
14. Agriculture Occupations
15. Public Service Occupations[22]

If a selection of one or more clusters is made in junior high school it can be narrowed and specialized later. The final year in high school should include internships or work-study experiences. There is security for the graduating student who knows when and where he can join the labor force. If more specialized education is required there are several options: community college, technical school (public or private), or the four year college or university. Students then relate academic skills to a job and further education becomes a more realistic expectation, interests and abilities being matched. Counseling can emphasize the satisfaction derived from good work attitudes. This approach to career education, known as the school-based model, includes: (1) career awareness in grades 1-6; (2) career exploration in grades 7-9; and (3) career preparation in grades 10-12 and beyond. A closer alliance between the public schools and the business community is required if this program is to succeed. School districts that have pioneered in the use of the school-based model include: Atlanta, Georgia; Los Angeles, California; Pontiac, Michigan; Hackensack, New Jersey; and Mesa, Arizona.

UNEMPLOYMENT

Recession in the economy creates a wave of problems in the inner city neighborhood. The National Advisory Commission on Criminal

Justice Standards and Goals suggests that unemployment rates in low-income areas average 50 to 70 percent above the national unemployment rate.[23] The national jobless rate hovers between 4 and 6 percent annually, the pattern varying within states or regions. There are seasonal fluctuations and an unemployment rate ranging between 3 and 15 percent is not unusual. The young are the first to have a hard time getting jobs in a declining economy. A return to peace, and the abolition of the compulsory draft law, increases the number of young adults trying to enter the labor force.

Many reasons have been advanced to explain the high level of unemployment among young people: (1) inadequate preparation in school; (2) the absence of information about available jobs; and (3) the unavailability of transportation to move people from their homes to the work site. Another viewpoint is that many youths cherish their leisure time and are unemployed or underemployed in order to follow other pursuits. More realistic reasons for unemployment tend to be: (1) lack of training; (2) lack of relevant work experience; (3) age; (4) unavailability of work in areas of individual interest; and (5) health problems.

The unemployed young adult must find a means of support. The most frequent source of assistance is family or friends. Others will resort to crime and delinquency when not working. Pandering, selling drugs, theft, and extortion are common sources of financial remuneration. Youth work programs sometimes begin with popular enthusiasm and then fade away. The 1930s saw the advent of the Civilian Conservation Corps and the National Youth Administration. World War II and the accompanying full employment throughout the country brought with it a reduced interest in youth unemployment. In the early 1960s the problems of rural migration to the city, automation, and growing unemployment revived interest. The passage of the Manpower Development and Training Act of 1962 and the Economic Opportunity Act of 1964 created work training programs for the unskilled. A successful urban work program requires: (1) a concentration of population; (2) the availability of training opportunities; and (3) a reasonable level of employment in the area. The National Advisory Commission on Criminal Justice Standards and Goals summarizes the results of work training programs funded through the Manpower Development and Training Act.

> First, minority youths are likely to benefit less from training than whites—an indicator of racial bias in the labor market. Second, remedial programs for severely disadvantaged inner city youths are expensive while consequent improvements in employability are not likely to be impressive. Third, minority individuals who can be trained without prior remedial education will usually find the programs offer access to better jobs, even when training is of less benefit to them than it is to whites. The overall conclusion is that where funding for manpower programs is limited, and where minority and other youth with fair academic records and abilities are destined for unemployment, under-employment, and perhaps crime, the first priority in the allocation of resources should be training in specific skills that will facilitate entry into better paying jobs.[24]

The community concerned about youth unemployment should determine the status of the local labor market. A helpful guide for ascertaining the economic situation has been developed by the Singer Manpower Training Division of Rochester, New York. The guidelines call for answers to the following questions from labor market analysts in the U.S. Department of Labor or the state employment service:

1. What is the present overall employment situation?
   a. Present unemployment rate?
   b. Present work force?
   c. Total employed?
   d. Total unemployed?
2. What is the projected trend in employment for the next year or two?
3. What is the expected growth in non-skilled, semi-skilled, skilled, and white collar occupations?
4. What will the competition be for non-skilled and semi-skilled jobs?
5. What are the semi-skilled and skilled occupations your department has identified for state and federally sponsored training programs?
6. What industries are expected to experience the most growth in terms of employment over the next year?

7. Who are the leading employers in the industries identified as having the most growth potential?[25]

STUDY QUESTIONS

1. Did your high school emphasize the success ideology? If so, did this influence your career objectives?
2. Explain the controversy surrounding compulsory school attendance laws. What is the mandatory age in your state? Has reform legislation been introduced in the past year?
3. Have the recommendations of the National Commission for the Reform of Secondary Education been implemented in your community?
4. Determine the current cost of school vandalism in your city. Identify the methods used to control this problem.
5. What are the causes of violence on school campuses? Has your state department of education conducted a study dealing with this problem? If so, compare the conclusions with those found in the California study.
6. What is the role of a school ombudsman?
7. Identify the duties of a teacher-probation-officer.
8. Do you favor the abolition of compulsory school attendance laws? Explain.
9. List the advantages and disadvantages of a school attendance review board.
10. Review existing alternative education programs in your community. Are such programs meeting the vocational needs of those enrolled?
11. Define career education. What is the school-based model?
12. Have work training programs been effective in reducing delinquency and unemployment in your home town?
13. Identify the occupational preference clusters.
14. What is the unemployment rate in your community? How might it be reduced?

NOTES

1. Lloyd E. Ohlin, *A Situational Approach to Delinquency Prevention,* U.S. Department of Health, Education, and Welfare, Social and Rehabilitation Service, Youth Development and Delinquency Prevention Administration (Washington, D.C.: U.S. Government Printing Office, 1970), p. 10.

2. Kenneth Polk and Walter E. Schafer, eds., *Schools and Delinquency* (Englewood Cliffs, N.J.: Prentice-Hall, 1972), pp. 22–27.

3. *Delinquency Prevention through Youth Development,* U.S. Department of Health, Education, and Welfare, Social and Rehabilitation Service, Youth Development and Delinquency Prevention Administration (Washington, D.C.: U.S. Government Printing Office, 1972), p. 26.

4. National Commission on the Reform of Secondary Education, *Reform of Secondary Education* (New York: McGraw-Hill Book Co., 1973).

5. Delos H. Kelly and William T. Pink, "Academic Failure, Social Involvement, and High School Dropout," *Youth and Society,* 4 (September, 1972): 47–59.

6. Jerald G. Bachman, Swayzer Green, and Ilona D. Wirtanen, *Youth in Transition,* vol. 3: *Dropping Out—Problem or Symptom?* (Ann Arbor, Michigan: Survey Research Center, Institute for Social Research, 1971).

7. Michael Lalli and Leonard Savitz, *Delinquency and City Life,* U.S. Department of Justice, Law Enforcement Assistance Administration, National Institute of Law Enforcement and Criminal Justice (Washington, D.C.: U.S. Government Printing Office, 1972), pp. 1–19.

8. *The Sacramento Bee,* 9 November 1973, p. A-1.

9. *San Francisco Sunday Examiner and Chronicle,* March 31, 1974, p. B-4.

10. *U.S. Congressional Record,* 94th Cong., 1st sess., vol. 121, no. 59 (April 17, 1975), pp. S6011–S6013.

11. California Task Force on the Resolution of Conflict, *A Report on Conflict and Violence in California's High Schools* (Sacramento: California State Department of Education, 1973).

12. "Labor Month in Review," *Monthly Labor Review,* Vol. 94, No. 5 (May, 1971), p. 2. See current issues of this U.S. Department of Labor publication for up to date information.

13. *Delinquency Prevention Through Youth Involvement,* U.S. Department of Health, Education, and Welfare, Social and Rehabilitation Service, Youth Development and Delinquency Prevention Administration (Washington, D.C.: U.S. Government Printing Office, 1972), p. 29.

14. National Advisory Commission on Criminal Justice Standards and Goals, *Report on Community Crime Prevention* (Washington, D.C.: U.S. Government Printing Office, 1973), p. 166.

15. Committee for Economic Development, *Education for the Urban Disadvantaged from Preschool to Employment* (New York: Committee for Economic Development, 1971), p. 45.

16. Richard A. Cloward and Lloyd E. Ohlin, *Delinquency and Opportunity: A Theory of Delinquent Gangs* (New York: The Free Press, 1960), pp. 111–112.

17. Arthur L. Stinchcombe, *Rebellion in a High School* (Chicago: Quadrangle Books, 1964), p. 5.

18. Ibid., p. 179.

19. Albert K. Cohen, *Delinquent Boys* (Glencoe, Ill.: The Free Press, 1955).

20. Christopher Jencks, *Inequality: A Reassessment of the Effect of Family and Schooling in America* (New York: Basic Books, 1972).

21. National Advisory Commission on Criminal Justice Standards and Goals, *Report on Community Crime Prevention* (Washington, D.C.: U.S. Government Printing Office, 1973), p. 154.

22. Ibid., p. 155.

23. Ibid., p. 117.

24. Ibid., p. 123.

25. *The Community and Criminal Justice: A Guide for Organizing Action,* prepared for distribution at the National Conference on Criminal Justice, January 23-26, 1973, Washington, D.C., p. 33.

IMPROVING JUVENILE JUSTICE

NATIONAL CRIME COMMISSIONS
EVALUATING SUCCESSFUL PROGRAMS
INFORMATIONAL RESOURCES

Concerned individuals in and out of the system can be effective if they have a viable grasp of contemporary issues. The preceeding chapters hopefully point the direction for further study. The presumption is for continued growth.

The juvenile justice system is frequently criticized. From the left, there is talk of oppression; from the right, fears of leniency. Polarized opinion does not create significant dialogue; it may win elections but it does not improve juvenile justice or bolster community protection. Walter Miller, in his study of ideology and criminal justice policy, states:

> One must bear in mind that both left and right have important parts to play. The left provides the cutting edge of innovation, the capacity to isolate and identify those aspects of existing systems which are least adaptive, and the imagination and vision to devise new modes and new instrumentalities for accommodating emergent conditions. The right has the capacity to sense those elements of the established order that have strength, value, or continuing usefulness, to serve as a brake on over-rapid alternation of existing modes of adaptation, and to use what is valid in the past as a guide to the future. Through the dynamic clash between the two forces, new and valid adaptations may emerge. . . . It does not seem unreasonable to ask of those engaged in the demanding task of formulating and implementing criminal justice policy that they accord to differing positions that measure of respect and consideration that the true idealogue can never grant.[1]

Fusing different viewpoints cannot always create successful prevention and control programs. These programs are predicated on knowledge, and the critical thing is knowing where to find the right information.

NATIONAL CRIME COMMISSIONS

Three national surveys have been studying the problem of crime and delinquency since 1931. The National Commission on Law Observance and Enforcement, established by President Herbert Hoover in 1929, became known as the Wickersham Commission because its chairman, George W. Wickersham, was a former Attorney General of the United States. Although established to study the matter of prohibition, two of the 14 volumes issued in 1931 were concerned with juvenile delinquency. Report No. 6, *The Child Offender in the Federal System of Justice*, was written by a progressive prison warden named Miriam Van Waters. Report No. 13, *Causes of Crime, Volume II*, was prepared by Clifford R. Shaw and Henry D. McKay, the founders of the Chicago Area Project.[2] The issues of crime and delinquency did not capture the interest of citizens and legislators in that depression era.

Not until 1967 was the second national survey published. Lyndon Johnson estabished the President's Commission on Law Enforcement and Administration of Justice in 1965. The work of the commission was divided into four major areas: police, courts, corrections, and assessment of the crime problem. Later, special task forces were formed to deal with special problems: drunkenness, juvenile delinquency and youth crime, narcotics, organized crime, and science and technology. *The Challenge of Crime in a Free Society* was the summary volume. *Task Force Report: Juvenile Delinquency and Youth Crime* contains the commission's recommendations, which have been accepted by a number of progressive criminal justice agencies. National interest in the problem of crime and delinquency has aided implementation of these recommendations.

The third national survey of criminal problems, completed in 1973, was the work of the National Advisory Commission on Criminal Justice Standards and Goals formed in 1971. The goal of the commission was to formulate national criminal justice standards and goals for crime reduction and prevention at the state and local level; it was funded by the Law Enforcement Assistance Administration. The six volumes published by the commission in 1973 are available from the U.S. Government Printing Office:

1. *A National Strategy to Reduce Crime*
2. *Report on Police*
3. *Report on Courts*
4. *Report on Corrections*
5. *Report on Criminal Justice System*
6. *Report on Community Crime Prevention.*

Hundreds of recommendations are made in these volumes. Communities should implement as many of them as possible before 1983. Although a separate volume is not devoted to juvenile delinquency as in 1967, there are many references to youth crime prevention. During 1974 and 1975 representatives of criminal justice agencies in each state met to determine which of the standards would be implemented. It is to be hoped that political ideologies will not spoil the cooperative mood necessary for law enforcement, the courts, and corrections to set workable goals for the next decade. The citizen will play a critical role in determining whether the goals of this commission are realistic by urging the community to adopt its standards. An important aim is the 50 percent reduction in high-fear crimes by 1983. These crimes are murder, rape, robbery, aggravated assault, and burglaries committed by strangers. The crime reduction goal is to be accomplished in two ways: (1) reforming the activities which involve the offender after he has been arrested; and (2) preventing a person from getting into trouble by encouraging community crime prevention.

EVALUATING SUCCESSFUL PROGRAMS

Effective control of juvenile delinquency requires the cooperation of all criminal justice agencies. They must respond to the priorities of the community they serve. This is best accomplished when each state and local government evaluates its criminal justice activities. The Omnibus Crime Control Act of 1968, as amended by the Crime Control Act of 1973, requires that the comprehensive state plan establish goals, priorities, and standards for crime reduction and prevention. The decisions made by criminal justice representatives, regarding the standards to be implemented from the National Commission, will appear in all comprehensive state plans beginning in fiscal year 1976. Legislation to improve state and local criminal justice activities cannot proceed without an articulation of accepted standards.

Each state should produce its reasons for rejecting the goals of the National Advisory Commission. Some of these might include the following: (1) rejection of the goal by one or more segments of its criminal justice system; (2) inadequate financial assistance for implementation of the goal; (3) unresolved ideological issues; and (4) these programs have been unsuccessful when attempted in the past. The recommendation adopted by the National Conference of State Criminal Justice Planning Administrators for program evaluation states:

> Evaluation shall be defined as determining whether the project or program accomplished its objectives, in terms of either preventing, controlling or reducing crime or delinquency or of improving the administration of criminal justice within the context of the state comprehensive criminal justice plan. Such evaluation shall include, whenever possible, the impact of the project or program upon other components of the criminal justice system.[3]

The most comprehensive evaluation program has been credited to the state planning agency in Virginia.[4] Materials dealing with evaluation procedures are being developed and greater effectiveness is anticipated (see Appendix D, General Bibliography, Evaluation). Program evaluations for individual states should be reviewed in order to determine whether the goals and priorities for reducing delinquency are being met. It is easy to accept standards but difficult to implement them.

INFORMATIONAL RESOURCES

Continuing study and research in matters relating to delinquency prevention and control requires familiarity with the subject indexes and journals in the field.

The following selected periodical indexes should be consulted when preparing a term project or position paper. Most of them will be found in the reference room of the college or university library:

1. Abstracts on Criminology and Penology
2. Abstracts on Police Science
3. Abstracts for Social Workers
4. Bibliographic Index
5. Crime and Delinquency Literature
6. Current Contents—Behavioral, Social and Educational Sciences
7. Current Contents—Clinical Practice
8. Current Index to Journals in Education
9. Document Retrieval Index
10. Education Index
11. Essay and General Literature Index
12. Index Medicus
13. Index to Legal Periodicals
14. Psychological Abstracts
15. Public Affairs Information Service Bulletin
16. Readers' Guide to Periodical Literature
17. Social Sciences Index
18. Sociological Abstracts

In addition, the following 100 journals, the majority in the behavioral and social sciences, provide information on juvenile delinquency:

1. Administrative Science Quarterly
2. Adolescence

3. American Bar Association Journal
4. American Behavioral Scientist
5. American Journal of Correction
6. American Journal of Orthopsychiatry
7. American Journal of Psychiatry
8. American Journal of Psychology
9. American Journal of Psychotherapy
10. American Journal of Public Health
11. American Journal of Sociology
12. American Psychologist
13. American Sociological Review
14. Annals of the American Academy of Political & Social Science
15. Behavioral Science
16. British Journal of Criminology
17. California Youth Authority Quarterly
18. Canadian Journal of Criminology and Corrections
19. Child Care Quarterly
20. Children Today
21. Civil Liberties Review
22. Clinical Social Work Journal
23. Community Mental Health Journal
24. Congressional Quarterly
25. Contemporary Psychology
26. Contemporary Sociology: A Journal of Reviews
27. Corrections Magazine
28. Crime and Delinquency
29. Crime Prevention Review
30. Criminal Justice and Behavior: An International Journal of Correctional Psychology
31. Criminal Law Bulletin
32. Criminology: An Interdisciplinary Journal
33. Day Care and Early Education
34. Developmental Psychology
35. Education and Urban Society
36. Federal Probation

37. Human Behavior
38. Human Organization
39. International Journal of Criminology and Penology
40. Journal of Abnormal Psychology
41. Journal of Applied Behavioral Science
42. Journal of Applied Psychology
43. Journal of California Law Enforcement
44. Journal of Child Psychology and Psychiatry
45. Journal of Consulting and Clinical Psychology
46. Journal of Correctional Education
47. Journal of Counseling Psychology
48. Journal of Criminal Justice
49. Journal of Criminal Law and Criminology
50. Journal of Criminal Law, Criminology and Police Science (discontinued January 1973)
51. Journal of Educational Psychology
52. Journal of Health and Social Behavior
53. Journal of Law Enforcement Education and Training
54. Journal of Marriage and the Family
55. Journal of Nervous and Mental Disease
56. Journal of Personality and Social Psychology
57. Journal of Police Science and Administration
58. Journal of Research in Crime and Delinquency
59. Journal of Social Issues
60. Journal of Systems Management
61. Journal of Urban Analysis
62. Judicature
63. Juvenile Court Digest
64. Juvenile Justice
65. Law and Order
66. LEAA Newsletter
67. Life-Threatening Behavior
68. Mental Hygiene
69. Monthly Labor Review
70. Pacific Sociological Review

71. People Watching
72. Police Chief
73. Prison Journal
74. Psychiatric Quarterly
75. Psychiatry
76. Psychoanalytic Quarterly
77. Psychoanalytic Review
78. Psychological Bulletin
79. Psychological Review
80. Public Administration Review
81. Public Interest
82. Quarterly Review of Studies on Alcohol
83. Social Casework
84. Social Forces
85. Social Problems
86. Social Research
87. Social Service Review
88. Social Work
89. Society Magazine
90. Sociological Methods and Research
91. Sociology and Social Research
92. Sociology of Education
93. Today's Education
94. Training and Development Journal
95. Urban Affairs Quarterly
96. Urban Education
97. Urban Life and Culture
98. Welfare in Review
99. Youth and Society
100. Youth Reporter

The U.S. Department of Justice recently published the *Library Book Catalog* which lists approximately 6,000 books, documents, and periodicals contained in its libraries (see Appendix D, General Bibliography). These are housed in the Law Enforcement

Assistance Administration, Federal Bureau of Prisons, and the Drug Enforcement Administration. The catalog is published in four separate sections:

1. *Author Catalog*—an alphabetical listing by author of the material currently held by the three libraries.
2. *Title Catalog*—a list of the three libraries' holdings arranged by title.
3. *Subject Catalog*—list of books and documents in the three libraries arranged under 7,352 subject entries.
4. *Periodicals Catalog*—a listing of approximately 450 periodicals subscribed to by the three libraries.

Marvin E. Wolfgang and associates, at the Center for Studies in Criminology and Criminal Law, University of Pennsylvania, have compiled an important resource for those interested in the etiology of crime and delinquency. Entitled *Criminology Index,* the two volumes are a convenient central source for every significant book and article published from 1945 to 1972.[5]

A body of knowledge exists for use in reducing the delinquency problem. A number of state legislatures are calling for passage of a bill of rights for children. Goals, priorities, and standards are being established by communities to fight delinquency. Concerned adults are forming state and national lobbies to assure passage of legislation offering services to children. The decade of the 70s contains, as perhaps never before, the potential strength of its increasingly sophisticated ideas.

STUDY QUESTIONS

---

1. Have political ideologies influenced the introduction of specific delinquency prevention and control programs in your locality? Explain.
2. Compare the juvenile delinquency issues accorded high priority in the publications of the three national crime surveys.

3. Identify the national crime commissions.
4. What is a high-fear crime?
5. How did your state determine whether to accept the recommendations of the National Advisory Commission on Criminal Justice Standards and Goals?
6. Define criminal justice program evaluation.
7. Which periodical indexes do you find most helpful when studying a delinquency issue?
8. Prepare a list of the ten periodicals which you consult when preparing a routine report on current issues in delinquency prevention and control. Why do you find this list most influential?
9. How do you propose to improve juvenile justice?

NOTES

1. Walter B. Miller, "Ideology and Criminal Justice Policy: Some Current Issues," *The Journal of Criminal Law and Criminology*. Reprinted by special permission of the *Journal of Criminal Law and Criminology*, Copyright © 1973 by Northwestern University School of Law, Vol. 64, No. 2.

2. The reports of the National Commission on Law Observance and Enforcement have been reprinted and are available from Patterson Smith Publishing Corporation, 23 Prospect Terrace, Montclair, New Jersey 07042.

3. National Conference of State Criminal Justice Planning Administrators, *State of the States on Crime and Justice: An Analysis of State Administration of the Safe Streets Act* (Frankfort, Kentucky: The National Conference, 1973), p. 62.

4. Ibid., p. 25.

5. See: Marvin E. Wolfgang, Robert M. Figlio, and Terrence P. Thornberry, *Criminology Index: Research and Theory in Criminology in the United States, 1945-1972*, 2 vols. (New York: Elsevier Scientific Publishing Company, Inc., 1975).

APPENDICES

APPENDIX A: CHILD ADVOCACY PROGRAMS, STATE AND LOCAL

ALABAMA

Preparation for Parenthood and Early Childhood Development Program, Macon County Board of Education, Tuskegee

ALASKA

Community Coordinated Child Care, Inc., Juneau

ARKANSAS

South End Family Service Agency, Little Rock

CALIFORNIA

Alameda County Mental Health Association—Tri-City Child Advocacy Project, Oakland

California Childern's Lobby, Sacramento

Children's Defense Fund, Monterey

Citywide Youth Council of San Francisco, Commission on Human Rights, San Francisco

Community Family Day Care Project, Pasadena

Family Development Center, Family Service Agency of San Francisco

Forum for Youth Services, San Mateo County Department of Health and Welfare, San Mateo

Institute for Child Advocacy, Central City Community Mental Health Center, Los Angeles

Kings County Youth Community Project, Hanford

Operation Early Success, Redwood City

Social Advocates for Youth, San Francisco

Youth Involvement Program, Children's Hospital, Los Angeles

COLORADO

Child Advocacy Coalition, Denver

Child Advocacy Group, Division of Psychiatry, Denver General Hospital, Denver

Children's Laws Section, League of Women Voters of Colorado, Boulder

The Connection, Youth Coalition, Denver

H.O.M.E. Parent and Child Centers, Inc., La Junta

SOURCE: Alfred J. Kahn, Sheila B. Kamerman, and Brenda G. McGowan, *Child Advocacy: Report of a National Baseline Study*, U.S. Department of Health, Education, and Welfare, Office of Child Development, Children's Bureau (Washington, D.C.: U.S. Government Printing Office, 1973), pp. 173–177.

CONNECTICUT

Connecticut Child Advocacy Center, Connecticut Child Welfare Association, Hartford

Family Advocacy Program, Catholic Family Services, Hartford

Family Service of New Haven, Inc., New Haven

FLORIDA

Parent and Child Center/Child Advocacy Project, Jacksonville

GEORGIA

American Friends Service Committee, Southern Regional Office, Atlanta

Athens-Clarke County Coordinated Child Care Program, Athens

Black Child Development Institute, Southern Project, Atlanta

Child Service and Family Counseling Center, Atlanta

Males in Day Care/Project Success Environment, Emory University, Atlanta

HAWAII

Research Demonstration Children's Center, University of Hawaii, Honolulu

ILLINOIS

Illinois Commission on Children, Springfield

Illinois Council of Youth, Springfield

INDIANA

Youth Advocacy Program of St. Joseph County, South Bend

KENTUCKY

Child Advocacy Component, Parent and Child Center, Leitchfield

Community Resources Development Unit, Kentucky Department of Child Welfare, Frankfort

Kentucky Commission on Children and Youth, Frankfort

Kentucky Juvenile Defender Program, Kentucky Youth Research Center, Frankfort

Southeast Caucus for Child Advocacy, Newport

MARYLAND

Martin Luther King, Jr., Parent and Child Advocacy Center, Baltimore

Working Together for Children—A Neighborhood Advocacy System, Prince George's County Public Schools, Upper Marlboro

MASSACHUSETTS

Action for Children's Television, Newton

Child Care Advocate, Department of Mental Health, Division of Children's Services, Boston

Coalition for Children, Newton

Massachusetts Committee on Children and Youth, Boston
Parent and Child Center—Child Advocacy Project, Dorchester

MINNESOTA
Children's Health Center, Inc., Minneapolis
Family and Children's Service, Minneapolis
Minnesota Youth Advocacy Corps, Minnesota State Department of Education, St. Paul
Planning Office, Minnesota Department of Public Welfare, St. Paul

MISSISSIPPI
Tougaloo Community Day Care Center, Tougaloo

MISSOURI
National Juvenile Law Center, St. Louis University School of Law, St. Louis

NEBRASKA
Citizen Advocacy Program, Capitol Association for Retarded Children, Lincoln

NEW HAMPSHIRE
Child and Family Services of New Hampshire, Manchester

NEW JERSEY
Citizen Advocacy Program, Trenton
Youth Services Agency, Newark

NEW MEXICO
Albuquerque Child Advocacy Demonstration, Unified Child Care Association, Albuquerque

NEW YORK
The Center on Human Policy, Syracuse University, Syracuse
Children-In-Crisis Project, Children's Aid Society, Buffalo
Citizens' Committee for Children of New York, New York City
Family Development Research Program, The Children's Center, Syracuse
Family Service Association of Nassau County, Inc., Mineola
Martin Luther King, Jr., Health Center, Community Health Advocacy Department, Montefiore Hospital, New York City
New York State Association for Retarded Children, Inc., New York City
Office of Children's Services, Judicial Conference, New York City
Parent Education in the Pediatric Clinic, Mt. Sinai Hospital School of Medicine, New York City
United Bronx Parents, Inc., New York City
Wiltwyck School for Boys, Inc., Comprehensive Neighborhood Program, New York City

NORTH CAROLINA

Child Advocacy Center, North Carolina Department of Mental Health, Durham

Child Advocacy System Project, Morganton (Learning Institute of North Carolina, Durham)

Child Development Program, Winston-Salem

Focus on Optimal Development, Durham City Schools, Durham

Governor's Commission on Child Advocacy, Raleigh

North Carolina Conference for Social Services, Raleigh

Western Carolina Center, Morganton

OHIO

Center for the Study of Student Citizenship, Rights and Responsibilities, Dayton

Demonstration Project in School Health and Nutrition, Dayton Board of Education, Dayton

Hough Parent and Child Center/Advocacy Component, Cleveland

OREGON

Child Welfare Association of Oregon, Portland

Portland Youth Advocates Runaway Program, Portland

PENNSYLVANIA

Child Advocacy in a Diverse Urban Community, Philadelphia

Philadelphia Urban League Child Advocacy Project, Philadelphia

SOUTH CAROLINA

Health and Nutrition Program, Beaufort County Schools, Beaufort

Youth Service Agency, Rock Hill

TENNESSEE

Citizens Advocacy Project, Tennessee Association for Retarded Children and Adults, Nashville

East Nashville–Caldwell Child Advocacy Project, Nashville

Family and Children's Service, Nashville

West Nashville Youth Service, Nashville

TEXAS

Child Advocacy Committee, Texas Association for Mental Health, Austin

Coordinated Child Care Council of Bexar County, Inc., San Antonio

Demonstration Project in School Health and Nutrition Services, Galveston Independent School District, Galveston

Hidalgo County Community Coordinated Child Care, Inc., Edinburg

Mexican-American Neighborhood Civic Organization Child Advocacy Project, San Antonio

South Austin Child Advocacy Project, Texas Association for Mental Health, Austin

VIRGINIA
Demonstration Project in Health and Nutrition, School Board of the City of Norfolk

WASHINGTON
Holly Park Child Advocacy Demonstration Project, Seattle
Youth Advocates, Seattle

WEST VIRGINIA
Parent and Child Center Program, Southwestern Community Action Council, Inc., Huntington

WISCONSIN
Child-Adolescent Services Program, Wisconsin Association for Mental Health, Madison
Dane County Mental Health Association, Madison
Freedom House, Madison
Governor's Committee on Children and Youth, Madison
Innovative Youth Services of Racine, Inc., Racine
Parent ACT (Advocates for Children Today), Milwaukee Mental Health Association, Milwaukee
Pathfinders, Milwaukee
Rock County Learning Disability Association, Janesville

NATIONAL ORGANIZATIONS
American Parents' Committee, Inc., Washington, D.C.
Child Welfare League of America, New York City
Children's Foundation, Washington, D.C.
Children's Lobby, New York City
Crusade against Hunger, National Council of Churches, New York City
Day Care and Child Development Council of America, Washington, D.C.
National Committee for Children and Youth, Washington, D.C.
National Welfare Rights Organization, Washington, D.C.
Robert F. Kennedy Fellows Program for the Rights of Children, Washington, D.C.

APPENDIX B: STUDIES OF POLICE DECISION MAKING IN THE DISPOSITION OF JUVENILE OFFENDERS: A BIBLIOGRAPHY

1. Barrett, David R.; Brown, William J. T.; and Cramer, John M. "Juvenile Delinquency: The Police, State Courts, and Individualized Justice." *Harvard Law Review* 79 (1966): 775–810.
2. Black, Donald J. "Production of Crime Rates." *American Sociological Review* 35 (1970): 733–748.
3. Black, Donald J. and Reiss, Albert J., Jr. "Police Control of Juveniles." *American Sociological Review* 35 (1970): 63–77.
4. Block, Richard L. "Fear of Crime and Fear of the Police." *Social Problems* 19 (1971): 91–101.
5. Ferdinand, Theodore N. and Luchterhand, Elmer G. "Inner-City Youths, the Police, the Juvenile Court, and Justice." *Social Problems* 17 (1970): 510–527.
6. Ferster, Elyce Z., and Courtless, Thomas F. "The Beginning of Juvenile Justice, Police Practices, and the Juvenile Offender." *Vanderbilt Law Review* 22 (1969): 567–608.
7. Goldman, Nathan. *The Differential Selection of Juvenile Offenders for Court Appearance.* New York, N.Y.: National Council on Crime and Delinquency, 1963.
8. Green, Edward. "Race, Social Status, and Criminal Arrest." *American Sociological Review* 35 (1970): 476–490.
9. Hohenstein, William F. "Factors Influencing the Police Disposition of Juvenile Offenders." In *Delinquency: Selected Studies,* edited by Thorsten Sellin and Marvin E. Wolfgang, pp. 138–149. New York: John Wiley & Sons, 1969.
10. Hudson, James R. "Police-Citizen Encounters That Lead to Citizen Complaints." *Social Problems* 18 (1970): 179–193.
11. Lichtenberg, Philip. *Police Handling of Juveniles.* U.S. Department of Health, Education, and Welfare, Social and Rehabilitation Service, Office of Juvenile Delinquency and Youth Development, 1966.

12. Marshall, James and Mansson, Helge. "Punitiveness, Recall and the Police." *Journal of Research in Crime and Delinquency* 3 (1966): 129–139.

13. McEachern, A. W. and Bauzer, Riva. "Factors Related to Disposition in Juvenile Police Contacts." In *Juvenile Gangs in Context: Theory, Research, and Action,* edited by Malcolm W. Klein, pp. 148–160. Englewood Cliffs: Prentice-Hall, 1967.

14. Monahan, Thomas P. "Police Dispositions of Juvenile Offenders: The Problem of Measurement and a Study of Philadelphia Data." *Phylon* 31 (Summer 1970): 129–141.

15. Piliavin, Irving, and Briar, Scott. "Police Encounters with Juveniles." *American Journal of Sociology* 70 (1964): 206–214.

16. President's Commission on Law Enforcement and Administration of Justice. *Task Force Report: Juvenile Delinquency and Youth Crime.* Washington, D.C.: U.S. Government Printing Office, 1967. See "Pre-Judicial Dispositions: Critique and Recommendations," pp. 16–21.

17. Sellin, Thorsten, and Wolfgang, Marvin E. *The Measurement of Delinquency.* New York: John Wiley & Sons, 1964. See "The Juvenile Aid Division of the Philadelphia Police," pp. 87–113.

18. Sullivan, Dennis C., and Siegel, Larry J. "How Police Use Information to Make Decisions." *Crime and Delinquency* 18 (July 1972): 253–262.

19. Terry, Robert M. "Discrimination in the Handling of Juvenile Offenders by Social Control Agencies." *Journal of Research in Crime and Delinquency* 4 (1967): 218–230.

20. Thornberry, Terence P. "Race, Socioeconomic Status and Sentencing in the Juvenile Justice System." *Journal of Criminal Law and Criminology* 64 (March 1973): 90–98.

21. Wattenberg, William and Bufe, Noel. "The Effectiveness of Police Youth Bureau Officers." *Journal of Criminal Law, Criminology, and Police Science* 54 (1963): 470–475.

22. Weiner, Norman L. and Willie, Charles V. "Decisions by Juvenile Officers." *American Journal of Sociology* 77 (1971): 199–210.

23. Werthman, Carl and Piliavin, Irving. "Gang Members and the Police." In *The Police: Six Sociological Essays,* edited by David Bordua, pp. 56–98. New York: John Wiley & Sons, 1967.

24. Williams, J. R., and Gold, Martin. "From Delinquent Behavior to Official Delinquency." *Social Problems* 20 (Fall 1972): 209–229.

25. Willie, Charles V., and Gershenovitz, Anita. "Juvenile Delinquency in Racially Mixed Areas." *American Sociological Review* 29 (1964): 740–744.

26. Wilson, James Q. "The Police and the Delinquent in Two Cities." In *Controlling Delinquents,* edited by Stanton Wheeler, pp. 9–30. New York: John Wiley & Sons, 1968.

APPENDIX C: STATE PLANNING AGENCIES

ALABAMA
Alabama Law Enforcement Planning Agency
501 Adams Avenue
Montgomery, Alabama 36104

ALASKA
Governor's Commission on the Administration of Justice
Goldstein Building Pouch AJ
Juneau, Alaska 99801

AMERICAN SAMOA
Territorial Criminal Justice Planning Agency
Office of the Attorney General
Box 7
Pago Pago, American Samoa 96902

ARIZONA
Arizona State Justice Planning Agency
Continental Plaza Building
5119 North 19th Avenue
Suite M
Phoenix, Arizona 85015

ARKANSAS
Commission on Crime and Law Enforcement
1009 University Tower Building
12th at University
Little Rock, Arkansas 72204

CALIFORNIA
Office of Criminal Justice Planning
7171 Bowling Drive
Sacramento, California 95823

COLORADO
Division of Criminal Justice
Department of Local Affairs
600 Columbine Building
1845 Sherman Street
Denver, Colorado 80203

CONNECTICUT
Governor's Planning Committee on Criminal Administration
75 Elm Street
Hartford, Connecticut 06115

DELAWARE
Delaware Agency to Reduce Crime
Room 405, Central YMCA
11th and Washington Streets
Wilmington, Delaware 19801

DISTRICT OF COLUMBIA
Office of Criminal Justice Plans and Analysis
Room 1200
711 - 14th Street, N.W.
Washington, D.C. 20005

FLORIDA
Governor's Council on Criminal Justice
307 East Seventh Avenue
Post Office Drawer 3786
Tallahassee, Florida 32303

GEORGIA
Office of the State Crime Commission
Bureau of State Planning and Community Affairs Office
270 Washington Street, S.W.
Atlanta, Georgia 30304

GUAM
Office of Comprehensive Law Enforcement Planning
Office of the Governor
Government of Guam
P.O. Box 2950
Agana, Guam 96910

HAWAII
State Law Enforcement and Juvenile Delinquency Planning Agency
1010 Richard Street
Kamamalu Building, Room 412
Honolulu, Hawaii 96813

IDAHO
Law Enforcement Planning Commission
State House, Capitol Annex No. 2
614 West State Street
Boise, Idaho 83707

ILLINOIS
Illinois Law Enforcement Commission
Suite 600
150 North Wacker Drive
Chicago, Illinois 60606

INDIANA
Indiana Criminal Justice Planning Agency
215 North Senate
Indianapolis, Indiana 46202

IOWA
Iowa Crime Commission
520 East 9th Street
Des Moines, Iowa 50319

KANSAS

Governor's Committee on Criminal Administration
525 Mills Building
Topeka, Kansas 66603

KENTUCKY

Commission on Law Enforcement and Crime Prevention
Room 130, Capitol Building
Frankfort, Kentucky 40601

LOUISIANA

Louisiana Commission on Law Enforcement and Administration of Criminal Justice
P.O. Box 44337, Capitol Station
Baton Rouge, Louisiana 70804

MAINE

Maine Law Enforcement Planning and Assistance Agency
295 Water Street
Augusta, Maine 04330

MARYLAND

Governor's Commission on Law Enforcement and Administration of Justice
Executive Plaza One, Suite 302
Cockeysville, Maryland 21030

MASSACHUSETTS

Committee on Law Enforcement and Administration of Criminal Justice
Room 1230
80 Boylston Street
Boston, Massachusetts 02116

MICHIGAN

Office of Criminal Justice Programs
Lewis Cass Building, 2nd Floor
Lansing, Michigan 48913

MINNESOTA

Governor's Commission on Crime Prevention and Control
276 Metro Square Building
7th and Robert
St. Paul, Minnesota 55101

MISSISSIPPI

Division of Law Enforcement Assistance
345 North Mart Plaza
Jackson, Mississippi 39206

MISSOURI

Missouri Law Enforcement Assistance Council
P.O. Box 1041
Jefferson City, Missouri 65101

MONTANA

Governor's Crime Control Commission
1336 Helena Avenue
Helena, Montana 59601

NEBRASKA

Nebraska Commission on Law Enforcement and Criminal Justice
State Capitol Building
Lincoln, Nebraska 68509

NEVADA

Commission on Crime, Delinquency and Corrections
Suite 41, State Capitol Building
Carson City, Nevada 89701

NEW HAMPSHIRE

Governor's Commission on Crime and Delinquency
3 Capitol Street
Concord, New Hampshire 03301

NEW JERSEY

State Law Enforcement Planning Agency
447 Bellevue Avenue
Trenton, New Jersey 08618

NEW MEXICO

Governor's Council on Criminal Justice Planning
P.O. Box 1628
Santa Fe, New Mexico 87501

NEW YORK

State of New York, Office of Planning Services
Division of Criminal Justice
250 Broadway, 10th Floor
New York, New York 10007

NORTH CAROLINA

North Carolina Department of Local Affairs
Law and Order Division
422 North Blount Street
Raleigh, North Carolina 27602

NORTH DAKOTA

North Dakota Combined Law Enforcement Council
State Capitol Building
Bismarck, North Dakota 58501

OHIO

Ohio Department of Urban Affairs
Administration of Justice Division
8 East Long Street
Columbus, Ohio 43215

OKLAHOMA

Oklahoma Crime Commission
5235 North Lincoln Boulevard
Oklahoma City, Oklahoma 73105

OREGON

Executive Department, Law Enforcement Council
306 Public Service Building
Salem, Oregon 97310

PENNSYLVANIA
Governor's Justice Commission
Department of Justice
P.O. Box 1167
Federal Square Station
Harrisburg, Pennsylvania 17108

PUERTO RICO
Puerto Rico Crime Commission
G.P.O. Box 1256
Hato Rey, Puerto Rico 00936

RHODE ISLAND
Governor's Committee on Crime, Delinquency, and Criminal Administration
265 Melrose Street
Providence, Rhode Island 02907

SOUTH CAROLINA
Law Enforcement Assistance Program
915 Main Street
Columbia, South Carolina 29201

SOUTH DAKOTA
State Planning and Advisory Commission on Crime and Delinquency
State Capitol Building
Pierre, South Dakota 57501

TENNESSEE
Tennessee Law Enforcement Planning Agency
Andrew Jackson State Office Building
Suite 1312
Nashville, Tennessee 37219

TEXAS
Criminal Justice Council, Executive Department
730 Littlefield Building
Austin, Texas 78701

UTAH
Law Enforcement Planning Agency
State Office Building, Room 304
Salt Lake City, Utah 84114

VERMONT
Governor's Commission on Crime Control and Prevention
43 State Street
Montpelier, Vermont 05602

VIRGIN ISLANDS
Virgin Islands Law Enforcement Commission
Charlotte Amalie, Box 280
St. Thomas, Virgin Islands 00801

VIRGINIA
Division of Justice and Crime Prevention
9th Street Office Building, Suite 101
Richmond, Virginia 23219

WASHINGTON
Law and Justice Planning Office
Planning and Community Affairs Agency
Office of the Governor
Olympia, Washington 98501

WEST VIRGINIA
Governor's Committee on Crime, Delinquency and Corrections
1706 Virginia Street East
Charleston, West Virginia 25311

WISCONSIN
Wisconsin Council on Criminal Justice
State Capitol
Madison, Wisconsin 53702

WYOMING
Governor's Planning Committee on Criminal Administration
P.O. Box 468
Cheyenne, Wyoming 82001

APPENDIX D: GENERAL BIBLIOGRAPHY

The first part of this Bibliography is an alphabetical listing of all the books referred to in the text, although references appearing in the detailed chapter notes are not repeated here. The second portion provides sources for further reading. These are ordered according to subject matter. The following subjects are listed: Children's Rights (Child Advocacy), including General References; The Golden Years, 1966–71: The U.S. Supreme Court and Juvenile Justice; Books for Children; Court Judges; Courts; Crisis Technique Training for Police; Curriculum Materials for Police and Social Studies Teachers; Employment of Ex-Offenders; Evaluation; Personality Traits and Typologies; Planning; Revenue Sharing; Runaways; Standard Juvenile Court Act; Statistics; Status (Non-Adult) Offenses; Undetected Delinquency; and Youth Service Systems.

In addition to the books and articles listed here, as well as in Appendix B and the chapter notes, the student is referred to the section on Informational Resources in Chapter 11, "Improving Juvenile Justice." Sources for up-to-date information on juveniles and the criminal justice system may be found there.

Referred Texts and Reports

Aichhorn, August. *Wayward Youth.* New York: Viking Press, 1935.

Bettelheim, Bruno. *Love Is Not Enough.* New York: Free Press, 1950.

Cloward, Richard A. and Ohlin, Lloyd E. *Delinquency and Opportunity: A Theory of Delinquent Gangs.* New York: Free Press, 1960.

Cohen, Albert K. *Delinquent Boys.* New York: The Free Press, 1955.

Federal Bureau of Investigation. *Uniform Crime Reports for the United States.* Washington, D.C.: U.S. Government Printing Office, issued annually each August.

Library Book Catalog. U.S. Department of Justice. Washington, D.C.: U.S. Government Printing Office, 1972.

National Advisory Commission on Criminal Justice Standards and Goals. *Report on Community Crime Prevention*. Washington, D.C.: U.S. Government Printing Office, 1973.

Pappas, Nick, ed. *The Jail: Its Operation and Management*. Washington, D.C.: U.S. Bureau of Prisons, 1971.

President's Commission on Law Enforcement and Administration of Justice. *The Challenge of Crime in a Free Society*. Washington, D.C.: U.S. Government Printing Office, 1967.

President's Commission on Law Enforcement and Administration of Justice. *Task Force Report: Corrections*. Washington, D.C.: U.S. Government Printing Office, 1967.

President's Commission on Law Enforcement and Administration of Justice. *Task Force Report: Juvenile Delinquency and Youth Crime*. Washington, D.C.: U.S. Government Printing Office, 1967.

Redl, Fritz and Wineman, David. *Children Who Hate*. New York: Free Press, 1951.

Report of the 1971 White House Conference on Youth. Washington, D.C.: Government Printing Office, 1971.

Report to the President, 1970 White House Conference on Children. Washington, D.C.: U.S. Government Printing Office, 1971.

Shaw, Clifford R. *Brothers in Crime*. Chicago: University of Chicago Press, 1938.

Shaw, Clifford R. *The Jack-Roller: A Delinquent Boy's Own Story*. Chicago: University of Chicago Press, 1930.

Shaw, Clifford R. *The Natural History of a Delinquent Career*. Chicago: University of Chicago Press, 1931.

Shaw, Clifford R. and McKay, Henry D. *Social Factors in Juvenile Delinquency*. A publication of the National Commission on Law Observance and Enforcement, No. 13, Vol. 2, June 26, 1931. Washington, D.C.: U.S. Government Printing Office, 1931.

Steffens, Lincoln. *The Shame of the Cities*. New York: Hill and Wang, 1957.

U.S. Department of Health, Education, and Welfare, Office of Human Development, Office of Youth Development. *Juvenile Court Statistics*. Washington, D.C.: U.S. Government Printing Office, issued annually.

Whyte, William. *Street Corner Society*. 2nd ed. Chicago: University of Chicago Press, 1955.

Recommended Reading

CHILDREN'S RIGHTS (Child Advocacy)
General References

Bremner, Robert H., ed. *Children and Youth in America: A Documentary History, Volume III: 1933–1970*. Cambridge, Mass.: Harvard University Press, 1974.

Davis, Samuel M. *Rights of Juveniles: The Juvenile Justice System*. New York: Clark Boardman Co., 1974.

Gottlieb, David, ed. *Children's Liberation*. Englewood Cliffs, N.J.: Prentice-Hall, 1973.

Holt, John. *Escape from Childhood: The Needs and Rights of Children*. New York: E. P. Dutton, 1974.

Weinstein, Noah. *Legal Rights of Children*. Reno: National Council of Juvenile Court Judges, 1974.

THE GOLDEN YEARS, 1966–1971: THE U.S. SUPREME COURT AND JUVENILE JUSTICE

Finklestein, M. Marvin; Weiss, Ellyn; Cohen, Stuart; and Fisher, Stanley Z. *Prosecution in the Juvenile Courts: Guidelines for the Future*. U.S. Department of Justice, Law Enforcement Assistance Administration, National Institute of Law Enforcement and Criminal Justice. Washington, D.C.: U.S. Government Printing Office, 1973.

Maxwell, John K., and Bridges, Barbara. *The Adjudication and Disposition Phases in Court Handling of Juveniles: An Annotated Bibliography*. Austin, Texas: University of Texas Law School, Criminal Justice Reference Library, 1972. A superior review of the resources, available from Tarlton Law Library, University of Texas Law School, 2500 Red River, Austin, Texas 78705.

Paulsen, Monrad G., and Whitebread, Charles H. *Juvenile Law and Procedure*. Reno, Nevada: National Council of Juvenile Court Judges, 1974.

Weinstein, Noah. *Supreme Court Decisions and Juvenile Justice*. Juvenile Justice Textbook Series. Reno: National Council of Juvenile Court Judges, 1973. This paperback is available from National Council of Juvenile Court Judges, Box 8978, Reno, Nevada 89507.

BOOKS FOR CHILDREN

Dorman, Michael. *Under 21: A Young People's Guide to Legal Rights*. New York: Delacorte Press, 1970.

Lobenthal, Joseph S., Jr. *Growing Up Clean in America*. New York: World Publishing Co., 1970.

COURT JUDGES

McCune, Shirley D., and Skoler, Daniel L. "Juvenile Court Judges in the United States, Part I: A National Profile." *Crime and Delinquency* 11 (April 1965): 121–131.

Smith, Kenneth Cruce. "A Profile of Juvenile Court Judges in the United States." *Juvenile Justice* 25, no. 2 (August 1974): 27–38.

Walther, Regis H., and McCune, Shirley D. "Juvenile Court Judges in the United States, Part II: Working Styles and Characteristics." *Crime and Delinquency* 11 (October 1965): 384–393.

COURTS

Alers, Miriam S. "Transfer of Jurisdiction from Juvenile to Criminal Court." *Crime and Delinquency* 19 (October 1973): 519–527.

Cicourel, Aaron V. *The Social Organization of Juvenile Justice*. New York: John Wiley & Sons, 1968. Highly critical of specific courts.

Emerson, Robert M. *Judging Delinquents: Context and Process in Juvenile Court*. Chicago: Aldine Publishing Co., 1969. Highly critical of specific courts.

Fox, Sanford. "The Reform of Juvenile Justice: The Child's Right to Punishment." *Juvenile Justice* 25, no. 2 (August 1974): 2–9.

Lemert, Edwin M. *Social Action and Legal Change: Revolution within the Juvenile Court*. Chicago: Aldine Publishing Co., 1970.

Rubin, Ted and Smith, Jack F. *The Future of the Juvenile Court: Implications for Correctional Manpower and Training*. Washington, D.C.: Joint Commission on Correctional Manpower and Training, 1968.

Younghusband, Eileen L. "The Dilemma of the Juvenile Court." *Social Service Review* 33 (March 1959): 10–20.

Attempts to improve existing court-administered services are discussed in the following articles by Donald Loughery and by Charles Shireman.

Loughery, Donald L., Jr. "Innovations in Probation Management: Catching Up with a Changing World." *Crime and Delinquency* 15 (April 1969): 247–258.

Shireman, Charles. "Innovations in Juvenile Court Probation." *Juvenile Court Judges Journal* 20, no. 2 (Summer 1969): 64–68.

CRISIS TECHNIQUE TRAINING FOR POLICE

Bard, Morton. *Training Police as Specialists in Family Crisis Intervention*. U.S. Department of Justice, Law Enforcement Assistance Administration, National Institute of Law Enforcement and Criminal Justice, Publication PR 70-1. Washington, D.C.: U.S. Government Printing Office, 1970.

———. "The Role of Law Enforcement in the Helping System." *Community Mental Health Journal* 7, no. 2 (June 1971): 151–160.

Katz, Myron, "Family Crisis Training: Upgrading the Police while Building a Bridge to the Minority Community." *Journal of Police Science and Administration* 1 (March 1973): 30–35.

Mann, Philip A. "Establishing a Mental Health Consultation Program with a Police Department." *Community Mental Health Journal* 7, no. 2 (June 1971): 118–126.

Reiser, Martin; Sokol, Robert J.; and Saxe, Susan J. "An Early Warning Mental Health Program for Police Sergeants." *The Police Chief* 39, no. 6 (June 1972): 38–39.

Stratton, John. "Crisis Intervention Counseling and Police Diversion from the Juvenile Justice System: A Review of the Literature." *Juvenile Justice* 25, no. 1 (May 1974): 44–53.

CURRICULUM MATERIALS FOR POLICE AND SOCIAL STUDIES TEACHERS

Becker, Harold K. "The Student and the Law." *The Police Chief* 39, no. 3 (March 1972): 75–77.

Coopersmith, Stanley. *Student Attitudes toward Authority, Law, and Police: How They Are Affected by the Law Education Program of Davis, California.* Davis, California: Institute of Governmental Affairs, University of California, 1971 (pp. 49–54).

Kobetz, Richard W., and Bosarge, Betty B. *Juvenile Justice Administration.* Gaithersburg, Md.: International Association of Chiefs of Police, 1973 (pp. 602–679).

Matz, Arthur O. "Laws for Youth Seminar." *Police* 16, no. 9 (May 1972): 3–4.

National Conference of Christians and Jews. *Learning to Cope with the C.O.P.S.: An Instructional Manual.* New York: National Conference of Christians and Jews, 1972.

Portune, Robert. *Changing Adolescent Attitudes toward Police: A Practical Sourcebook for Schools and Police Departments.* Cincinnati: W. H. Anderson Co., 1971 (pp. 129–264).

Rafky, David M., and Sealey, Ronald W. "The Adolescent and the Law: A Survey." *Crime and Delinquency* 21 (April 1975): 131–138.

Rubin, Ted. *Law as an Agent of Delinquency Prevention.* U.S. Department of Health, Education, and Welfare, Social and Rehabilitation Service, Youth Development and Delinquency Prevention Administration. Washington, D.C.: U.S. Government Printing Office, 1971 (pp. 40–51).

Tilton, Dennis S. "Law in the Classroom." *Juvenile Justice* 23, no. 2 (November 1972): 37–41.

EMPLOYMENT OF EX-OFFENDERS

Spergel, Irving A. *Community Problem Solving: The Delinquency Example.* Chicago: University of Chicago Press, 1969 (pp. 44–49). A discussion of stigmatization.

U.S. Civil Service Commission. "Employment of the Rehabilitated Offender in the Federal Service." *Federal Probation* 35 (September 1971): 52–53.

For further information on employment of ex-offenders, contact the National Clearinghouse on Offender Employment Restrictions, 1705 DeSales Street, N.W., Washington, D.C. 20036.

EVALUATION

Adams, Stuart. *Evaluative Research in Corrections: A Practical Guide.* U.S. Department of Justice, Law Enforcement Assistance Administration, National Institute of Law Enforcement and Criminal Justice. Washington, D.C.: Government Printing Office, 1975.

Directory of Federal Juvenile Delinquency and Related Youth Development Programs: A Handbook for Juvenile Delinquency Planners. The Interdepartmental Council to Coordinate All Federal Juvenile Delinquency Programs. Washington, D.C.: U.S. Government Printing Office, 1973.

Evaluation in Criminal Justice Programs: Guidelines and Examples. U.S. Department of Justice, Law Enforcement Assistance Administration, National Institute of Law Enforcement and Criminal Justice. Washington, D.C.: U.S. Government Printing Office, 1973.

Evaluation of Crime Control Programs in California: A Review. Sacramento: California Council on Criminal Justice, 1973.

PERSONALITY TRAITS AND TYPOLOGIES

Halleck, Seymour. *Psychiatry and the Dilemmas of Crime.* New York: Harper & Row, 1967 (pp. 134–138).

Quay, Herbert C. *Juvenile Delinquency: Research and Theory.* Princeton, N.J.: D. Van Nostrand Co., 1965 (pp. 139–169).

Trojanowicz, Robert C. *Juvenile Delinquency: Concepts and Control.* Englewood Cliffs, N.J.: Prentice-Hall, 1973 (pp. 57–60).

PLANNING

Howlett, Frederick W., and Hurst, Hunter. "A Systems Approach to Comprehensive Criminal Justice Planning." *Crime and Delinquency* 17 (October 1971): 345–354.

Klein, Malcolm; Kobrin, Solomon; McEachern, A. W.; and Sigurdson, Herbert R. "System Rates: An Approach to Comprehensive Criminal Justice Planning." *Crime and Delinquency* 17 (October 1971): 355–372.

Skoler, Daniel L. "Comprehensive Criminal Justice Planning—A New Challenge." *Crime and Delinquency* 14 (July 1968): 197–206.

REVENUE SHARING

Advisory Commission on Intergovernmental Relations. *Revenue Sharing—An Idea Whose Time Has Come.* Washington, D.C.: U.S. Government Printing Office, 1970.

Hardcastle, David A. "General Revenue Sharing and Social Work." *Social Work* 18, no. 5 (September 1973): 3–8.

RUNAWAYS

Ambrosino, Lillian. *Runaways.* Boston: Beacon Press, 1971. A handbook prepared to assist youngsters who are runaways experiencing crises associated with the event.

Bock, Richard, and English, Abigail. *Got Me on the Run.* Boston: Beacon Press, 1973.

Suddick, David E. "Runaways: A Review of the Literature." *Juvenile Justice* 24, no. 2 (August 1973): 47–54.

STANDARD JUVENILE COURT ACT

"Standard Juvenile Court Act—Text and Commentary." *National Probation and Parole Association Journal* 5 (October 1959): 330.

A copy of the Standard Juvenile Court Act, 6th edition, is available from the National Council on Crime and Delinquency, 411 Hackensack Avenue, Hackensack, N.J. 07601.

STATISTICS

U.S. Department of Justice, Law Enforcement Assistance Administration. *Sourcebook of Criminal Justice Statistics: 1973.* Washington, D.C.: U.S. Government Printing Office, 1974.

STATUS (NON-ADULT) OFFENSES

Arthur, Lindsay G. "Status Offenders Need Help, Too." *Juvenile Justice* 26, no. 1 (February 1975): 3–7.

Board of Directors, National Council on Crime and Delinquency. "Jurisdiction over Status Offenses Should Be Removed from the Juvenile Court." *Crime and Delinquency* 21 (April 1975): 97–99.

Ferster, Elyce Z., and Courtless, Thomas F. "The Beginning of Juvenile Justice, Police Practices, and the Juvenile Offender." *Vanderbilt Law Review* 22 (April 1969): 567–608.

Fox, Sanford J. *The Law of Juvenile Courts in a Nutshell.* St. Paul, Minnesota: West Publishing Co., 1971 (pp. 38–42).

Sellin, Thorsten, and Wolfgang, Marvin E. *The Measurement of Delinquency.* New York: John Wiley & Sons, 1964 (pp. 55–86).

UNDETECTED DELINQUENCY

Gold, Martin. "Undetected Delinquent Behavior." *Journal of Research in Crime and Delinquency* 3 (January 1966): 27–46.

———. *Delinquent Behavior in an American City.* Belmont, Ca.: Brooks/Cole Publishing Co., 1970.

Hardt, Robert H., and Bodine, George E. *Development of Self-Report Instruments in Delinquency Research: A Conference Report.* Syracuse, N.Y.: Syracuse University Youth Development Center, 1965. An excellent introduction to undetected delinquency.

YOUTH SERVICE SYSTEMS

Better Ways to Help Youth: Three Youth Services Systems. U.S. Department of Health, Education, and Welfare, Social and Rehabilitation Service, Youth Development and Delinquency Prevention Administration. Washington, D.C.: U.S. Government Printing Office, 1973.

The Challenge of Youth Service Bureaus. U.S. Department of Health, Education, and Welfare, Social and Rehabilitation Service, Youth Development and Delinquency Prevention Administration. Washington, D.C.: U.S. Government Printing Office, 1973.

Duxbury, Elaine. *Youth Service Bureaus in California.* Progress Report no. 3, January 1972. Sacramento: Department of the Youth Authority, 1972. Analyzes questions of coordination and diversion.

Early successful youth service bureaus are described in the following four sources:

Canlis, Michael N. "Tomorrow Is Too Late!" *California Youth Authority Quarterly* 21, no. 1 (Spring 1968): 9–16.

Keech, James; Bilodeau, Frank; and Egan, Maurice. "Changing Delinquent Behavior (YSB Style)." *Canadian Journal of Corrections* 10, no. 2 (April 1968): 311–320.

Moore, Eugene A. "Youth Service Bureaus—Local Community Action Program Prevents Delinquency." *Judicature* 52, no. 3 (October 1968): 117–119.

Norman, Sherwood. *The Youth Service Bureau: A Key to Delinquency Prevention.* Paramus, N.J.: National Council on Crime and Delinquency, 1972 (pp. 179–231).

The President's Commission reports (see alphabetical listing under President's) contain discussion of youth service systems as follows:

Challenge of Crime, pp. 79–89

Task Force Report: Juvenile Delinquency, pp. 9–22

Task Force Report: Corrections, pp. 22–23.

The White House Conference reports (see alphabetical listing under *Report*) also contain information about youth service systems:

Report, 1970, p. 381

Report, 1971, pp. 183–184.

INDEX